FRAMING IMMIGRANTS

FRAMING IMMIGRANTS

NEWS COVERAGE, PUBLIC OPINION, AND POLICY

CHRIS HAYNES, JENNIFER L. MEROLLA, AND

S. KARTHICK RAMAKRISHNAN

Russell Sage Foundation • New York

The Russell Sage Foundation

The Russell Sage Foundation, one of the oldest of America's general purpose foundations, was established in 1907 by Mrs. Margaret Olivia Sage for "the improvement of social and living conditions in the United States." The foundation seeks to fulfill this mandate by fostering the development and dissemination of knowledge about the country's political, social, and economic problems. While the foundation endeavors to assure the accuracy and objectivity of each book it publishes, the conclusions and interpretations in Russell Sage Foundation publications are those of the authors and not of the foundation, its trustees, or its staff. Publication by Russell Sage, therefore, does not imply foundation endorsement.

Library of Congress Cataloging-in-Publication Data

Names: Haynes, Chris, 1977– author. | Merolla, Jennifer Lee, 1975– author. | Ramakrishnan, S. Karthick (Subramanian Karthick), 1975– author.
Title: Framing immigrants : news coverage, public opinion, and policy / Chris Haynes, Jennifer Merolla, S. Karthick Ramakrishnan.
Description: New York : Russell Sage Foundation, [2016] | Includes bibliographical references and index.
Identifiers: LCCN 2016007688 (print) | LCCN 2016022185 (ebook) | ISBN 9780871545336 (pbk. : alk. paper) | ISBN 9781610448604 (ebook)
Subjects: LCSH: Mass media and immigrants. | Immigrants—Press coverage. | Emigration and immigration—Press coverage.
Classification: LCC P94.5.I48 H39 2016 (print) | LCC P94.5.I48 (ebook) | DDC 305.9/06912—dc23
LC record available at http://cp.mcafee.com/d/1jWVIp410q3zqb3ypEVd7dPhOy UrKrjKqenPhOCYYCqejqtPhO-qekTzhOyMrjKqenPhOCYYOyrhhKUqen6m7AjqKNJ VZgl6CAvU02rzjifY01dIcf3CmhP_nVZxZVNXHTbFEFIsyyOM-evVqWtAklrFIYG 7DR8OJMddECQjt-hsd7bOabatTztPpesRG9pxZHgU-JK8RcUDt5OZNPzPNKRaJwE -JK8RcCSn1RPoA6xoQg8rfjh0Xm9Ewd78VWXMV5ZxZBBMSCUr6VoTFLVy

The paper used in this publication meets the minimum requirements of American National Standard for Information Sciences—Permanence of Paper for Printed Library Materials. ANSI Z39.48-1992.

Text design by Suzanne Nichols.

RUSSELL SAGE FOUNDATION
112 East 64th Street, New York, New York 10065
10 9 8 7 6 5 4 3 2 1

To our families, who come from various immigrant generations and backgrounds

Contents

List of Illustrations

About the Authors

Chris Haynes is assistant professor of political science at University of New Haven.

Jennifer Merolla is professor of political science at University of California, Riverside.

S. Karthick Ramakrishnan is professor and associate dean of the School of Public Policy at University of California, Riverside.

Acknowledgments

Tᴴɪs ʙᴏᴏᴋ got its humble beginning as a fifteen-minute presentation at the Politics of Race, Immigration, and Ethnicity Consortium, or PRIEC, as many of us call it. PRIEC is a series of "unconferences" held around the country that dispense with the usual setup of themed paper panels and assigned discussants. Instead, scholars get fifteen minutes to present their work in progress and then receive immediate feedback from audience members. Back in January 2010, when Jennifer was a professor at Claremont Graduate University and Chris was still a graduate student at UC–Riverside, we presented the results of a survey experiment that tested whether calling someone an "illegal immigrant" or an "undocumented immigrant" was consequential for public opinion. Indeed, we got the idea for this experiment design at a prior PRIEC meeting, during which Matt Barreto (then a professor at the University of Washington–Seattle) had suggested that the term "illegal" evokes more restrictive opinion than a term like "undocumented." We got excellent feedback from the audience for our 2010 presentation and soon thereafter we began plans for an article. Finishing the article took a little longer than we expected (Millan was born in May of that year, and Luca a few weeks later). But we persevered and finally managed to submit the piece in early 2012. Thanks to the helpful feedback of Jeff Isaac and various reviewers, it was published in the September 2013 issue of *Perspectives on Politics*.

While working on the *Perspectives* piece, we realized that we had a lot more to say about immigrant framing, particularly with respect to issue frames and the possible interplay between news frames and their effects on opinion. By the fall of 2013, immigration had become a hot topic once again: President Obama had announced Deferred Action for Childhood Arrivals (DACA) in 2012, Mitt Romney had lost his bid for the presidency in part because of his support for immigration restriction, and soon thereafter many Republican leaders were calling for their party to support comprehensive immigration reform. Those reform efforts had gotten off to a promising start in early 2013, but ground to a halt in the

House of Representatives by the time our article came out. We thus made a fairly reasonable calculation that immigration would remain a contentious policy issue for the foreseeable future and that what we now envisioned as our book on immigrant framing would remain relevant by the time of its publication.

We are thrilled to be at this stage, three years and significant career changes later (Chris started a new job at the University of New Haven, Jennifer joined the political science department at UC–Riverside, and Karthick became associate dean at UC–Riverside's new School of Public Policy), with a book that we hope will better inform scholars and the larger public on the ways in which immigrants and immigration policy are framed in news coverage and the potential consequences of such frames for public opinion.

As we reflect back on our journey, we owe thanks to many people and institutions that helped us along the way. This book would not have been possible without the generous support of various funding agencies, including the Blais Foundation, the Leer Foundation, and the Chief Justice Earl Warren Institute on Law and Social Policy. These grants helped to support the data collection for our survey experiments. In some cases (the 2007, 2008, and 2010 Cooperative Congressional Election Studies and the 2011 and 2012 YouGov studies), our questions were included as part of a larger project with other collaborators, and we are especially grateful to Kevin Esterling, David Lazer, Michael Neblo, Adrian Pantoja, and Jean Schroedel for making space for our project on those surveys.

We also owe significant gratitude to the institutions that gave us the time, space, and resources to work on these projects: Claremont Graduate University, the University of California–Riverside, and the University of New Haven, as well as the Russell Sage Foundation, the Woodrow Wilson International Center for Scholars, the Center for Comparative Immigration Studies at UC–San Diego, and the Center for the Study of Democratic Institutions at Vanderbilt University.

We also extend our gratitude to the several scholars who offered their thoughts, encouragement, critiques, and provocative questions on our work. A deep and sincere thanks to Marisa Abrajano, John Aldrich, Matt Barreto, Larry Bartels, Ben Bishin, Ted Brader, Josh Clinton, John Geer, Zoltan Hajnal, Jennifer Hochschild, Vincent Hutchings, Jane Junn, Cindy Kam, Dave Lewis, Ben Newman, Francisco Pedraza, Efren Perez, Spencer Piston, Gabriel Sanchez, Gary Segura, Ali Adam Valenzuela, and Elizabeth Zechmeister. We would in particular like to thank those who carefully read early versions of chapters and gave constructive feedback, including Loren Collingwood, Alexandra Filindra, Joel Fetzer, Bernard Fraga, Seth Goldman, Eric Gonzalez Juenke, and Betina Wilkinson. A special thank-you as well goes to Jamie Druckman, not only for providing intellectual inspiration and helpful feedback but also for providing some data from his work on framing and the DREAM Act to assess the strength of different frames. We are also grateful to Jeffrey Isaac and his staff at *Perspectives on Politics*, who, as we noted earlier, published the article that forms the basis of some sections of this book. We are indebted as well to the anonymous reviewers at Russell Sage who read the full manuscript and helped us to make it appealing for a much broader audience.

The ideas in this book benefited greatly from opportunities to present at various conferences and meetings, including the American Political Science Association, the Midwest Political Science Association, the Western Political Science Association, and the Politics of Race, Immigration, and Ethnicity Consortium. We also benefited from presenting at faculty workshops and seminars at the Russell Sage Foundation, the University of California–San Diego, the University of California–Riverside, and Vanderbilt University.

We owe a huge thank-you to our research assistants Paul Monteon (UC–Riverside) and Matthew Serio (University of New Haven), who have made our work immeasurably easier. We also acknowledge the editorial staff at the Russell Sage Foundation, and especially Suzanne Nichols for her enthusiasm, dedication, and guidance in bringing this book to fruition.

Most of all, we want to thank our families for providing the love, support, and understanding we needed to complete this book.

From Chris: To my parents, Stephen and Sandra, who provided unconditional love and support through good and challenging times. To my grandparents, who sacrificed their lives and comforts so that, two generations later, I would have the opportunity to pursue my dreams.

From Jennifer: To my parents, grandparents, and parents-in-law, for their unwavering support throughout the years. To my two amazing children, Luca and Siena, who were born during the time span of our studies: you enrich my life in ways that defy measurement. And last but not least, to my partner Andy, whose love, encouragement, and support are what enable me to juggle the delicate balance of work and family.

From Karthick: A big thanks to my parents, whose migrant journeys and household conversations fed my early interest in politics; to Brinda, who remains a thoughtful, loving, and critical partner; and to Omji and Millan, who make every day a new adventure.

1

Introduction

IMMIGRATION HAS been a hotly debated and highly contested policy issue in the United States for over a decade. This was perhaps most evident in the summer of 2012, as the country eagerly waited for the Supreme Court to weigh in on the constitutionality of SB1070, an Arizona law that was widely condemned (or praised, depending on one's perspective) for harassing undocumented immigrants and making it easier to detain and deport them. Proponents and opponents of Arizona's law relied on various arguments and frames to make their case to the American public: Democrats and immigrant-serving organizations denounced the law as unconstitutional and racially motivated, while conservatives and Republicans, such as presidential nominee Mitt Romney, praised Arizona's law as a necessary response to policy challenges and called it a model for the rest of the country.[1]

In addition to arguing for the constitutionality of Arizona's law, conservative advocates also framed the issue in terms of immigrant criminality. Indeed, the criminality frame was central to the passage of SB1070 in the first place: in 2010 Republican lawmakers in Arizona comp of a spike in violent crime by unauthorized immigrants, and Jan Brewer even went so far as to claim that Mexican gangs w "headless bodies" in the Arizona desert.[2] Neither claim true: subsequent fact-checking by researchers and med vealed that violent crime near the Arizona border h up, and no one was able to verify any headless bo ert.[3] And yet these arguments about immigrant c remained an integral part of conservative disco authorized immigration, presenting it as a cris tion. The Arizona legislature drew heavily or passed SB1070, a law that challenged more edent whereby the federal government wa immigration enforcement.[4] Based on thi on enforcement, the Obama administratio

1

of Arizona, and by the summer of 2012 the Supreme Court was getting ready to issue a ruling on the law's constitutionality during one of its final sessions.

Just as the country was waiting on the Arizona cliff-hanger, the White House introduced another game-changing policy that shaped the national discourse on immigration, this time in a pro-integration direction. On June 15, President Barack Obama, speaking from the Rose Garden, announced a new program—Deferred Action for Childhood Arrivals, or DACA—that would provide temporary work permits and deportation protection for those undocumented immigrants who had come to the United States as children. In arguing for the importance of his administrative action, President Obama laid out a strong case to prevent the deportation of young undocumented immigrants, noting that "it makes no sense to expel talented young people, who, for all intents and purposes, are Americans—they've been raised as Americans; understand themselves to be part of this country—to expel these young people who want to staff our labs, or start new businesses, or defend our country simply because of the actions of their parents—or because of the inaction of politicians."[5] Clearly, in the summer of 2012, the president's actions and rhetoric on deportation relief stood in sharp contrast to Arizona's law that was awaiting a Supreme Court ruling.

It was in this context of a highly contentious national debate over immigration that the Quinnipiac University Poll asked respondents to weigh in on two very different approaches to addressing the issue of illegal immigration. One question in the survey gauged public support for "an Arizona-type law in their state, requiring police to check the immigration status of someone they have already stopped or arrested if they suspect he or she is in the country illegally." Meanwhile, another question gauged voter support for President Obama's policy "in which young illegal immigrants who came to the country as children will be able to obtain work permits and will not face deportation."[6] The results of this survey were remarkable: by a 64–32 margin, respondents supported Arizona's pro-deportation law, while at the same time supporting President Obama's deportation relief program by a 55–39 margin (see figure 1.1). A majority of Americans were seemingly holding contradictory opinions [on] immigration policy—favoring protective policies like DACA, on the [one] hand, while also favoring pro-deportation policies like Arizona's [SB] 1070.

[Al]though these contradictory attitudes may seem puzzling at first, [they] make more sense when we take a closer look at how each question [was ask]ed. The question on Arizona's policy refers to people who are [stoppe]d" or "arrested," inviting the respondent to think of immigration [in a parti]cular law enforcement context. On the other hand, the question [about Preside]nt Obama's policy mentions "children" who "will be able to

Figure 1.1   Public Opinion on Deportation and Deportation Relief, 2012

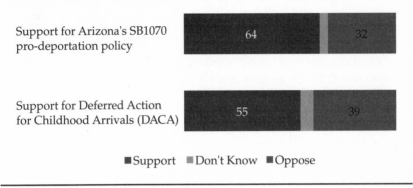

| Support for Arizona's SB1070 pro-deportation policy | 64 | 32 |

| Support for Deferred Action for Childhood Arrivals (DACA) | 55 | 39 |

■Support   ■Don't Know   ■Oppose

Source: Quinnipiac University Poll, 2012, Q40 and Q38.

obtain work permits," invoking a very different image and context for the survey respondent. Of course, these questions also vary in other ways—they make references to different levels of government (state versus federal), and while one makes no mention of elected officials, the other mentions Obama. In other words, there are too many variations in the frames to assess which ones might be most important in shaping people's attitudes on deportation. Nevertheless, the survey evidence shown in figure 1.1 strongly suggests that the framing of immigration policy is consequential for public opinion.

The key argument we advance in this book is that the different frames that individuals are exposed to on immigration have important effects on shaping opinions on particular policies that affect the undocumented population. Given that public opinions on specific policies are not very well developed, the door is open for political elites to play an important role by strategically deploying certain frames. Furthermore, in our contemporary media environment, where people have an array of choices on what type of news to consume, their exposure to immigration policy frames is likely to vary depending on the ideological slant of the news outlet. Given the combination of underdeveloped opinions on immigration and the modern media environment, it is imperative for us to begin understanding public opinion on immigration through the lens of framing.

In this book, we study both the supply of media frames and their effects on public opinion as they relate to the undocumented or illegal immigrant population in the United States. As we discuss later in this chapter, the "immigration debate" in the United States over the last decade has focused significant attention on policies affecting the undocumented population, ranging from deportations to comprehensive immigration reform, the DREAM (Development, Relief, and Education for Alien Minors) Act, and DACA. Despite prominent and multifaceted policy debates, scholarship on media framing and public opinion on immigration remains relatively constrained: media studies tend to focus on the racialization of the immigration debate and the characteristics and qualities of immigrants in particular, while most scholarly treatments of public opinion still focus on the general question of whether immigration to the United States should be increased, decreased, or kept the same. The nuances and particularities of policy are often missing from these accounts, something we seek to rectify in this book as we provide an in-depth look at framing and opinion on three types of policies: mass deportations, comprehensive immigration reform, and piecemeal measures targeting immigrant children, such as the DREAM Act. For our news framing analysis, we conduct in-depth content analysis of both print and cable media outlets that vary by ideological slant from 2007 to 2013. We then assess the impact of some of these media frames on public opinion through a variety of survey experiments that were conducted from 2007 to 2014.

Framing the Fight over Immigration Policy

The United States is a nation of immigrants. It is also a country that fights about immigration. This is perhaps the simplest way to characterize long-standing debates on immigration policy in the United States, discussions that reflect both the centrality of immigration to the country's development and its very divisiveness. Indeed, as scholars such as Rogers Smith remind us, the long-running fight over immigration reflects a more basic, underlying tension in America's civic ideals, with traditions of liberal egalitarianism existing alongside, and often doing battle with, traditions of "ascriptive hierarchy," including racism, sexism, and nativism.[7] Contentious frames on immigration are thus reflective of a larger pattern of heated debates in the United States over immigration, race, and inequality.

For much of American history, arguments over immigration policy have focused on the desirability or undesirability of letting in particular groups of people: Benjamin Franklin raised the alarm in 1760 on German immigration to Pennsylvania when it was a British colony, the Know-Nothing Party railed against Catholic immigration in the 1840s, and the United States built its national immigration policy with a series of restrictions on Asian migration that started in 1875, expanded through the next fifty years, and remained largely in place until 1965.[8] It was only with the 1965 Immigration and Nationality Act—which abolished national-origin quotas and established family unification and employment qualification as the primary means for people to legally migrate to the United States—that U.S. policies on immigration moved away from national-origin restrictions toward a more general framework on who is allowed to enter the country, who is allowed to remain here, and who can become a U.S. citizen.

While the 1965 reforms to immigration law made significant headway in addressing long-standing problems of racial and national-origin exclusion in U.S. immigration policy, it also created a new set of problems, notably the growth of the unauthorized, or "illegal," immigrant population in the United States, who now number nearly 12 million.[9] As other scholars have noted, the 1965 immigration law created, for the first time, numerical limits on migration from the Western Hemisphere. Around the same time, Congress also abolished the Bracero Program, which had provided a way for millions of agricultural workers from Mexico to work in the United States as migrant laborers from the 1940s through the early 1960s.[10] Soon thereafter, the population of undocumented immigrants in the United States soared dramatically, as large numbers of employers had grown reliant on immigrant labor, primarily from Mexico, and immigrants themselves had established fairly strong networks of migration connecting home regions to particular places in the United States. As we elaborate later in this book, the 1986 Immigration Reform and Control Act sought to address this growing problem by providing legalization to over 1 million immigrants and introducing federal employer sanctions. These reforms brought only a temporary reprieve, however, to the problem of unauthorized migration: the number declined from 4 million in 1986 to about 2.5 million in 1989, but subsequently rose to 8 million by 2000 and exceeded 11 million by 2005.[11]

Since the 1960s, then, illegal immigration has become one of the most salient and pressing problems of immigration policy in the United States. In this book, we focus on the last decade of federal efforts to address the problem, including attempts not only at legalization and regularization but also at greater border enforcement and deportation.

In the summer of 2001, President George W. Bush proposed a comprehensive fix to the nation's immigration policies, including a path to legalization on par with the 1986 amnesty law signed by President Ronald Reagan. The September 11, 2001, attacks effectively postponed such efforts as the national debate focused centrally on the wars in Afghanistan and Iraq and domestic security measures such as the PATRIOT Act. In 2005 the Bush administration flagged comprehensive immigration reform as an important policy priority for the president's second term, lending public support for bipartisan efforts under way in Congress in 2006 and 2007. Those efforts failed, however, as the issue became polarized along partisan lines and support for immigrant legalization plummeted among Republican legislators. Many conservative media outlets and party activists branded any legalization effort as an amnesty, evoking memories of the prior round of immigrant legalization under the

1986 Immigration Reform Control Act. While the 1986 act had garnered bipartisan support in Congress and won the signature of Ronald Reagan, conservative activists had managed to make "amnesty" a pariah twenty years later, and they pushed Republican leaders to introduce bills that were entirely focused on enforcement. Thus, federal legislation on immigration ground to a halt in Congress, either because of opposition in the Republican-controlled House of Representatives or because of filibusters by Republicans in the Senate.

By 2010, even the most popular aspect of immigration reform—the DREAM Act, which would have granted a path to citizenship to those who came to the United States illegally as young children—failed to pass Congress.[12] There was a glimmer of hope for immigration reform after the 2012 elections, as Mitt Romney lost the presidential race owing in significant part to his dismal standing among Latino and Asian American voters. Many Republican leaders pushed for immigration reform as a way to repair the party's national fortunes, and about a dozen Republican senators voted in favor of a comprehensive reform package in 2013. However, these efforts met stiff resistance in the U.S. House, and immigration policy became stalemated in Congress once again.[13]

Importantly, the framing of immigration policy figured heavily in congressional debates on legalization and in related media coverage. Thus, for example, pro-immigrant activists tended to portray legalization as an opportunity or pathway to citizenship that would be earned after immigrants paid their taxes, learned English, and stayed clear of legal trouble during an extended period of temporary legal status. On the other hand, conservative activists denounced any legalization effort as an "amnesty" that would reward those who broke the country's laws and encourage more to do the same. The casting of amnesty in a negative light was perhaps surprising, as many Republican legislators had voted in favor of the 1986 amnesty and Ronald Reagan, a Republican president and conservative hero, had signed the bill into law. As we show in this book, however, anti-immigration activists have since succeeded in portraying the prior amnesty as a legislative mistake and policy failure, encouraging even more illegal immigration to the United States since its passage. In addition to "pathways" and "amnesties," immigration reform provided many other framing opportunities to proponents and opponents alike.

Importantly, framing efforts on immigration were not confined to congressional legislation or the activities of interest groups—they often played out in extensive news coverage on immigration. A major part of this book is devoted to examining these immigration policy frames as they play out in news and editorial coverage, in both newspapers and news television networks. We examine variation in the use of such frames over time and across news outlets, particularly between mainstream sources and those that are more clearly conservative or liberal. Finally, we rely on survey experiments to examine the potential causal effects of these frames on American public opinion.

Of course, frames in communication may serve important purposes even if they do not have strong effects on public opinion. First, news media may adopt certain frames to make themselves understood to their readers and viewers. Representatives may choose certain words or phrases to send important signals to interest groups and issue constituencies (for example, using terms like "illegal alien" and "amnesty" to appeal to particular groups or to differentiate themselves more clearly from each other). Other elites, such as issue experts, may use particular frames (such as "unauthorized immigrants") that are more reflective of dominant usage in scholarly communities. Finally, elected officials and advocates may adopt particular frames in the belief that they could be consequential for opinion, as was clearly evident in the case of President Obama's Rose Garden speech, in which he justified his decision to defer the deportation of thousands of young "undocumented" immigrants.[14]

Looking ahead, our book is motivated by two sets of key questions:

1.   How are policies toward undocumented immigrants framed in news media, and how does this framing vary across outlets?

2.   Are the frames consequential for public opinion, and do these effects vary among different types of respondents?

To answer these questions, we analyze a set of original survey experiments between 2007 and 2014 and conduct content analyses of news coverage during the same time period. Our content analysis uses both quantitative and qualitative coding strategies in analyzing news coverage from liberal, mainstream, and more conservative media outlets. For print media, we use the *New York Times, New York Post, Washington Post,* and *Washington Times.* For cable media, we use CNN, MSNBC, and Fox News. To connect frames to public opinion, we rely on a host of survey experiments conducted between 2007 and 2014, which we describe in more detail in chapter 2. We rely on survey experiments because they provide a much cleaner test of causality than trying to link changes in media coverage of immigration to aggregate polling data.

Our Contribution

While immigration policy has taken on several new and interesting dimensions in the last decade, much public opinion research on immigration still analyzes American views on immigration policy in a fairly blunt manner: the extent to which immigration is an important issue to voters; whether immigration is generally a good thing or bad thing for the coun-

Figure 1.2   Views Among American Voters on Whether Immigration Should Be Kept at Its Present Level, Increased, or Decreased, 1999–2013

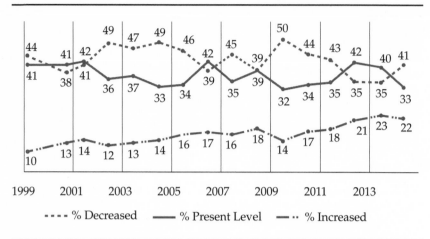

    ---- % Decreased   —— % Present Level   —·· % Increased

Source: Gallup surveys (Saad 2014).

try; and whether Americans want to increase, decrease, or maintain the current levels of immigration into the country. Certainly, these are important questions to help get a general sense of where Americans stand on immigration: survey evidence from the last two decades shows a steady increase in the proportion of Americans who wish to have more immigrants coming into the United States (figure 1.2) and a strong, steady sense that immigration is generally good for the United States (figure 1.3). Surveys have also shown immigration policy to be a relatively low-salience issue, but one in which the public's attention does respond to political developments, such as the legislative push for comprehensive immigration reform in 2007 and Arizona's passage of its immigration enforcement law in 2010.[15]

In addition, much research has explored the factors that may influence public opinion along these dimensions, including the influence of such factors as perceptions of economic threat, beliefs about Americanism, and the framing of racial and ethnic cues.[16] There is also now a fairly extensive literature on public perception toward immigrants, including group stereotypes and beliefs about their effects on American society.[17] However, opinion studies of immigration policy still primarily use either fairly standard, blunt measures—such as whether immigration generally or immigration by a particular group should be increased or decreased— or more tangential measures to immigration policy, such as stereotypes about immigrants and whether English should be declared the official language of the United States.[18] As we show in this book, these measures

Figure 1.3   Views Among American Voters on Whether Immigration Is a Good Thing or a Bad Thing for the United States, 2001–2014

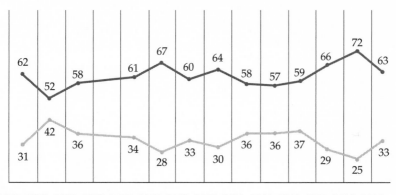

2001 2003 2003 2005 2005 2007 2009 2009 2011 2011 2011 2011 2013 2013

——— % Good Thing   ——— % Bad Thing

Source: Gallup surveys (Saad 2014).

do not fully capture the policy debate and media discourse on immigration policy in the past decade.

There are some newer studies that look at media framing on particular immigration policies, such as legalization and the DREAM Act, as we discuss in subsequent chapters. However, these studies typically look only at a handful of frames on one or two issues.[19] Furthermore, there are few efforts to link public opinion on immigration to actual media coverage, with work by Marisa Abrajano, Johanna Dunaway, and their colleagues as notable exceptions.[20] In this book, we not only look at the content of media coverage across many different dimensions of immigration policy but also explore how different frames present in the media influence public opinion.

The crux of our argument is that while many forces shape opinion on immigration, the framing of policy information plays an integral role. One key element in the new media environment is the diversity of voices present in the media. We argue that the ways in which immigrants and immigration policy are described will vary across liberal, mainstream, and conservative media outlets. More specifically, conservative outlets should be more likely to use terms like "illegal" to describe those without legal status. We consider these frames akin to "equivalency frames," as initially introduced by Amos Tversky and Daniel Kahneman and later typologized by Jamie Druckman.[21] Druckman contrasts these frames, in which different phrases are used to describe logically equivalent conditions, to "issue frames," in which different aspects of a condition or policy are emphasized or deemphasized. For example, advocates on the right were quick to brand comprehensive immigration reform as "amnesty," while those on the left attempted to use language reflecting an opportunity of citizenship for those who have already been contributing to U.S. society. We expect conservative, liberal, and mainstream media outlets to also vary in their use of issue frames.

Drawing from the literature on framing in public opinion, we argue that these different frames in communication are consequential for public opinion on different dimensions of immigration policy. For example, framing people as "illegal immigrants" should lead to less support for progressive immigration policy compared to frames that use terms such as "undocumented" or "unauthorized." Similarly, on issue framing, the amnesty frame should lead to less support for comprehensive immigration reform compared to the opportunity frame. Throughout the book, we explore the effects of a variety of frames that are relevant across many different dimensions of immigration policy, including comprehensive immigration reform, the DREAM Act, and enforcement policies. We elaborate on our expectations as we introduce the frames that are prevalent (and not so prevalent) across these dimensions. We also explore whether the effects of these frames vary depending on one's partisanship (and media viewership), ethnicity and family immigration history, and level of education. That is, we look at whether certain groups of individuals may be more accepting of or more resistant to certain frames.

Looking Ahead

In the chapters that follow, we provide a detailed look at media framing on immigration policy and the effects of many of those frames on American public opinion. In chapter 2, we provide a deeper look at framing, starting with a general overview of framing in the social science literature before proceeding closer to our enterprise—an examination of framing immigrants and immigration policy in news coverage and public opinion. We present a more focused discussion of how frames work to influence opinion, different types of frames, and the factors that may cause some individuals or groups to react differently to media framing on immigration. Importantly, we also discuss the ways in which we analyze the framing of immigration in news coverage and how we propose to test the potential effects of many of these frames using a wide variety of survey experiments.

Next, in chapter 3, we focus on immigrant legalization, which has been a critical component of various immigration reform attempts in the past decade. We begin this chapter by discussing the historical precedent for immigrant legalization (then labeled an "amnesty") in 1986, the legislative and policy developments that led to the proposal of comprehensive immigration reform in 2006 and 2007, and the rhetorical attempts by moderate Republicans and Democrats to use terms that avoided mentions of "amnesty." After discussing the historical and institutional contexts, we present a content analysis of media coverage of comprehensive immigration reform across print and cable news. As expected, the tone of the legalization coverage mirrored the ideological leanings of the news source, but we also have some unexpected findings: economic frames and family frames received the most frequent coverage, while the legality frame received considerably less coverage. Next, we focus attention on how the term "amnesty" is invoked in news coverage of comprehensive immigration reform; we find that mentions of amnesty have declined over time, although they remain fairly high in conservative news sources such as Fox News. Finally, we examine the potential ways in which these different frames affect public opinion on legalization policy. We find, through analysis of various survey experiments conducted between 2007 and 2014, that the amnesty frame has the strongest and most consistent effect on reducing support for immigrant legalization. We also find significant differences in support for legalization, based on how long undocumented immigrants have lived in the United States. Interestingly, however, news coverage does not draw much attention to length of stay in the United States, and our survey experiment findings suggest that pro-immigration advocates may be able to shift public opinion by focusing their messaging efforts on the long-term resident population of undocumented immigrants. Finally, we also find significant effects for the law-abiding versus law-breaking frame, and again, the comparative paucity of these mentions in news coverage suggests opportunities for immigration conservatives to tilt public opinion in their favor by consistently relying on the law-breaking frame.

After comprehensive immigration reform failed in 2007, proponents of reform turned to piecemeal strategies by taking more popular aspects of reform and trying to pass them separately. The DREAM Act was one such piece of legislation in that it sought to provide citizenship to children who came to the United States in an undocumented status and had served in the military or graduated from college. In chapter 4, we first provide a historical overview of the DREAM Act, from its promising start as the most popular component of immigration reform in 2006 to its failure to pass Congress in 2010 despite having Democrats in control of Congress and the presidency. Next, we provide a content analysis of how the DREAM Act was covered in the news. In particular, we pay attention to the relative prominence in news stories of frames that emphasized the consideration of the act's beneficiaries as those who came to the United States as young children or as those who had no choice in the matter of having a legal way to enter and stay in the United States. We also consider the extent to which the term "amnesty" was invoked in news coverage of the DREAM Act, and whether this varied by the ideology of the news source. Overall, we find consistent differences between conservative and mainstream sources: Fox News and conservative print sources were more likely to mention "amnesty" in their coverage of the DREAM Act, and mainstream sources were more likely to provide empathetic news coverage, with more episodic (human interest) framing. Finally, we examine whether these various issue frames made any difference for voter opinion. We find that the amnesty frame reduced support for the DREAM Act, particularly among independents and Republicans. We also find that the child frame was especially effective in moving Republican opinion on the DREAM Act in the early years, when the issue was less well known among the general public. By 2012, however, and with the president's DACA program gaining national attention and prominent Republican opposition, the child frame was much less effective in swaying Republican opinion on the DREAM Act.

After devoting chapters 3 and 4 to permissive solutions to the problem of illegal immigration, we turn our attention in chapter 5 to deportations as a proposed solution. First, we provide a historical overview of deportations and other enforcement-heavy solutions. Next, we provide a content analysis of how these issues have been covered in print and cable news. For border security and deportations, we pay close attention to whether the issue of terrorism is raised in conjunction with immigration. Finally, we examine variations in the use of counterframes in news coverage of immigration enforcement, ranging from the deep roots put down by many illegal immigrants in the United States to the disruptive harm of deportations to families and, potentially, to the economy. In contrast to findings in our other chapters, we find that pro-deportation coverage is more common than con-deportation coverage, regardless of the ideological leaning of the news outlet. We also find that the rule of law is the most common frame in news coverage of deportations, followed by public safety. By contrast, con-deportation frames, such as family disruption and economic costs, receive much less news coverage.

Interestingly, we find in our analysis of the survey experiment data that public support for mass deportations is significantly lower among those who are exposed to the economic costs frame. We also find that support for deportation is lower when respondents are cued to think about long-term residents as opposed to more recent arrivals. Given the relative dearth of news coverage on both these dimensions (the economic costs of deportation and length of stay), our findings indicate potential opportunities for pro-immigrant advocates to shift public opinion against mass deportations. Our findings also indicate that much existing news coverage, with its tendency to focus on legality and public safety, tends to favor more restrictive opinion on immigrant deportation.

Finally, while most of our book is focused on policy frames, we also draw attention to the ways in which news media describe immigrants without legal status. Thus, in chapter 6, we ask: How are these immigrants labeled in news media coverage? Does the use of these terms vary over time and across ideology of news source? And what effects might the use of these terms have on voter support for public policies on immigration?

This chapter examines the sharp lines drawn between conservative advocates on immigration reform who insist on using the term "illegal," liberal advocates who argue that the term "illegal" should be dropped in favor of more neutral terms such as "undocumented," and still other experts insisting that the term "unauthorized" more accurately captures the population that would benefit from a legalization program. Next, we analyze the prevalence of these terms across print, network television, and cable news and find that the term "illegal" is used most of the time, regardless of news source. However, we do find that the frequency of the term receded among avowedly liberal news outlets after 2008 and among mainstream outlets after 2012. By contrast, we find much stronger differences in the use of the terms "undocumented" and "illegal" by elected officials, with Democrats much more likely to use the former and Republicans much more likely to rely on the latter. We end this chapter by analyzing a series of survey experiments on whether variations in these equivalency frames have any effect on voter support for public policies such as legalization, the DREAM Act, and deportation. Finally, in our concluding chapter, we highlight the key findings across the chapters, discuss their implications, and indicate potential avenues for future research on this topic.

Overall, our findings support the contention that there is a wide degree of variation in media frames on immigration across liberal, mainstream, and conservative media outlets. However, this variation is much more noticeable in how news media describe policy issues than in how they describe the immigrants themselves. The vast majority of media coverage uses the term "illegal" to describe those without legal status. We found very little use of terms such as "undocumented" or "unauthorized" in our content analysis. However, we do find more variation in the use of different issue frames. For example, conservative outlets are more likely to use the term "amnesty" for any program that provides some measure of deportation. We also find that coverage of the legal and economic facets of immigration varies considerably by the ideological orientation of the news outlet.

Our analysis of frames in both news coverage and public opinion reveals important findings that may not be apparent in separate analyses of each. For example, we find in our survey analysis that duration of immigrant stay in the United States has a strong and consistent effect on public opinion, increasing support for legalization and decreasing support for deportation. And yet our content analysis reveals that news and opinion coverage of immigration makes little mention of how long undocumented immigrants have been in the United States. This suggests that, akin to Frank Luntz's recommendation to legalization opponents that they consistently invoke amnesty when they discuss immigration, pro-legalization advocates might have better luck in moving public opinion if they consistently emphasize that their policies would benefit long-term immigrant residents.[22]

Another major finding in our book is that the amnesty frame has a strong and fairly consistent effect in reducing support for immigrant legalization, even when it involves policies that benefit immigrants who arrived in the United States as children, like the DREAM Act. Indeed, we find that mentioning amnesty dramatically reduces support for the DREAM Act even when the child frame is included. Not only does amnesty wipe out any boost associated with describing policies as benefiting young children, but people exposed to these dueling frames are much less likely to support the DREAM Act than those in the control condition, who are exposed to neither frame. Furthermore, on legalization, the DREAM Act, and deportations, we find that negative frames are generally more effective than positive frames; this finding is consistent with work in public opinion on negativity bias.[23]

Finally, contrary to the beliefs of many proponents and opponents of immigration reform, we find that the difference between using "illegal" and using "undocumented" makes little difference with respect to opinion on policy: those who are asked about "illegal immigrants" are just as supportive of legalization measures as those asked about "undocumented immigrants." Importantly, however, we do find that those with immigrant family backgrounds sometimes react against the use of the term "illegal," expressing even greater support for legalization and greater opposition to deportation when they are exposed to the term. Finally, we find much greater effects that are based on how policies are framed. In some cases, such as opinion on legalization, our policy frames make the difference between adopting a restrictive stance or a neutral stance. In other cases—namely, support for the DREAM Act—the effects are even stronger, accounting for the difference between a restrictive stance and a progressive stance.

As this book goes to press, immigration policy is once again on the national agenda, with candidates from both parties making immigration a frequently discussed topic in the 2016 presidential campaign. If this book had been written three years ago, many would have considered our detailed attention to restrictive policy proposals and negative rhetoric on immigration to be outdated. The Republican Party's massive electoral losses in 2012 were blamed largely on the party's restrictive policy stances and harsh rhetoric on immigration. Many Republican officials and conservative opinion leaders in 2013 called for the party to moderate its rhetoric on immigration and to back comprehensive immigration reform. The Republican National Committee even went so far as to generate an extensive study, *The Growth and Opportunity Project*, which laid out a road map for Republicans to win the presidency by ramping up outreach to Latinos and immigrant voters.[24]

Within a year of the report's publication, however, it was apparent to many House Republicans that immigration restriction would continue to be a powerful impulse among primary voters. As we discuss more fully in chapters 3 and 4, the electoral logic of winning House primaries led to the defeat of "pro-amnesty" leaders like Eric Cantor and killed any hopes of immigration reform. This political dynamic carried through to the 2016 presidential primaries, with restrictionist candidates like Donald Trump vaulting to the top of the Republican pack after a series of incendiary comments on immigration, while pro-legalization candidates like Marco Rubio and Jeb Bush struggled to gain traction among primary voters.

Thus, as we have seen many times over the past decade, the problem of unauthorized immigration has returned as a salient issue for American voters, with proposed solutions ranging from permissive measures that provide a pathway to citizenship to more punitive measures that focus on border enforcement and deportation. As our study indicates, these proposed solutions will continue to offer significant framing opportunities on immigration policy—for proponents as well as opponents—with significant consequences for public opinion and electoral politics.

2

Media Framing and Effects on Public Opinion

W E BRIEFLY sketched out our argument in chapter 1 for the importance of frames to understanding public opinion on immigration policies. In this chapter, we dig more deeply to develop our theoretical arguments and present the methodological approaches we take to testing them. To refresh, the crux of our argument is that while many forces shape opinion on immigration, the framing of policy information plays an integral role. First, we argue that the ways in which immigrants and immigration policy are described will vary across liberal, mainstream, and conservative media outlets. Second, we expect to find that different frames in communication are consequential for public opinion on different dimensions of immigration policy.

We begin this chapter by presenting a richer discussion of framing. After clearly defining what frames are, we discuss how they are used by social movement organizations, politicians, and the media to advance their causes. We then discuss how the increase in partisan media has created in media discourse a more diverse collection of frames, which we expect to vary according to the ideological slant of the media source in question. To explore how this plays out in the domain of immigration policies, we detail our methodological approach to testing variation in frames across news sources.

After discussing the supply of frames by elites, we turn to a discussion of the general literature on intergroup attitudes and the impact of various cues on public opinion toward and evaluations of racial and ethnic minorities. We then turn to a more focused discussion of the influence of frames on public opinion in general and on immigration policy more specifically. Highlighting the particular types of frames we are looking at, we discuss how we expect them to influence opinions. Much of our focus is on equivalency and issue frames, though we also look at episodic and thematic frames. In addition to discussing general expectations, we

16

also argue that the effect of different frames may vary according to one's partisan identification, especially in an era of increased polarization, and family immigration history, given that the issue will be higher in relevance to those who are first- and second-generation in the United States. Finally, we discuss our methodological approach to testing the effects of frames on public opinion: analysis of survey experiments conducted from 2007 to 2014.

Types of Frames

Framing Theory

In his classic work *Frame Analysis*, the sociologist Erving Goffman conceived of a frame as a cognitive structure that helps individuals to make sense of their surroundings.[1] Frames structure what individuals perceive to be most salient in understanding the world. These understandings, in turn, help organize their experiences and ultimately influence behavior. Given that frames are open to different cognitive interpretations, framing theory helps us understand how people might see the same information or setting and come to very different conclusions about it.

Many sociologists have explored how this plays out at the individual level across a variety of domains. In looking at a Latino public housing project in Boston, Mario Small shows that what matters most to whether individuals participate in the community are the frames through which they view the neighborhood.[2] Those who frame participation as being linked to the community's history of political activity are more likely to participate, while those who view the community as just another housing project are less likely to. Frames might also help us to understand differences in educational and employment achievement, both within and across groups. For example, using in-depth interviews, Alford Young finds that African American men of different education levels have very different visions of a good life and frame a good job in different ways.[3] In seeking to explain the exceptional achievement of Asian American immigrant children, even among those whose parents have limited economic resources, Jennifer Lee and Min Zhou argue that certain frames, like a success frame and a good education frame, are important, but that these frames are shaped and reinforced by the selectivity of the immigrants authorized by immigration laws to enter the country, the ethnic cultural institutions and support networks that develop to support the frames, and the gateway institutions and stereotypes that further reinforce them.[4]

Given that frames help individuals make sense of the world, it is no surprise that social movement organizations, political elites, and other relevant actors try to influence the frames that make it into public discourse. Scholars often refer to these as "frames in communication," or "media frames," by which they mean "the words, images, phrases, and presentation styles that a speaker (e.g., a politician, a media outlet) uses when relaying information about an issue or event to an audience . . . The chosen frame reveals what the speaker sees as relevant to the topic at hand."[5]

Before turning to our narrower focus of media framing, we briefly discuss how frames are used by social movements to mobilize supporters to their cause, for the light it sheds on the frame-building process. One important theoretical framework has been frame alignment theory, which builds off of work by Goffman but also connects to frames in communication. "Frame alignment" refers to "the linkage of individual and social movement organization (SMO) interpretive orientations, such that some set of individual interests, values and beliefs and SMO activities, goals, and ideology are congruent and complementary."[6] According to this theory, successful mobilization by social movement organizations can occur only when frame alignment is present, and it involves four different processes. One important process is "frame bridging," or the linking of frames that are ideologically congruent but may be structurally unconnected on a particular issue; frame bridging serves to tap into a broader pool of support. A second process is "frame amplification," which involves the "clarification and invigoration of an interpretive frame that bears on an issue."[7] Frame amplification highlights either values relevant to the issue, such as social justice, or belief frames that speak to the seriousness of the problem, identify the cause of the problem, or shape beliefs about the target. A third process is "frame extension"—extending frames outside of their initial conceptualization to attract a broader group of support. Finally, "frame transformation" requires the specification of new values or reinterpretation of old ones.

A wide array of scholars have applied this theoretical construct to understanding both successful and unsuccessful mobilizations by social movement organizations (and countermobilization efforts) across an array of areas, such as the abortion movement, the peace movement, terrorist organizations, and local environmental contamination responses.[8]

Political elites are another set of actors who try to advance their favored frames in the public arena, often after testing out frames with focus groups.[9] Democratic and Republican Party elites often vie to be the first to frame a particular issue, since they perceive that such frames are more likely to stick in the public's mind. Once a bill is introduced, opponents try to develop frames to kill it. To give just a few examples, on the issue of comprehensive immigration reform, as we discussed in the introduction, opponents were quick to brand it as an amnesty. Looking beyond immigration, framing has been an important part of legislative fights on tax policy (for example, whether the term "estate tax" or "death tax" is used) as well as on health policy, perhaps most famously with former Republican vice-presidential candidate Sarah Palin decrying the Affordable Care Act of 2010 as sanctioning "death panels" for the elderly.[10] Whether or not these frames are consequential for public opinion, political elites certainly believe in the importance of framing policies to attract supporters.

Media Framing

Both social movement organizations and political elites ultimately try to get their favored frames adopted and amplified in media coverage, since that is the way in which most potential audiences are exposed to information. And as we noted in chapter 1, while public opinion does not directly move with whatever slant the news is taking, the news media play an influential role in shaping *what* and *how* people think about an issue.[11] Much of this influence works through frames.[12]

In turning more specifically to different types of media frames, we focus on three types in this book: episodic versus thematic frames, equivalency frames, and issue frames. An "episodic frame" is a way of presenting "an issue by offering a specific example, case study, or event-oriented report."[13] By contrast, a "thematic frame" is a way of presenting an issue in a broader context, using generalities and abstractions instead of more concrete, real-life examples. Alternative, nontechnical terms for episodic and thematic frames are "human-interest stories" and "general stories," respectively, and we occasionally use these terms throughout the book. The following is an example of an episodically framed article from the *Washington Post* (episodic terms in bold):

> **Residents of a Bethesda condominium complex** who waged a relentless campaign for weeks to prevent the deportation of a beloved building engineer were ecstatic to hear yesterday that Immigration and Customs Enforcement has granted a deferral to **Marco Antonio Rua,** permitting him to remain in the country. . . .
>
> **"Here's my statement—yaaayyyyy!!!" said Marcia Weinberg,** a board member at the condominium and a resident. **"I am also proud of America, because at times like this, you can get very upset and angry, and I knew America was better** than the way it was being shown and the way it was showing itself. This gives me a renewed faith in my country and its sense of righteousness and also in its compassion.[14]

Contrast this episodic story from the *Washington Post* to the impersonal portrayal of deportation in many conservative outlets, such as the following thematic example from the *Washington Times,* which presents the deportation in a much more abstract, removed, and generic style (thematic terms in bold):

The Border Patrol and ICE [U.S. Immigration and Customs Enforcement] are the two chief immigration law enforcement branches of the federal government. **Border Patrol agents' jurisdiction runs along the nation's international boundaries,** and many of the illegal immigrants they apprehend are returned—usually straight to Mexico—rather than put in formal removal proceedings. . . .

ICE, meanwhile, generally handles removals, which are more formal proceedings complete with potential penalties. Mr. Smith's committee obtained **documents that show 72,000 people caught** by the Border Patrol and sent to ICE under the Border Patrol's Alien Transfer Exit Program are being **included in the ICE statistics.** Administration officials told the committee they have been including **those numbers in their official count since 2011.**[15]

Thus, while episodic news coverage on immigration tends to focus on stories of particular individuals or families, thematic news coverage tends to focus on statistics like numbers of border apprehensions and deportations. As we discuss later in this chapter, the style of a frame can have important consequences for public opinion.

Also, on any given policy, various considerations along different dimensions may be highlighted. Scholars typically refer to these as issue frames. Elite decisions to frame issues in different ways can alter the weight that individuals give to some considerations, which can then lead to alternate responses.[16] One example that has been studied in the framing literature is whether the KKK should be allowed to hold a rally. If the issue is framed as one of public safety, then people are less supportive of letting the KKK hold a rally; however, if the issue is framed as one of free speech, then people are more supportive.[17]

The media have a wide variety of issue frames available to employ on the issue of immigration. For example, in discussing comprehensive immigration reform, media coverage might focus on the economic costs of unauthorized migration. Below is an example from the appearance of former congressman Alan West (R-FL) on a March 2013 segment of *Your World with Neil Cavuto* on Fox News: "When you look at our economic situation here in the United States of America, are we going to be capable of having another six million or seven million people that are going to be more so dependent on the federal government and social welfare type of policies and programs."[18] Alternatively, a more positive frame might focus on immigration reform as a way of keeping families together, as indicated by the following segment from the MSNBC show *Up with Chris Hayes:* "Rep. Steven Hosford (D-NV): 'I think that's what adds to the hypocrisy of those on the other side who advocate for a guest worker program, who also say they stand for family values. I believe our immigration policy should keep families together. . . . They should promote the parents taking care of their kids and kids being able to pursue their education and career goals and serving in the military."[19]

In these examples, listeners may become less supportive of permissive immigration policies when exposed to the economic cost frame compared to their response to the family frame.[20] These different types of issue frames may connect to values or beliefs, as in frame amplification, or they may introduce new ways of looking at an issue, as in frame transformation.

Finally, the media can frame logically equivalent information in different ways. Often, this entails a positive or negative presentation of the same information. In everyday parlance, we might describe a glass as half-full or half-empty. With respect to public policy,

> Examples of equivalency communication frames include alternative descriptions, such as "90% employment" versus "10% unemployment." . . . These are similar to emphasis or issue communication frames insofar as both put the respondent's focus on specific considerations (e.g., free speech or public safety; unemployment or employment). However, equivalency frames employ materially identical descriptions (e.g., 90% employment = 10% unemployment; from a rationality perspective, the frames should not matter), whereas emphasis frames focus on qualitatively different yet potentially relevant considerations (e.g., free speech or public safety).[21]

In referencing particular groups, the media might refer to "the poor" or to "those on welfare." Those who oppose abortion might be labeled "pro-life" or "anti-abortion." Some refer to the most recent overhaul of health care as "the Affordable Care Act," while others label it "Obamacare." On the issue of immigration, the media might describe those without legal status as "illegal immigrants," "illegal aliens," "undocumented immigrants," or "unauthorized immigrants." All of these different terms are logically equivalent but prime different associations.

In the next section, we turn to a more focused discussion of the literature on media coverage of immigration, how we expect frames on immigration to vary across different news outlets, and our methodology for making this assessment. We then discuss ways in which frames work to influence opinion and the factors that may cause some individuals or groups to react differently to media framing on immigration.

The Supply of Media Frames

Scholarship on the supply of immigration frames in the media generally falls into one of two groups. One group is primarily concerned with vividly describing media coverage of immigration and then critically analyzing this coverage to examine its implications for race relations and policymaking in the United States.[22] One example is Leo Chavez's *Shadowed Lives*, an account of how the media and other institutions have systematically painted immigrants, and particularly Mexican immigrants, in very negative, foreign, and un-American terms. The second, and larger, group focuses more on explaining the variation in coverage across news organizations and over time, offering three primary theoretical explanations for this variation in volume and content.

First are "demand-driven" or "economic" explanations grounded in previous work on other political issues.[23] These scholars argue that the media's coverage of immigration is but a reflection of their target audiences' preferences.[24] Another strand of research focuses on the role of selection bias. These explanations attribute variation to choices made by journalists and editors.[25] Scholarship in this area finds that immigration coverage varies tremendously (that is, in tone, issues frames, and restrictive language) depending on the news anchor and the news organization and even after controlling for the difference between news and opinion stories.[26] Finally, a newer line of research examines the role of immigrant agency and the political opportunity structure. This explanation examines the confluence of the level of immigrant political participation with the types of opportunities afforded them by the political system given their legal status. Scholars like Irene Bloemraad, Els de Graauw, and Rebecca Hamlin find that the media tend to dedicate more media coverage to immigrant groups whose entry into the United States is valorized and who are active in politics, while Caitlin Patler and Roberto Gonzales find that social movement organizations can overcome these barriers and provide important counternarratives to shape media coverage.[27] Finally, Karthick Ramakrishnan and Andrea Silva find that electoral developments and White House–Congress dynamics can overshadow the importance of the ground realities of immigrant and asylee flows in shaping immigration coverage.[28]

While scholars continue to work on developing more comprehensive models explaining variation in immigration coverage, few studies have described and explained the media's coverage of specific immigration policies or explicitly focused on the coverage of undocumented immigrants. Instead, most work focuses on the broader issue of immigration and the plight of all immigrants. Additionally, almost all previous research uses the newspaper medium as the sole data source to test theories that apply to other media (cable, Internet, broadcast, radio) that are subject to a number of different forces and constraints and thus may behave very differently. Moreover, most published works are based on content analyses of immigration stories drawn for a period of time of less than a year. In this book, we build on these prior works on media coverage and make the following contributions:

1. Ours is the first study to comprehensively examine variation in coverage of specific immigration *policies* rather than immigration as a larger issue.

2. We pay considerable attention to cable news outlets, which prior scholarship has shown to be significantly related to partisan opinion.

3. We focus on various dimensions of framing, such as tone, episodic framing, and policy-specific framing, rather than simply coding for "anti-immigrant" or "pro-immigrant" news coverage.

Our Expectations on News Coverage

When it comes to news coverage of a socially and politically divisive issue like immigration, we expect news coverage of undocumented immigrants and immigration policy to vary according to the ideological leanings of the news source. Much has been written on the ideological polarization of news coverage in the United States, particularly with the decline of network news and the growth of cable news.[29] There are strong debates over whether ideologically tilted news coverage has an independent effect on public opinion or whether Americans largely self-select into watching news that reflects their political beliefs or otherwise choose to opt in or out of partisan news coverage.[30] Regardless of the selection mechanism, however, there is broad agreement that news coverage in the United States has grown more ideologically divided over time, with a particularly strong divergence in television news after the launch of Fox News in 1996.[31]

Thus, we might generally expect news coverage of immigration policy and of undocumented immigrants to vary according to the ideological leanings of the news source. Of the print media outlets we examine, we expect the *New York Post* and *Washington Times* to have more restrictive news coverage than the *New York Times* and *Washington Post*, because the *New York Post* and the *Washington Times* are generally considered more conservative print outlets while the latter two are considered mainstream outlets.[32]

When it comes to cable news, however, we do not expect these general expectations to hold across the outlets we consider (CNN, Fox, and MSNBC), at least not in the earlier part of this news period (2007 and 2008). While Fox News is generally reputed to be a conservative news channel, CNN featured conservative voices like Glenn Beck from January 2006 through October 2008 and Lou Dobbs from August 2000 through November 2009.[33] In particular, Lou Dobbs's controversial conservative coverage of issues like immigration and the "birther" issue mobilized so much protest from groups such as Presente.org, Media Matters, and the Southern Poverty Law Center that CNN decided to buy out the remainder of Dobbs's contract for an $8 million severance payment in November 2009.[34] Finally, MSNBC is now known as a left-leaning news channel after the election of 2009, when the network allied itself more closely with the positions of the Obama White House and in critical opposition to conservative movements such as the Tea Party.[35] However, this was less true prior to Obama's 2009 election, when the network commonly featured well-known conservatives such as Tucker Carlson, the host of *Tucker*, and Patrick Buchanan, an outspoken conservative critic of illegal immigration and social progressivism.

Thus, for CNN and MSNBC, we would expect to see changes in news coverage on immigration before 2009 for MSNBC and after 2010 for CNN, with coverage that is net permissive at MSNBC after 2009 and more split prior to 2009, and coverage that is split at CNN after 2010 and more conservative prior to 2010. Finally, we expect Fox News to have the most restrictive coverage throughout this period. Of course, we use "restrictive" and "permissive" here as shorthand for a more detailed set of codes and classifications, which we elaborate on in the next section.

Content Analysis Methods

To investigate our expectations, we conducted content analyses examining immigration news stories from the *New York Times, Washington Post, New York Post, Washington Times,* CNN, MSNBC, and Fox News. We included the *New York Times* and *Washington Post* because they are the premier national sources of news coverage on matters of public policy, with the *New York Times* in particular setting the agenda for news coverage by other newspapers across the country.[36] We also include stories from the *New York Post* and *Washington Times* because of their relative uniqueness among large-circulation newspapers in having a conservative tilt to their news coverage (as opposed to editorials and opinion columns). Finally, we drew data from the largest and most frequently watched cable news organizations—Fox News, CNN, and MSNBC.

In terms of time period, we draw news stories from 2007 to 2014 to mirror the period in which we conduct our survey experiments and those years when immigration was a major item on the agenda. The population of immigration stories depends on the question under consideration. We draw stories specifically on immigration and the DREAM Act to evaluate questions on the DREAM Act; on immigration and the path to citizenship for questions on legalization; and on immigration and deportation for questions on deportation. However, we look at all immigration stories to explore questions on the terms used to describe immigrants without legal status.

For our coding strategy, we employ both quantitative and qualitative content analysis. We use quantitative content analysis to explore frames that contain key phrases or words (such as "amnesty," "pathway to citizenship," "undocumented immigrant," and "illegal alien"). However, many important questions do not lend themselves as easily to simple quantitative content analysis. For example, coding the tone of immigration coverage necessitates reading words, phrases, and passages in their entirety and in context. Certain issue frames can also be much more accurately identified using qualitative coding, since many policy frames can be difficult to distinguish using keyword search strategies (for example, distinguishing between the economic benefits and economic costs of immigration policies when searching for a term like "unemployment"). Given the more intensive nature of qualitative coding, we code all news stories (the universe) up to fifty stories per year for any given source, and we code a sample when they exceed that number.[37]

Finally, while the coding strategy on particular policies varies across chapters, a number of codes are applied throughout the book. including tone (positive or negative), episodic versus thematic framing, equivalency framing (for example, whether immigrants without legal status are referred to as illegal or undocumented or unauthorized immigrants), and issue framing (for example, whether children are mentioned when discussing the DREAM Act or whether the rationale given to support legalization is to strengthen families or accrue the economic benefits of legalization).

"Tone" is defined as the extent to which a news story or broadcast segment casts the issue at hand in a favorable or unfavorable light. Following along the lines of Druckman and Parkin, for our qualitative samples we code tone by counting the number of positively and negatively slanted terms or phrases that appear within each immigration story.[38] Stories with more than 55 percent positive terms and phrases are coded as positive and assigned a value of 1. Stories with more than 55 percent negative terms and phrases are coded as negative and assigned a value of −1. Finally, stories falling in between are coded as neutral, at 0. For example, a segment on legalization could be coded as positive in tone if it uses positively toned words such as "children," "family," and "future" or if it invokes positive emotions such as hope, enthusiasm, and happiness. Alternatively, a negatively toned segment might include words that violate well-known norms, such as "illegal," "cutting in line," "violating the rule of law," and "amnesty," or invoke emotions such as fear, anxiety, or anger. Previous research finds that tone can influence the way a news story is interpreted by the reader or viewer. Among other outcomes, differences in tone can significantly influence reader engagement, probability for persuasion, emotional reactions, and overall issue preferences and opinions.[39]

In our analysis, we code episodic and thematic framing using qualitative content analysis. Based on our sample of stories, episodic frames are coded as 1 if the coverage discusses real-life examples of immigrants whose lives have been affected by the current "illegal" immigration policy context, and thematic frames are coded as 0 if the coverage provides generic and relatively impersonal accounts of the policy area, with greater attention to broader strokes than to specific stories.[40]

Finally, because the remaining frames in our analysis vary across chapters, we introduce them, detail their coding, and lay out our expectations later in the book. In the next section, we turn to the effects of cues on intergroup attitudes and, more specifically, the effect of frames on public opinion.

Intergroup Attitudes

Before we delve more deeply into framing effects and how they affect attitudes toward policies related to undocumented immigrants, we briefly take a step back to situate our study in the much broader literature on intergroup attitudes. Not only are the substantive questions and findings in this line of work broadly connected to our area of focus, but this literature also helps motivate our methodological approach to looking at the effects of frames on public opinion about immigration policies.

A long line of work in social psychology tells us that people have a natural tendency to categorize themselves and others into groups—to conceive of "us" versus "them."[41] Much experimental research in social psychology shows that individuals project more positive evaluations onto members of their in-group and more negative evaluations onto out-groups even when those groups are randomly assigned in the lab.[42] Furthermore, individuals of a dominant group project more negative attitudes toward racial and ethnic minorities who strongly identify with their group compared to their attitudes toward those who weakly identify.[43]

If we turn more specifically to work that has looked at attitudes toward racial and ethnic minorities, in some respects there has been progress in racial attitudes over time. In focusing on attitudes toward African Americans, Howard Schuman and his colleagues show that white attitudes on a host of measures related to racial equality, such as support for integrated schools, equal job opportunities, and equal housing accommodations, have improved dramatically over time.[44] At the same time, whites are generally less supportive of particular policies that would lead to the realization of such principles.

This gap between principles and policy has led many social scientists to conclude that bias still persists, even if whites have learned that old-fashioned racial beliefs are no longer acceptable to express, or that it is important to express support for equality in the abstract.[45] This tendency to support equality in principle but exhibit negative racial attitudes or behaviors has been captured in various theoretical constructs, such as symbolic racism, racial resentment, and aversive racism.[46] More generally, in their work on aversive racism, Samuel Gaertner and John Dovidio demonstrate through a series of experiments how biased attitudes and behaviors toward African Americans do not emerge when norms are well defined, but do emerge when norms are ambiguous or conflicting or when a nonracial justification is salient.[47]

An important implication of racial attitudes going underground is that cues from the environment can have a strong effect on whether negative attitudes toward out-groups are manifest in public opinion. One strand of work has explored how intergroup relations, especially with respect to a dominant group relative to an out-group, may sour under conditions of threat. Group threat theory, which was developed to explain attitudes of whites toward African Americans, argues that the dominant group becomes more negative toward a minority group as the minority increases in size.[48] The mechanism supporting this argument is that as a minority's size increases in the population, members of the dominant group perceives a threat to their social and economic privileges and resources. We see some of this play out in the domain of immigration. Scholars have found that the public comes to hold more restrictive attitudes toward immigrants in states with a larger influx of new immigrants.[49]

With respect to particular types of threats, scholars also argue that when certain threats are salient, or primed, for the individual, he or she may have more negative attitudes toward racial and ethnic minorities, as well as toward out-groups in society. A long line of work on authoritarianism shows that authoritarian attitudes, which include negative attitudes and behaviors toward racial and ethnic minorities, surface when threat is salient.[50] A fair amount of scholarship has looked at linkages between particular threats and opinions toward immigrants and immigration policies. Jennifer Merolla and Elizabeth Zechmeister find that when terrorism is salient, individuals come to have more negative attitudes toward immigrants and are less supportive of progressive immigration policies.[51] Others also find that when economic or cultural threat is salient, individuals hold more negative attitudes toward immigrants.[52] John Duckitt and Chris Sibley, as well as Maureen Craig and Jennifer Richeson, show, in comparative perspective, that some of the linkage between threat and negative immigration attitudes is driven by how right-wing authoritarians and those high in social dominance orientation react to different dimensions of threat.[53] Many of these works create contexts of threat through experimental approaches in which participants read articles about a hypothetical situation or about news that makes salient certain threat conditions.

A long line of work has also explored how the priming of race and race-related constructs brings negative racial attitudes to the surface. Simply varying the race of a suspect can lead to strong effects on criminal justice attitudes. For example, describing juvenile offenders as black instead of white leads individuals to view the juveniles as significantly more similar to adults in the extent to which they are to blame for their actions and to express more support for severe sentencing.[54] Black defendants in murder trials who are rated as looking more stereotypically black receive the harshest sentences.[55] Furthermore, even though expressing the old-fashioned connection between African Americans and apes is no longer publicly acceptable, the public continues to make associations between African Americans and apes: making ape imagery and race salient in an experimental context increases the endorsement of violence against black suspects in criminal cases.[56] These are but a few examples of work that looks at the effects on public opinion of priming race and racial constructs.

Fewer scholars have looked at the effects of varying the target on attitudes toward immigration policies. Ted Brader, Nicholas Valentino, and Elizabeth Suhay, in an Internet experiment on the effect of positive and negative media frames on immigration, find that opposition is higher when the frames are discussed with respect to Latino rather than white European immigrants and when the description is consistent with stereotypes (low-wage jobs).[57] Natalie Masuoka and Jane Junn, also varying the race-ethnicity of the immigrant pictured in a story about immigration, find that whites hold more restrictive preferences in the control group compared to when Asian immigrants are depicted.[58]

Other scholarship has explored how some constructs are automatically linked in individuals' minds. For example, many scholars have documented an association between African Americans and crime, and some have shown the association to be automatic.[59] Work by Jennifer Eberhardt and her colleagues has shown that this association even works the other way: having subjects think of crime can lead to thoughts of African Americans.[60] In the domain of Latinos and immigration, the terms "Latino," "illegal," and "criminal" are also closely linked in public opinion.[61]

If scholars have studied the many factors that lead to negative attitudes toward racial and ethnic minorities and societal out-groups, they have also studied ways to improve intergroup relations—including increased social contact. In *The Nature of Prejudice*, Gordon Allport argued that intergroup contact could lessen whites' prejudice against African Americans.[62] A long line of scholarship has shown that increased intergroup contact can reduce prejudice against a variety of groups, including racial and ethnic minorities, gays and lesbians, religious groups, the physically disabled, the mentally disabled and ill, and the elderly.[63] However, some scholars warn that while positive and even neutral contact can lead to lower prejudice, negative social interactions may not have this effect.[64] Furthermore, initial intergroup contact can often increase anxiety and stress, leading to impaired cognitive functioning.[65] The studies in social contact theory have used a mixture of observational and experimental approaches.

Other strategies that may improve intergroup relations are recategorizing group identity, asking individuals to take the perspective of a racial or ethnic minority, and connecting racial discussions with vivid imagery. The Common In-group Identity Model of Samuel Gaertner and his colleagues proposes that recategorization into a broader, or superordinate, social category can reduce intergroup bias.[66] For example, they show that whites express less bias toward minorities who categorize themselves as part of a superordinate group that includes whites relative to when minorities categorize themselves as part of a unique group that does not include whites. Other studies show that asking individuals to think about a black target's psychological experiences, or taking their perspective, can also mitigate automatic expressions of racial bias.[67] Finally, racial claims accompanied by vivid imagery of disaster can change beliefs in the justness of the system. Colette Eccleston, Cheryl Kaiser, and Lindsay Kraynak find that participants exposed to images of the Hurricane Katrina disaster combined with racism explanations for the government's poor response to it come to see the system as less just.[68]

One important takeaway from this very brief review is that a dominant group's attitudes toward a minority group in society can be greatly affected by cues in the environment, whether those be racial or ethnic primes, the size of the group, the salience of particular threats, vivid imagery, or attempts at recategorization. We would therefore expect that different ways of framing information would also play an important role in affecting attitudes toward policies related to undocumented immigrants. Furthermore, scholars have typically taken an experimental approach to exploring the effects of different cues on attitudes toward racial and ethnic minorities; this approach enables them to hold constant many features save the particular cue they want to isolate. Later in this chapter, we discuss in greater detail why we take this approach ourselves; here suffice it to say that the experimental approach follows from a very long tradition of work on intergroup relations in social psychology (as well as more recent work in political science and sociology). Now we turn to looking more specifically at how another type of cue, media frames, influences public opinion on immigration policy attitudes.

The Effects of Frames on Public Opinion

To what extent do media frames influence public opinion on immigration policies? That is, does this variation in the coverage of frames that we expect to find across outlets matter for the opinions people hold? Furthermore, do the effects of frames vary across different subgroups of individuals or given different providers of the frames? In this section, we discuss framing effects in more detail and use this literature to develop our expectations.

There are many different pathways through which frames might alter public opinion. When asked for their opinions on an issue, individuals take into account a host of both positive and negative considerations, and how they aggregate those considerations, in turn, affects the opinion they report.[69] For example, when an individual is asked whether the number of immigrants admitted into the United States should be increased, decreased, or kept at the same level, an individual might have three negative considerations and two positive considerations pop into his head; if he weights them similarly, the result is a net negative response: the number of immigrants should be decreased, he says.

There are a few different ways in which framing affects public opinion that are related to these various considerations an individual takes into account when forming an opinion. First, the information in a frame might induce learning by providing new information to citizens about an issue. Thus, an individual might change the content of his or her beliefs (or considerations), and that change, in turn, might change the individual's opinions on the policy. Second, media coverage may prime an issue by bringing associated beliefs and feelings to the forefront of consideration. Finally, media coverage can increase the weight of certain considerations—that is, media coverage might cause an individual to give these considerations greater relevance by making them seem more important than others. This enhanced weight should then have a greater effect on overall attitudes on a given policy issue.[70]

Most scholars have found support for the proposition that frames affect the weight given to relevant considerations across issues as varied as welfare and poverty, affirmative action, AIDS policy, campaign finance, land development, and a KKK rally.[71] For example, Thomas Nelson, Rosalee Clawson, and Zoe Oxley find that the importance people attribute to free speech on the issue of whether a KKK should hold a rally is higher in a free speech frame than it is in a public order frame.[72] In a study on frames related to poverty, James Druckman also demonstrates that frames work primarily by influencing the importance and weight of relevant beliefs in opinions on poverty.[73] In a more recent study, Ivy Cargile, Jennifer Merolla, and Adrian Pantoja show similar effects for increasing the weight of relevant beliefs in immigration policy attitudes when using frames related to the economy, cultural threat, and national security.[74]

Scholars also find that media frames have some effects, if more limited, on belief content. For example, Druckman and Nelson show that a free speech frame influences beliefs about the impact of free speech on campaign finance reform.[75] Nelson and Oxley find that individuals change some beliefs about the impact of the environment on land development in an environmental frame, though an economic frame does not change their beliefs about the economic impact on land development.[76] However, in another study, they show that individuals react against a welfare frame with respect to belief content.[77] Thus, the findings for the persuasion effects of media frames are a bit mixed. It could be that persuasion effects are more likely for novel considerations.[78] For example, in the 2014 study of Cargile and her colleagues, they found evidence only of a positive economic frame on immigration changing belief content, and this frame is much less prevalent in media coverage.

In sum, there are many different ways in which frames in media coverage may alter public opinion, and a mixture of these paths often occurs simultaneously. This is especially true when public opinion on a given issue is not stable or well formed.[79] Some work has explored the mechanisms through which frames influence opinions, and other work looks at the direct effects of different frames on public opinion.[80] It is this latter approach that we follow in this book, since we generally embed different frames in survey questions. In the next section, we discuss the impact of different types of frames on public opinion on immigration policies.

Different Types of Frames

As indicated earlier, episodically framed stories mention concrete examples, cases, or events associated with the news topic, while thematically framed stories include broad generalizations and statistical information. In a series of experiments, Iyengar has found that thematically framed stories lead to more support for government policies meant to address issues such as poverty, crime, and racial equality compared to episodically framed stories.[81] One reason is that in reading a story that focuses on an individual rather than broader trends, individuals may be more likely to blame the individual rather than the system more generally. However, other research suggests that episodic framing is effective when individual case histories are presented.[82] Since the population we are dealing with, the undocumented, is generally perceived as an out-group within the American political context, episodically framed stories about this population may work in ways similar to how they work in the domains Iyengar examined—evoking blame for the individual rather than the system.[83] Thematic framing that focuses on more general trends may be more effective and result in higher support for permissive policies (such as a pathway to citizenship or the DREAM Act) and lower support for restrictive policies (such as deportation).

Equivalency framing effects occur when differently worded but logically equivalent phrases cause individuals to alter their opinions. A classic example of an equivalency framing effect is the "Asian Disease Problem," explored in research by Tversky and Kahneman.[84] They find that respondents are more likely to opt for a risk-averse choice of treatment when it is framed in the domain of gains (choosing, say, the certainty of saving two hundred lives over a one-third chance of saving six hundred lives) and more likely to choose the more risk-seeking choice when it is framed in the domain of losses (declining the certainty of four hundred deaths over a one-third probability that none of the six hundred will die), even though all choices have the same expected outcomes. These types of frames are likely to alter opinion either by priming associated beliefs or by increasing the weight given to different considerations; however, they should not change belief content, since the information is essentially the same across the different frames.

Here we ask whether the terms used to describe those without legal status matters for immigration policy opinions. That is, does it matter for opinions if the term "illegal immigrant," "illegal alien," "undocumented immigrant," or "unauthorized immigrant" is used? All of these terms are logically equivalent in the sense that they are referring to immigrants without legal status. However, the term "illegal immigrant" carries more negative associations. Masuoka and Junn argue that drawing distinctions between "illegal" and "legal" directs attention "to the values of fairness, the importance of law, and protection of national identity as justification for more punitive immigration policies."[85] Furthermore, use of the term "illegal" in the United States connotes criminal behavior, so using it to describe those without legal status makes immigrants criminals in the minds of some individuals.[86] As we noted earlier, research shows that the terms "Latino," "illegal," and "criminal" are closely linked in public opinion.[87] Terms such as "undocumented" or "unauthorized" may not bring to mind the values violations just noted, and using them would also be unlikely to prime associations with criminals. Meanwhile, the term "illegal alien" has all of the negative associations with "illegal" as well as the associations with another negative term, "alien," which represents the ultimate outsider. Across these different terms, we would expect that attitudes on immigration policy will be most restrictive when the term "illegal alien" is used, followed by "illegal immigrant," with attitudes most positive when "undocumented" or "unauthorized" are used to describe those without legal status.

To date, few studies have examined how the use of different words describing immigrants without legal status can affect policy preferences.

One such study is a survey wording experiment by Benjamin Knoll and his colleagues, who find null effects among a sample of Iowa voters between using the terms "illegal" and "undocumented" on support for various legalization programs.[88] It is unclear, however, whether these results generalize to the national electorate, to other types of immigration policies, or to the other terms discussed here—such as the "unauthorized" label favored by many social scientists or the "illegal alien" label sometimes used by those on the right.

Finally, we explore issue framing, or "situations where, by emphasizing a subset of potentially relevant considerations, a speaker leads individuals to focus on these considerations when constructing their opinions."[89] These types of frames are not always logically equivalent. To refresh from the example provided earlier on whether the KKK should be allowed to hold a rally, if the issue is framed as one of public safety, people are less supportive, while if it is framed as one of free speech, they are more supportive.[90] Issue framing can alter opinions via any of the pathways discussed in the prior section.

When dealing with immigrant legalization, for example, the economic cost frame might cause people to weight economic considerations more heavily when constructing their opinions on legalization and make them less supportive of comprehensive reform. Meanwhile, those who are presented with a more positive frame of our nation as a history of immigrants may weight different considerations, such as their own family's immigration experience, in constructing their opinions, and the result may be more support for the policy. We expect that slight variations in the framing of immigration policies should lead to different opinion reports, since public opinion is not well crystallized on detailed immigration policies and the parties do not have a clear reputation on the issue.[91] This should particularly be the case in the absence of strong counterframes. In this book, we examine a wide variety of issue frames across different policies related to undocumented immigration, introducing the specific frames and our expectations for each of them in each empirical chapter.

With respect to existing work on framing and immigration policy attitudes, as we noted earlier, Brader, Valentino, and Suhay find that opposition to immigration is higher with a negative frame when it is associated with Latino rather than white European immigrants and when the description is consistent with stereotypes (for example, low-wage jobs).[92] A few studies have looked more specifically at different issue frames. Cargile, Merolla, and Pantoja find that social and national security frames (whether positive or negative) are associated with more support for restrictive policies related to undocumented immigrants, while economic frames (whether positive or negative) are associated with less support.[93] However, on progressive immigration policies, they find higher support among those exposed to a positive economic frame compared to a negative one (while there were no differences for the other frames). A recent study by Druckman, Peterson, and Slothuus examines competing frames on the DREAM Act and finds that support is positively affected when a strong pro-frame is pitted against a weak con-frame, and vice versa, in a context with and without party cues in a nonpolarized partisan environment.[94] There is no change in opinion when two strong frames or two weak frames are pitted against each other in the absence of party cues, but partisans do follow their own party cues when they are provided in a nonpolarized environment. In a polarized partisan environment, individuals follow the party cue regardless of the strength of the frame. While these studies shed some light on the effect of different frames on immigration policy attitudes, they touch on only a handful of frames used in the immigration debate and a handful of policies. In this book, we explore a wide range of frames on legalization, the DREAM Act, and deportation policies.

Factors That May Moderate Reactions to Frames

Of course, not all frames are equally effective, nor do all individuals necessarily react the same to frames. With respect to individual-level factors that may moderate reaction to different frames, some individuals may be more susceptible and some less susceptible to framing effects, while others may even reject framing effects. We focus primarily on partisan identification (and Fox News viewership) and one's family immigration history, though we also look at whether one identifies as Latino and educational attainment.

With respect to partisanship, a long line of literature shows that individuals process information through a partisan lens.[95] They may therefore follow information that is consistent with their predispositions and reject information that runs counter to those predispositions.[96] As John Zaller notes, in order to resist information, individuals often need to have additional contextual information to identify whether it is consistent or not with their partisanship.[97] The literature on framing effects also finds that individuals with strong values may reject frames that run counter to their dispositions, though they are less likely to do so when exposed to novel frames.[98] If we apply these theories to frames on immigration, we expect to find that partisan groups react differentially to frames. Terms like "illegal alien" and "illegal immigrant" are more often used by elites and media on the right side of the political spectrum, so they may be especially effective among Republicans and Fox News viewers and resisted by Democrats and non-Fox viewers. On the flip side, terms like "undocumented" or "unauthorized" are more often used by those on the left, so such terms may be more effective among Democrats and non-Fox viewers. Of course, the Democratic Party has been a bit more divided on immigration and therefore does not send clear signals on the issue, so the effects among Democrats may be weaker. A similar process would be present for issue frames. If partisans have the cueing information necessary to identify whether a frame is consistent or inconsistent with their values, then they may accept or reject the frames. However, if the frame is more novel, partisans may react similarly to the frames. Knoll and his colleagues find some evidence of partisanship moderating reaction to frames with respect to the ethnicity of the immigrant.[99] More specifically, Republicans who care about the issue of immigration have more punitive attitudes when asked about a "Mexican undocumented" immigrant than an "undocumented" immigrant.

In addition to partisanship, race may also matter. Masouka and Junn argue that susceptibility to political communication, including frames, is moderated by one's position in the American racial hierarchy.[100] More specifically, whites, as the dominant group in the American racial hierarchy, are more influenced by political communication that paints immigrants in a negative light than minorities are. On the issue of immigration, given that Latinos are often perceived as linked to illegal immigration, exposure to such negative frames may activate in-group identity and make Latinos even more supportive of progressive immigration reform.[101] In their book, Masuoka and Junn find that Latinos have the most positive attitudes on a variety of policies related to undocumented immigration and do not see much of a distinction between legal and illegal immigration. However, Masuoka and Junn did not directly test whether Latinos react differently to the terms used to describe those without legal status or to different issue frames. We would expect Latinos, like individuals with strong predispositions, to be more likely to react against the "illegal" frames as well as issue frames that paint immigrants in a negative light. Unfortunately, our studies do not have large enough samples of Asians or African Americans to explore whether these groups also react against "illegal" or negative media frames on immigration. In addition, we consider how an individual's family immigration history in the United States affects his or her susceptibility to framing effects. In general, we would expect immigrants in the first and second generations to behave similarly to Latinos. Studies show that being an immigrant contributes to positive evaluations of immigrants generally.[102] Thus, newer immigrant groups may also reject frames that paint immigrants as "illegal" or issue frames that depict immigrants in a negative light.

Finally, scholars have also looked at how levels of political knowledge affect reactions to frames. Some studies have found that those low in knowledge are more susceptible to framing effects, while others have found the opposite.[103] Druckman and Nelson have shown that those higher in knowledge are more susceptible to framing effects when scholars take into account prior attitudes, since they are better able to access associated beliefs that may be relevant to a given frame.[104] Although we do not have indicators for political knowledge in many of our studies, we do have a proxy of educational attainment.[105] Another relevant dimension of education on the issue of immigration is the possibility that individuals with lower levels of education face greater labor market competition from immigrants than high-status persons and therefore display more restrictionist sentiments.[106] These individuals are likely to be more susceptible to negative framing of immigrants.

In addition to individual-level factors, the effects of frames may be moderated by contextual factors. One influential factor is the strength of the frame, with stronger frames being more likely to affect opinions than weaker frames.[107] Some studies suggest and find that negative frames are stronger than positive frames.[108] Another important factor is whether the frame is novel: individuals are more likely to be affected by frames they have not encountered before than by those they have already received in the more general information environment.[109] On some of the policies we consider, we look at the latter, with the expectation that novel frames on immigration policy will be more effective in influencing opinion. We detail these more novel frames in each empirical chapter. In one of our studies, we also assess the strength of different frames.

Related to the strength of the frame is the source: frames from credible sources are more likely to influence opinions than frames delivered by noncredible sources.[110] Furthermore, whether or not people follow a frame will depend on whether it is attached to a partisan source; individuals are more likely to follow a frame attached to their own party and to resist frames coming from other parties.[111] Individuals may even follow weak frames in polarized political environments.[112] One additional element relevant to source cues is being exposed to a frame from an unexpected source. For example, the frame of immigration reform as a path to citizenship would be more unexpected coming from Republican leaders than from Democratic leaders, thereby making the former more persuasive.[113]

Survey Experiment Methods

To empirically assess the effects of different frames on public opinion, we turn to survey experiments. Our basic approach is to randomly expose respondents to different frames on immigration policies and then measure their policy opinions. The value in this approach is that we know exactly what frames individuals are exposed to. Coupled with random assignment, this approach gives us a high degree of internal validity. An alternative approach would be to track the data from our content analysis to public opinion data on the various policies. The difficulty with this approach for establishing causal relationships is that identical survey questions are not repeated consistently enough on particular policies. Even if they were, we still do not know exactly what frames people have been exposed to, since we do not always have information on what media source they are using, if any, and at what point in time they are getting exposed to the media. This problem is exacerbated if we find wide variation in the coverage on immigration across different media outlets, as we would expect. This approach may be more feasible when the media cover immigration policies in similar ways.

Some of the experiments we use are simple survey wording experiments in which we vary a few words within a question. For example, when looking at comprehensive immigration reform, we refer to it as either a "path to citizenship" or as an "amnesty." As another example, across many different policy areas we vary the terms we use to describe those without legal status as "undocumented," "unauthorized," "illegal aliens," or "illegal immigrants."

In other experiments, we randomly assign individuals to receive a statement about a particular policy and measure their levels of support or opposition. On deportations, for example, respondents are randomly assigned to read different justifications for or against the policy and are then asked for their level of support or opposition to the policy. Some justifications focus on legal arguments, others highlight economic considerations, and still others focus on family considerations. Finally, in another study, we use another common methodology for assessing framing effects: respondents read a newspaper article on immigration in which we vary episodic and thematic frames, and then we ask them a battery of immigration policy questions following exposure (or not) to the article.

We conducted a total of seven experimental studies, most with representative samples and a few with convenience samples, from 2007 to 2014. First, we embedded survey experiments in the 2007, 2008, and 2010 Cooperative Congressional Election Studies (CCES), which were conducted online through YouGov during the fall elections.[114] The sample sizes for our battery of immigration questions were as follows across the three surveys: $n = 2,188$ (2007); $n = 1,581$ (2008); and $n = 1,352$ (2010). The sample drawn for each CCES study is a stratified national sample.[115] We present basic demographic information and political predispositions for the samples in table 2.1. The ages and educational attainment of the survey respondents across the three years of data are fairly well aligned with those of the U.S. electorate, although the proportion of whites in the sample is higher than the U.S. average and the proportion of males is higher in the 2007 data.[116] The distribution of partisanship and ideology is similar to the American National Election Study (ANES), though our

Table 2.1   Respondent Characteristics Across Experimental Studies, 2007–2013

	2007	2008	2010	2011	2012	2013	2014
White	85.3%	80.1%	78.4%	50.0%	69.5%	78.0%	79.5%
Black	3.7	8.7	9.2	—	10.5	8.3	10.7
Hispanic	3.9	6.1	5.3	50.0	12.8	6.1	5.5
Asian	0.8	1.1	2.3	—	2.0	9.7	6.0
Native American	0.8	1.2	0.81	—	0.4	1.2	0.8
Mixed	1.5	1.1	2.4	—	3.0	—	—
Other	4.0	1.8	1.7	—	1.7	0.8	0.8
Male	61.5	42.8	46.8	50.2	48.7	54.2	48.0
Female	38.5	57.2	53.2	49.8	51.3	45.8	52.0
No high school	1.7	3.2	2.0	7.9	6.1	1.0	1.3
High school graduate	14.7	34.2	25.2	47.1	40.5	31.9	19.3
Some college	19.7	24.4	26.0	19.9	21.3	6.8[a]	7.0
Two-year college	9.1	8.4	7.7	5.8	7.4	14.7	13.9
Four-year college	27.7	20.6	26.9	12.6	16.0	36.5	31.7
Postgraduate degree	27.2	9.2	12.3	6.6	8.8	9.8	26.9
Mean age (years)	55.6	48.0	51.8	43.8	45.9	32.5	47.3
Democrats	37.2%	35.0%	32.8%	38.4%	36.6%	42.2%	36.8%
Independents[b]	32.7	32.5	36.0	34.5	36.3	42.6	37.6
Republicans	30.2	32.5	31.2	27.1	27.1	15.3	25.6
Mean ideology[c]	3.06	3.23	3.34	3.18	3.36	3.36	4.09
Total N	2,188	1,581	1,352	800	1,300	4,147	1,160

Source: For 2007 to 2012, YouGov; for 2013, Mechanical Turk; for 2014, Survey Sampling International (SSI).
[a]For the Mechanical Turk and SSI surveys, this category is "technical or trade certificate."
[b]This category also includes "other" and "don't know."
[c]Measured on a seven-point scale from "extremely liberal" to "extremely conservative."

samples have a slightly higher percentage of Republicans and a slightly lower percentage of independents.

In addition to the CCES data sets, we were able to place experiments on two original online experimental studies, also conducted by YouGov, one that was fielded June 9 to June 21, 2011, and another that was in the field July 20 to August 8, 2012. For the 2011 study, 400 whites and 400 Latinos were sampled. We use the data weighted to be representative of the national population on all dimensions, except race-ethnicity.[117] In 2012 a total of 1,300 respondents were interviewed, with an oversample of 400 Latinos. We also use the weighted data for this study, and it does adjust for race and ethnicity.[118] Table 2.1 also shows the sample descriptives for these studies.

In 2013 we ran an online experimental study using Amazon's Mechanical Turk. The study was in the field in the summer of 2013, and a total of 4,147 respondents were interviewed. Mechanical Turk's sample is not as representative as the samples from YouGov, as can be seen in table 2.1. However, the sample is more reflective of the national population than a college population would be and is appropriate given that our primary purpose is to estimate the effect of an experimental treatment.[119] Finally, we ran an online experimental study with panelists from Survey Sampling International from March 8 to March 10, 2014. A total of 1,160 individuals participated in the study. The invitation was sent to a sample intended to reflect the national population, though we ended up with a slightly more educated and conservative sample compared to our other studies.

Conclusion

Since public attitudes toward policies that affect the undocumented population are unstable and inconsistent, the ways in which policies are framed in a diverse media environment can be especially consequential for shaping opinion. To understand public opinion about immigration policies, then, we need to first get a handle on the supply of media frames to which the public is exposed. We also need to assess the extent to which these frames affect public opinion. This is the central strategy of our book.

With respect to the supply of elite cues, we expect to find variation in the relative presence of different types of frames in coverage of legalization, the DREAM Act, and deportation policies depending on the ideological slant of the media outlet. More specifically, we expect more conservative outlets, such as the *Washington Times,* the *New York Post,* and Fox News, to have a higher prevalence of restrictive issue coverage and restrictive equivalency frames (for example, making references to "illegal immigrants" and "illegal aliens") when compared to more mainstream outlets like the *New York Times* and the *Washington Post.* For CNN and MSNBC, we expect to see changes in news coverage over time, as each network changed in important ways between 2008 and 2010. MSNBC became a decidedly more liberal network after the fall of 2008, when it hired Rachel Maddow to anchor its prime-time news show, while CNN forced out Lou Dobbs in November 2009 after boycott campaigns by national Latino organizations. We assess these expectations using both quantitative and qualitative content analyses conducted between 2007 and 2014.

We also expect to find these diverse frames to be consequential in shaping public opinion on immigration policy. More specifically, we expect to find that more restrictive frames lead to less support for legalization and the DREAM Act and more support for deportation policies. We expect the opposite to be the case for permissive frames. Furthermore, given prior research, we expect restrictive frames to be generally more effective than permissive frames, although more novel permissive frames, especially those coming from unexpected sources, may also prove effective in moving public opinion. Finally, we expect individuals to be more susceptible to frames that align with their partisanship or values and to reject frames that run counter to them.

3

Comprehensive Immigration Reform

T HE ISSUE of unauthorized immigration has been a prominent feature of immigration policy since 1965, when the United States ended its temporary worker program for Mexican nationals (the Bracero Program) and instituted a policy that favored skilled workers and those with family in the United States.[1] Even though the Bracero Program was no longer operative, there was continued high demand for Mexican labor, particularly in agriculture and the construction industry. Consequently, unauthorized immigration to the United States grew rapidly, and ever since the 1960s the United States has engaged in various schemes of enforcement and legalization to solve the problem, including a watershed bill in 1986—the Immigration Reform and Control Act (IRCA), which legalized over 2.5 million immigrants.[2] Even after the 1986 legalization, the problem of unauthorized immigration continued apace, however, owing in part to weak provisions for employer sanctions, networks of recruitment among families and sending regions, and the ongoing economic and political power of the United States with respect to Mexico and other Central American countries.[3]

Today there are an estimated 12 million unauthorized immigrants in the United States, most of whom are long-term residents of the United States and unlikely to return to their home countries in mass numbers.[4] Even as other important aspects of immigration policy vie for congressional attention—such as the shortage of workers with advanced degrees in science and engineering and the need for improvements in temporary agricultural worker programs—much of the public's attention has been focused on the problem of illegal immigration. Thus, even though legislative efforts such as the comprehensive immigration reform bills of 2006, 2007, and 2013 dealt with various topics such as refugees, asylum claims, family visas, and high-skill workers, much of the floor debate and related media coverage centered on the issue of illegal immigration.[5]

Amid the policy debates, advocates and elected officials have attempted to shape public opinion and legislative outcomes in their favor, paying increasing attention to the framing of policy in news coverage and popular discourse. However, while advocates may believe that policy frames on particular aspects of immigration policy have consequences for public opinion, these effects have rarely been tested in experimental settings. In this chapter, we pay specific attention to large-scale immigrant legalization, as has been attempted in Congress in various guises from 2006 to the present. First, we introduce the historical context for immigrant legalization, from the first massive legalization of immigrants in 1986 to the 2006 and 2007 efforts at comprehensive immigration reform in Congress. Even though these efforts had strong backing from the Bush White House, a set of deep partisan splits emerged on immigration that continued through the 2008 presidential campaign and beyond.

In the next section, we provide a content analysis of how immigrant legalization was covered in the news. In particular, we pay attention to the ways in which the policy of legalization has been covered, from being seen as rewarding criminal behavior and threatening U.S. jobs to being portrayed as a pragmatic and family-friendly solution to a thorny and persistent problem. We also consider the extent to which the term "amnesty" is invoked in news coverage of immigrant legalization compared to phrases such as "a pathway to citizenship." We also consider the extent to which news coverage references the length of stay of the undocumented, in addition to whether coverage is more episodic or thematic. To refresh, we expect to find that the frames used to cover legalization vary by the ideology of the news source, such that restrictive frames will be employed more often in conservative outlets and more progressive frames in mainstream and especially liberal outlets.

Finally, we examine whether these issue frames make any difference for public opinion, using experimental data collected over several years. In general, we expect that more restrictive frames, like amnesty, a focus on criminal behavior, and lawbreaking, will lead to less support for legalization when compared to frames that are more positive in nature, such as a pathway to citizenship, the economic benefits of immigration, and the importance of keeping families together. We also expect individuals to be more supportive of legalization in cases where the unauthorized have been in the United States for a longer period of time.

Contemporary Attempts at Immigrant Legalization

As we noted in chapter 1, the Bush administration had immigration reform high on its legislative agenda in early 2001, but the September 11 attacks scuttled any hopes for legislation that would legalize the millions of undocumented immigrants living in the United States. Within a few years, however, it was apparent that the White House's desire for immigration reform had been delayed, not deterred. In early 2004, President Bush signaled his interest in a renewed push for immigration reform, including temporary work status for existing unauthorized immigrants that could eventually lead to green cards and citizenship.[6] His proposal did not make much headway during his reelection year, but soon afterward the Bush administration again made a concerted push for comprehensive immigration reform, with his adviser Karl Rove seeing the issue as something that could potentially help Republicans win over Latino voters for a generation or more.[7] By then, however, the president's standing within the Republican Party had diminished considerably. Not only was Bush a lame-duck party leader, but he had also lost significant political capital among conservative Republicans for his support for Medicare expansion and his administration's inability to push for Social Security privatization in early 2005.[8] Thus, in response to the administration's call for immigration reform, the conservative Immigration Reform Caucus in the House entered into open rebellion, with the caucus organizer, Tom Tancredo (R-CO), leading the charge.[9] Soon Tancredo enlisted the help of Jim Sensenbrenner (R-WI), who spearheaded an enforcement-only bill (HR 4437) that quickly passed the House in late 2005. The measure provoked a series of immigration protests throughout the country and faced significant opposition in the Senate, which was trying to fashion a bipartisan package that would include a mix of enforcement and legalization.[10] The reform efforts in 2006 ended in a stalemate: the Senate had passed comprehensive immigration reform, and the House had passed an enforcement-only measure, and neither would budge on creating a bill that could pass both chambers.

The next opportunity for immigration reform came within a year: Democrats won control of the House and Senate after the 2006 midterm elections, and Latino mobilization on immigration was seen as playing a supportive role.[11] This time the House easily passed a comprehensive immigration measure that included a pathway to citizenship, and given the Senate's support for immigration reform in 2006, it seemed likely that the bill would soon become law. In the summer of 2007, however, conservative activists rallied strongly against the measure, with groups such as NumbersUSA and FAIR, along with conservative radio talk hosts, putting enormous pressure on Senate Republicans to uphold a filibuster on the House reform package. As noted in a feature story in the *New York Times:*

FAIR rallied talk show hosts. The Center for Immigration Studies churned out studies of the bill's perceived flaws. Numbers USA jammed the Capitol's phones.

Their success became the stuff of lore. They "lit up the switchboard for weeks," said Senator Mitch McConnell of Kentucky, the Republican leader, explaining his decision to oppose the bill. "And to every one of them, I say today: 'Your voice was heard.'"[12]

Despite this setback in the Senate, advocates for immigrant legalization were not deterred. During the 2008 Democratic presidential primaries, candidates Hillary Clinton and Barack Obama largely agreed on the need to pass comprehensive immigration reform.[13] Latino organizations continued to put pressure on Obama during the summer campaign to maintain his commitment to a citizenship pathway and secured his pledge to start working on immigration from the "very first day" of his administration.[14] And even though John McCain had walked back his sponsorship of immigration reform legislation during the 2008 Republican primaries, he subsequently sought to reassure Latino organizations in the summer of 2008 that he would continue to support a pathway to citizenship.[15] With the collapse of the stock market in late 2008, however, and the larger economic downturn, plans for comprehensive immigration reform receded to the margins once again. The Obama administration focused its efforts on economic recovery and passage of the Affordable Care Act, with immigration getting only sporadic attention. As we shall see in chapter 4, some pieces of immigration reform, such as the DREAM Act, remained viable during Obama's first term, but the overall prospects for a broader legalization were slim to none.

The 2012 elections provided a fresh boost to immigration reform. Mitt Romney maintained a fairly restrictive position on immigration, arguing for greater border enforcement and allowing states like Arizona to pass their own enforcement laws and opposing the White House decision to provide deportation relief to young undocumented immigrants through executive action (for more on the DACA program, see chapter 4). In the aftermath of Romney's defeat—particularly among Latinos, whom he lost to Obama by nearly forty points—national Republican Party leaders began calling for the party to move swiftly in favor of immigration reform as a way to win back some of these voters and remain viable in the 2016 presidential election and beyond. Even conservative opinion leaders on immigration such as the Fox News commentators Sean Hannity and Bill O'Reilly dropped their prior opposition to immigrant legalization and started calling for comprehensive immigration reform at the national level.[16] Thus, as President Obama held an immigration rally in late January 2013 and a bipartisan group of senators worked on a comprehensive reform package intended to draw broad support, it seemed like the time for immigrant legalization had finally come. Importantly, this group was careful to avoid any charges that their plan for legalization was a replay of the 1986 amnesty. As one of the bill's coauthors, Marco Rubio (R-FL), noted, the Senate bill set out a lengthy set of requirements and required a decade or more of waiting before undocumented immigrants could qualify for citizenship.[17]

By the summer of 2013, however, momentum on federal legislation had slowed down once again, continuing a decade-long pattern of fits and starts on immigrant legalization. Although the Senate had passed a comprehensive bill, S744, in June 2013 by an overwhelming margin (68–32) and with the support of fourteen Republican senators, it was declared "dead on arrival" in the House.[18] While previously House Republican leaders such as Paul Ryan (R-WI) and Eric Cantor (R-VA) had expressed support for various aspects of immigrant legalization, the House Republican Caucus rallied against the Senate bill and sought instead to pass a bill focused entirely on immigration enforcement. Prospects for immigrant legalization grew even dimmer as House incumbents worried about conservative challengers in Republican primaries, and these hopes got extinguished completely after Eric Cantor lost his primary election in June 2014—based, in part, on his prior support for immigration reform.[19] Thus, while immigrant legalization had moved in fits and starts between 2006 and 2013, it ground to a complete halt by the summer of 2014, with any future prospect of its passage highly unlikely with Republicans still in control of the U.S. House of Representatives.

With an understanding of the historical context surrounding attempts at legalization, we now turn to the meat of the chapter: exploring how legalization has been framed in media coverage, how this coverage has varied across outlets, and the effect of these frames on public opinion.

Framing Legalization in the News

There is general agreement that news coverage in the United States has grown more ideologically divided over time, particularly in the realm of cable television news after the creation of the Fox News network in 1996.[20] Thus, we might expect news coverage of immigrant legalization to vary according to the ideological leanings of the news source, with conservative outlets opposing legalization, liberal outlets in favor, and mainstream outlets occupying an intermediate space. As we shall see, however, news framing on immigrant legalization is not simply a matter of signaling support or opposition; it often involves other dimensions such as the decision on whether or not to use human interest stories in news segments, or whether or not to invoke considerations such as economic costs and benefits, family ties, and the rule of law. Here we demonstrate the variations along these different framing dimensions in news stories on immigrant legalization and the discernible patterns, if any, over time and across news outlets. In subsequent chapters, we do a similar analysis of news framing with respect to the DREAM Act and mass deportations.

We anticipate that conservative print sources such as the *Washington Times* and the *New York Post* will have more restrictive news coverage than more mainstream outlets such as the *Washington Post* and the *New York Times*. We do not expect such clear-cut differences with respect to cable news outlets. In particular, we expect that the pre-2010 tenure of the conservative and restrictionist host Lou Dobbs would have biased CNN's immigration coverage in a more restrictive bent. However, we might also expect some ideological deviation for MSNBC prior to the 2009 election, when it still chose to regularly feature well-known conservatives such as Tucker Carlson and Patrick Buchanan. Thus, for CNN and MSNBC, we would expect to see changes in news coverage on legalization over time, with coverage that is more permissive at MSNBC after 2009 and more balanced prior to 2009, and coverage that is more conservative prior to 2010 at CNN and more balanced thereafter. Finally, we expect Fox News to have the most restrictive coverage throughout this period.

So how do these different ways of framing legalization correspond to news coverage? We analyzed the content of news stories on immigrant legalization in mainstream and conservative daily newspapers from 2007 through 2013.[21] Additionally, we analyzed legalization stories from each of the three major cable news networks (CNN on the mainstream side, Fox News on the conservative side, and MSNBC, which transitioned from mainstream to liberal during this time period). We retrieved a total of 409 legalization stories from CNN, 187 from Fox News, 125 from MSNBC, 1,080 from the *Washington Post*, 335 from the *Washington Times*, 160 from the *New York Times*, and 72 from the *New York Post*. To analyze these stories we employed both a quantitative content analysis for the full set of stories and a qualitative content analysis for a sample of the stories, as we note in our discussion of the various frames.

The Volume of Coverage

To provide a broader view of the media's presentation of immigrant legalization, we begin by presenting results on the volume of coverage drawn from the quantitative content analysis of legalization stories from the five news organizations from January 1, 2007, through December 31, 2013.

First, what stands out is the unevenness in the volume of legalization coverage over the seven-year period. Specifically, 2007 and 2013 stand out as the most voluminous years by far (with 585 and 916 stories, respectively), with 2010 also registering a markedly higher level of coverage than the remaining years (see table 3.1). Overall, 2007 and 2013 ac-

Table 3.1   The Volume of Legalization Stories in Seven News Sources, January 1, 2007, to December 31, 2013

	2007	2008	2009	2010	2011	2012	2013	All
Total stories	585	188	157	312	153	207	916	2,518
CNN	146	9	16	55	13	14	156	409
Fox News	39	4	2	45	11	6	80	187
MSNBC	11	0	1	13	6	4	90	125
Washington Post	194	125	94	139	96	120	312	1,080
Washington Times	126	33	18	33	9	26	90	335
New York Times	57	15	24	22	14	31	139	302
New York Post	12	2	2	5	4	6	49	80

Source: Authors' quantitative content analysis of news data.

count for a majority of legalization stories during the seven-year period (54 percent), and this figure rises to nearly three-quarters (72 percent) when we add 2010 coverage. These year-specific patterns make sense when we consider the policy dynamics in Congress: immigration reform made the most legislative progress in 2007 and 2010. In 2007 comprehensive immigration reform (CIR) passed the House but, after several months of consideration in the Senate, failed to break a filibuster. The year 2013 saw a reverse pattern, with CIR passing easily in the Senate but "bleeding a slow death" in the U.S. House (the Senate bill eventually died in 2014, garnering another 422 news stories).[22] Finally, 2010 also saw an uptick in coverage of immigrant legalization, although most coverage discussed CIR in light of attempts to pass the DREAM Act as more comprehensive efforts failed to gain traction.

Looking beyond aggregate coverage to reports in particular sources, some important variations emerge. Among our cable news sources, CNN's coverage in 2007 was on par with its coverage in 2013 (146 versus 156 stories, respectively), while for MSNBC and Fox News immigrant legalization got most coverage in 2013. Indeed, coverage at Fox News was twice as high in 2013 as in 2007, while for MSNBC it was eight times higher. This dramatic time variation in coverage, particularly between CNN and MSNBC, seems surprising at first blush. As we noted earlier, however, CNN had shows hosted by Glenn Beck and Lou Dobbs in 2007, and both of them made immigration a high priority. While CNN continued to cover immigration after Beck left in 2008 and Dobbs left in 2009, the volume of its coverage was significantly lower. By contrast, MSNBC added several shows between 2008 and 2012, leading to an overall increase in news coverage that included immigration.[23] In our print sources, which were not subject to such dramatic programmatic changes, differences in the volume of coverage between 2007 and 2013 were less noticeable.

Table 3.2   The Tone of Legalization Coverage in Seven News Sources, 2007, 2010, 2012, and 2013

	All Four Years Combined	2007	2010	2012	2013
Washington Times	−0.42	−0.67	−0.19	−0.13	−0.50
Washington Post	0.40	0.32	0.29	0.56	0.47
Fox News	−0.40	−0.35	−0.64	−0.17	−0.28
CNN	0.13	−0.37	0.28	0.07	0.41
MSNBC	0.66	−0.27	0.69	0.50	0.82
New York Times	0.00	−0.16	−0.13	0.06	0.18
New York Post	−0.06	−0.17	−0.20	0.17	−0.04

Source: Authors' qualitative content analysis of news data.
Note: Reported are the average (mean) values of individual stories, ranging from −1 (negative tone) to 1 (positive tone).

The Tone of Coverage

With a better sense of the volume of coverage of immigration issues, we now begin our exploration of the content of the coverage by looking at the tone of legalization stories; here we find systematic differences across media outlets. By tone, we mean the extent to which a news story or segment on immigrant legalization casts the issue in a favorable or unfavorable light. Given the polarizing nature of the immigration issue and the tendency for the news outlets in question to hew to this ideological divide, we expect legalization stories in the more conservative outlets to be negatively toned, liberal outlets to be positively toned, and mainstream outlets to fall somewhere in between. In line with previous scholarship, we code tone by counting the number of positively and negatively slanted terms or phrases that appear within each immigration story.[24] Stories with more than 55 percent positive content were coded as positive and assigned a value of 1. Stories with more than 55 percent negative content were coded as negative and assigned a value of −1. Finally, stories falling in between were coded as neutral, at 0. Thus we have a three-point measure of tone that runs from −1 to 1.[25]

In table 3.2, we show the average tone of legalization coverage across cable and print news outlets from 2007, 2010, 2012, and 2013. If we look at the combined measure of tone across all years, we find that the liberal MSNBC had the most positive coverage (with a mean score of 0.66 on a scale of −1 to 1), while the conservative outlets had the highest net negative coverage (with Fox News at −0.40 and the *Washington Times* at −0.42, although the *New York Post* was close to neutral, with a mean rating of −0.06). Meanwhile, the mainstream outlets fell somewhere between Fox News and MSNBC, with CNN and the *New York Times* being close to net neutral and the *Washington Post* being more positive. Thus, as expected, we find that ideologically conservative outlets such as Fox News and the *Washington Times* presented a much more negative tone in their immigrant legalization coverage than liberal outlets like MSNBC and mainstream sources like CNN and the *Washington Post*.

Differences in tone were related, in turn, to a few key factors: (1) the presence or absence of particular language (for example, "amnesty" or "pathway"); (2) the use of episodic versus thematic frames; and (3) the inclusion of different arguments either supporting or opposing immigrant legalization.

Amnesty Versus a Pathway to Citizenship   As we discussed earlier in this chapter, the immigrant legalization debate in Congress was strongly polarized along party lines when it was introduced in 2005, in contrast to prior attempts at comprehensive immigration reform that had significant Republican support. Framing played a part in the growing Republican resistance: the frequent mentions of the term "amnesty" cast immigrant legalization in a very negative light. The rhetorical shift in the use of "amnesty" was partly due to the growth of conservative, anti-immigrant groups following Ronald Reagan's signing of the 1986 Immigration Reform and Control Act (IRCA), which granted amnesty to over 1 million undocumented immigrants.[26] While groups like the Federation for American Immigration Reform (FAIR) had existed well before 1986, the Center for Immigration Studies (CIS) and NumbersUSA were born out of the legislative fight over the 1986 law. Since then, NumbersUSA has largely been credited with growing the grassroots of the immigration restriction movement, while CIS has provided the intellectual framework for the argument against amnesty through a series of policy reports, conferences, and briefings.[27] It is not surprising, then, that when immigration reform was back on the legislative agenda in 2005, the conservative pollster Frank Luntz advised Republicans to consistently refer to any kind of immigrant legalization as "amnesty," noting, "If it sounds like amnesty, it will fail. . . . Amnesty, by definition, rewards criminal behavior and is therefore unacceptable."[28]

Some might argue that "amnesty" versus "opportunity" is not an instance of issue framing (each frame highlighting a different aspect of a policy) but rather an instance of equivalency framing (different terms are used to explain the same phenomenon). It is important to recognize, however, that advocates on the two sides—those who view legalization as amnesty and those who view it as an opportunity or "pathway to citizenship"—talk about the legalization process in fundamentally different ways. As Luntz's memo indicates, the amnesty frame is intended to get Americans to focus on the rule of law and on acts of lawbreaking by undocumented immigrants. It is also intended to get voters to focus on the

1986 amnesty, which was seen as a relatively quick process for undocumented immigrants to gain legalization. Meanwhile, proponents of immigration reform, including Republicans like Senator Marco Rubio, discuss the pathway to citizenship as a much longer process in an attempt to get voters to focus on what immigrants need to do in order to gain citizenship rather than on the kinds of immigration laws they may have violated many years ago. They are therefore not equivalent. Indeed, as Rubio's extensive interview on *Meet the Press* in April 2013 indicated, the opportunity frame explicitly seeks to deflect the amnesty frame's focus on lawbreaking and forgiveness and to evoke the more positive idea of individuals working with the system to gain citizenship. When asked if his immigration reform bill was an amnesty, Rubio responded, "Well, first of all, *amnesty is the forgiveness of something.* In fact, there will be consequences for having violated the law. And they'll be reasonable consequences" (our emphasis). Later in the interview, Rubio noted that "all this bill does is give people access to the legal immigration system. It allows them to earn an access to the legal immigration system. And so what we are doing is we are creating an alternative to that path that exists now."[29]

Given greater party polarization on immigration, as well as growing ideological polarization in news coverage, we would expect that conservative news outlets will be much more likely than mainstream news outlets or liberal news outlets to use the term "amnesty." By contrast, we would expect mainstream news outlets to be much more likely to use the term "path(way) to citizenship"—the phrase used by the members of Congress who were sponsoring legislation on comprehensive immigration reform in 2007 and 2013. Indeed, we find strong evidence in support of these expectations. We draw all findings for this section from the quantitative content analysis of stories including the word "amnesty" with no mention of a "path(way) to citizenship," and vice versa for stories mentioning a "path(way) to citizenship" (see table 3.3).[30] Thus, we end up with the percentage of immigrant-based stories on legalization that are "amnesty only" or "pathway only."

Looking first at the "amnesty only" measure, we continue to find a clear ideological divide between the more conservative news organizations and the more mainstream news organizations (see table 3.3). While the word "amnesty" was mentioned in about one-quarter of immigration news stories on Fox News and in the *Washington Times*, this was the case for fewer than one-tenth of the immigration stories in the more liberal sources (the *Washington Post* and MSNBC). As we would expect, CNN, the more neutral outlet, fell in between at 15 percent, though this still seems high for a neutral outlet. As we noted earlier, CNN's former association with the anchor Lou Dobbs may have had something to do with this unusually high percentage.[31]

Table 3.3   Legalization Stories in Seven News Sources Mentioning "Amnesty" or "Path(way)," 2007–2013

	CNN	FOX	MSNBC	Washington Post	Washington Times	New York Times	New York Post
"Amnesty" mentioned; no mention of "pathway"	15%	23%	7%	3%	24%	7%	13%
"Pathway" mentioned; no mention of "amnesty"	27	19	47	21	21	38	29
Neither term mentioned	24	27	20	70	30	35	49
Both terms mentioned	34	32	26	6	27	20	13
Any mention of "amnesty"	49	55	33	9	51	27	26
Any mention of "pathway"	61	51	73	27	48	58	42

Source: Authors' quantitative content analysis of news data (see chapter 3, note 30).

Table 3.4   CNN Immigrant Legalization Stories Mentioning "Amnesty" or "Path(way)," Dobbs Era (2007–2009) and Post-Dobbs Era (2010–2013)

	During Dobbs Era	During Post-Dobbs Era	Overall
Any mention of "amnesty"	76%	30%	49%
"Amnesty" mentioned; no mention of "pathway"	29	5	15
Any mention of "pathway"	57	65	61
"Pathway" mentioned; no mention of "amnesty"	10	40	27

Source: Authors' quantitative content analysis of news data (see chapter 3, note 30).

To explore this possibility, we reanalyzed the data by dividing our measure into a Dobbs era (2007–2009) and a post-Dobbs era (2010–2013). In short, the results are stark (see table 3.4). Consistent with expectations, we find that CNN's inclusion of the "amnesty" term in its immigrant legalization coverage plummeted after 2009. During Dobbs's time at CNN, 29 percent of CNN's immigration segments included the word "amnesty," with no mention of a "path(way) to citizenship." This compares to only 5 percent after Dobbs's departure. Overall, the data indicate a clear ideological cleavage in the news coverage of immigrant legalization.

Much like "amnesty"-heavy coverage, immigrant legalization coverage that includes references to a "path (or pathway) to citizenship" has a distinctly ideological hue. There is a clear divide in the percentage of immigration stories including the phrase "path(way) to citizenship" with no mention of "amnesty," but it only appears when we compare the most liberal news organization (MSNBC) with the rest of the news organizations (see table 3.3). While 47 percent of MSNBC's legalization coverage mentioned the "path(way) to citizenship" without mentioning "amnesty," this was the case for only 27 percent, 21 percent, 19 percent, and 21 percent of legalization coverage from CNN, the *Washington Post*, Fox News, and the *Washington Times*, respectively.[32]

Finally, we reanalyze the data by dividing our measure of CNN into the Dobbs era and the post-Dobbs era. Just as with the "amnesty" findings, the results are stark (see table 3.4). Consistent with expectations, we find that CNN's inclusion of the term "path(way) to citizenship" without mentioning "amnesty" rose sharply after 2009. During Dobbs's time at CNN, only 10 percent of the network's immigration segments included the phrase "path(way) to citizenship" with no mention of "amnesty," compared to 40 percent after his departure.

We now shift to look at changes over time in the mentions of "amnesty" and "pathway to citizenship." Two findings, in particular are most striking. First, beginning with differences in the percentage of legalization stories in which only one of the two terms is mentioned, we find that stories in which only "amnesty" is mentioned fell precipitously from 21 percent in 2007 to 7 percent in 2011 and remained flat through December 31, 2013 (see table 3.5). In raw numbers, this equates to a steep drop from 123 stories in 2007 to 51 stories in 2013. This means that of the 26 percent of legalization stories in 2013 containing the "amnesty" term, 20 percent were in stories also containing the permissive "pathway to citizenship" frame.

Second, we find that the drop in the percentage of stories containing only the "amnesty" frame was accompanied by a steep rise in the percentage of stories containing only the "pathway" frame. Specifically, legalization stories mentioning a "path(way) to citizenship" without mentioning "amnesty" rose from 13 percent in 2007 to 27 percent in 2010, to 39 percent in 2013. In raw numbers, this represents an increase from 76 stories in 2007 to 84 stories in 2010, then up to 361 stories in 2013. Overall, while the data indicate a clear ideological cleavage, other factors—such as volume and news anchor—also played a large role in shaping the news coverage of immigrant legalization.

Episodic Human-Interest Accounts Versus Thematic General Accounts   Differences in tone between mainstream and conservative news sources correlate strongly with the frequent use of concrete, episodically framed stories in the former and more thematically framed stories in the latter. As we noted in chapter 2, episodically framed stories present real-life examples of people whose lives are affected by current policy, while thematically framed stories use broader strokes to provide relatively impersonal accounts of the policy area, with less attention to specific cases.[33] Our ideological framework does not offer clear predictions as to how conservative media as opposed to liberal media employ episodic and thematic frames in their legalization coverage. To evaluate any differences in coverage across outlets with respect to these frames, we use data from our qualitative content analysis. In particular, we coded news stories about immigrant legalization from 2007, 2010, 2012, and 2013 in the *Washington Post*, the *Washington Times*, the *New York Times*, the *New York Post*, CNN, MSNBC, and Fox News (see table 3.6).

We find that media coverage of legalization is dominated by thematic stories. However, the more conservative media in our analysis—the *Washington Times* (4.2 percent), the *New York Post* (0.0 percent), and Fox News (3.6 percent)—engaged in less episodic framing than the more mainstream outlets—CNN (14.9 percent), the *Washington Post* (11.7 per-

Table 3.5 Change in Percentage of Legalization Stories Mentioning "Amnesty" or "Path(way)" from 2007 to 2013

	2007	2008	2009	2010	2011	2012	2013	All
Any mention of "amnesty"	49%	17%	22%	21%	15%	20%	26%	28%
Any mention of "pathway"	41	20	33	39	26	32	59	44
"Amnesty" mentioned; no mention of "pathway"	21	10	9	9	7	7	6	10
"Pathway" mentioned; no mention of "amnesty"	13	13	20	27	18	19	39	26
Neither term mentioned	39	72	60	52	67	66	35	47
Both terms mentioned	28	7	13	12	8	13	20	18

Source: Authors' quantitative content analysis of news data (see chapter 3, note 30).

Table 3.6   **Episodic Human-Interest Framing in Immigrant Legalization Stories in Seven News Sources, 2007, 2010, 2012, and 2013**

	All Four Years Combined	2007	2010	2012	2013
Washington Times	4.2%	2.4%	6.5%	12.5%	0.0%
Washington Post	11.7	10.7	9.5	11.1	13.3
Fox News	3.6	9.7	2.4	0.0	23.1
CNN	14.9	14.3	11.3	7.1	20.7
MSNBC	10.6	0.0	23.1	0.0	10.6
New York Times	12.7	10.9	13.6	22.6	8.0
New York Post	0.0	0.0	0.0	0.0	0.0

Source: Authors' qualitative content analysis of news data.

cent), and the *New York Times* (12.7 percent)—and the more liberal MSNBC (10.6 percent).

Upon close inspection of the stories, it becomes clear why this is the case. Many of the episodic, or "human interest," stories depict the undocumented more positively, as illustrated in this example from MSNBC (episodic terms in bold):

> [What's] helpful to keep in mind is that dreamers, what we did successfully by coming out and sharing **our stories** and saying we are undocumented and unafraid, because that's what we learned in school. That is what we learned about the values of America, freedom of speech, freedom of following our dreams, but dreamers are **part of families, and our parents were courageous enough to leave everything behind, seeking a better life, to come to this country, and that is what we are fighting for**. And I think when it comes to sharing **our stories,** part of the work that we are doing, as organizers, right, as the foot soldiers, as you referred to organizers, is sharing the **stories of our families, of our parents,** because it is those **stories** that need to be reflective of the policy debate that we are having about immigration reform, and it is not only about the students.[34]

Compare this episodic segment from MSNBC to the more process-oriented, impersonal segment about legalization in the following example from Fox News of thematic framing. Notice the use of typical thematic markers, including generalities and statistics (thematic terms in bold):

> Let's just go back to 1986 and look at what happened when we promised the amnesty to **two million to three million,** and we were supposed to do all those second- and third- and fourth-order things that we ended up not

doing. So now we have a **situation where it could be twelve million,** what have you. And when you look at our **economic situation** here in the United States of America, are we going to be capable of having another **six million or seven million** people that are going to be more so dependent on the federal government and **social welfare type of policies and programs.**[35]

In short, the tone of legalization stories (negative tone for conservative media, more positive for mainstream and liberal media) is often linked to differences in the style of the frame. It could be that legalization stories that offer the audience a more concrete glimpse into the lives of the un-documented, perhaps mediated by increases in empathy, can be inter-preted as more positive in tone than the more impersonal, thematically framed accounts.[36] However, the examples so far differ not only in style but also in tone. In our experimental section, we hold tone constant and look at the effect of style on attitudes toward legalization.

Length of Stay in the United States   In addition to more general framing techniques such as episodic and thematic framing, there are frames spe-cific to immigration that are relevant to debates on legalization. In the 1986 Immigration Reform and Control Act, years spent in the United States was one of the criteria used to determine eligibility for legalization: an applicant needed to have arrived prior to January 1, 1982, and to have been residing continuously since then in the United States in order to be eligible for legal status. More recent attempts to provide a way for the unauthorized immigrant population to achieve legal status have not only excluded recent arrivals but also required that people spend ten years in a registered provisional status before they can apply for legalization and a subsequent pathway to citizenship.[37] This kind of time requirement, albeit less onerous for those who have "green cards," has been part of our system of immigration and naturalization for decades; as Elizabeth Cohen has shown, the argument for time as a basis for political member-ship was a central component of early Anglo and American conceptions of citizenship.[38]

Given the importance of time requirements in legislative debates on legalization and in long-standing principles on naturalization, we might expect "length of stay" to be a significant aspect of news coverage on im-migrant legalization. Furthermore, in line with other expectations by ide-ology of news source, we would expect conservative news sources to be less likely than mainstream or liberal news sources to play up lengthy stay requirements in immigration reform legislation. To measure the per-centage of legalization stories that mention the number of years that im-migrants have spent in the United States across media outlets, we em-ployed a quantitative content analysis. Specifically, we employed a Lexis-Nexis term search to identify legalization stories that included terms related to years in the United States.[39] The following is an example from CNN's Rick Sanchez of how such information can be conveyed.

But let's—can we just look at this from a commonsensical standpoint, if that is even possible in this country anymore? **There are people who have been in this country,** and the real sticking point in this bill is going to be— you and I both know this—is it not about how big the wall is. It's about legalization. It's about this question, Ruben. Who is allowed and should have a path to citizenship and who shouldn't? **A little old lady here who has been for forty years cleaning someone's house in Houston or in Dallas. A guy who came here when he was one [year] old,** and his parents may have been illegal, but in the meantime, he has gone on with his own dough to a junior high school and has now got a four-year degree and has opened up his own business.[40]

Most striking is that regardless of news organization and medium, there was little mention of the number of years that undocumented immigrants have spent living in the United States (see table 3.7). In terms of the percentage of legalization news stories including some discussion of length of stay, only the liberal MSNBC (1.1 percent) and the more mainstream *Washington Post* (9.7 percent) and *New York Times* (1.9 percent) broke the 1 percent mark. All other news organizations were below 1 percent on this measure. In raw terms, the *Washington Post* (ten stories) and *Washington Times* (three stories) ran the most stories that included a mention of years in the United States.

While we were confident that the quantitative search yielded accurate results about the prevalence of legalization stories mentioning the length of time undocumented immigrants had lived in the United States, we also coded for the appearance of this frame in our more detailed qualitative content analysis. In short, the qualitative findings are almost identical to those of the quantitative search. Overall, mention of the years spent in the United States frame was largely absent from the legalization coverage in all five news organizations (see table 3.8). In every organization's coverage over the four years sampled (2007, 2010, 2012, and 2013), only the mainstream *Washington Post* (9 percent) included the years in the United States frame in more than 2 percent of its legalization stories.

When we use our more detailed qualitative coding of legalization stories to look at patterns over time in the use of this frame, three findings stand out. First, we find that the media's inclusion of length of stay in its legalization coverage was minimal. In each year, with the exception of 2013, no more than 1.9 percent of all legalization stories included a reference to the length of time undocumented immigrants lived in the United States. Second, we find that 2013 stands out as a high point in terms of the inclusion of the length of stay in legalization stories. Specifi-

Table 3.7 Immigrant Legalization Stories Mentioning Years Residing in the United States, by News Source and Year

	CNN	Fox News	MSNBC	Washington Post	Washington Times	New York Times	New York Post	All	N
2007	0.0%	0.0%	0.0%	7.1%	2.4%	0.0%	0.0%	1.3%	230
2010	0.0	0.0	0.0	0.0	0.0	0.0	0.0	0.0	187
2012	0.0	0.0	0.0	0.0	0.0	9.7	0.0	3.2	94
2013	0.0	0.0	1.5	17.8	0.0	0.0	0.0	2.4	373
All	0.0	0.0	1.1	9.7	0.7	1.9	0.0	1.7	884
N	174	140	94	103	141	103	141	—	—

Source: Authors' quantitative content analysis of news data (see chapter 3, note 39).

Table 3.8 Immigrant Legalization Stories in Seven News Sources Mentioning Years Residing in the United States, 2007–2013

	CNN	Fox News	MSNBC	Washington Post	Washington Times	New York Times	New York Post
Years in the United States (percentage)	0.0%	0.0%	1.0%	9.0%	0.7%	1.9%	0.0%
Years in the United States (raw count)	0	0	1	10	1	3	0

Source: Authors' qualitative analysis of results from table 3.7.

cally, 3.3 percent of immigrant legalization stories in 2013 mentioned length of stay. Finally, this small bump in mentions was driven by the coverage of the *Washington Post,* which mentioned years in the United States in 17.8 percent of its legalization stories in 2013.

Pro and Con Frames About Legalization Policy   Frames that mention particular considerations for or against legalization policies are another important part of media coverage of the issue. Similar to other policies, the legalization debate comprises a number of frames both in favor of and opposed to the legalization of "illegal" immigrants. In this section, we identify four salient considerations as they have been discussed in the literature on immigration policy and report the extent to which they appear in legalization stories across news organizations and time. Using a quantitative search within the legalization stories, we coded for whether an article uses terms related to the following legalization frames: economic effect, familial dimension, rule of law, and impact on crime (safety).[41] Owing to the limitations of the quantitative content analysis, we cannot characterize whether the economic frame is permissive (legalization provides economic benefits) or restrictive (legalization burdens Americans with additional costs). However, given the nature of the debate and the search terms used, we assume that the familial frame is permissive for legalization and that the rule of law and crime frames are restrictive or against legalization.[42] Given that the quantitative content analysis cannot distinguish between the more permissive economic benefits frame and the more restrictive economic costs frame, and to check our assumptions about the other frames, we also investigated their use in our qualitative content analysis.[43]

Before turning to our findings, we provide examples of each frame. The following excerpt from the political pundit Patrick Buchanan, from *Hardball* on MSNBC, illustrates the restrictive economic costs frame:

> Look, you got thirty-six million immigrants in the country. You got twelve million to twenty million illegals in the country. They are **directly competitive with African American folks and Mexican Americans,** half of whom don't even graduate from high school. And of the half that does graduate, they don't go to college. **They're in construction jobs, all kinds of jobs.** Illegal immigrants and immigrants are competing with working folks. They're not competing with Chris Matthews, Robert Reich, and Pat Buchanan. And **it's an enormous increase in the labor supply, and that drives down the price of labor, which is wages.**[44]

MSNBC's Thomas Roberts provides an example of the more permissive economic benefits frame:

MSNBC policy analyst Ezra Klein is going to join the show later on. He makes this great economic argument about immigration reform in a recent blog post, saying that where he talks about immigration or immigrant entrepreneurs outpacing American ones. And giving—how **giving undocumented residents legal status will then turn them into taxpayers here.** This is on top of other studies, sir, which have also shown that **immigration reform would drastically boost our economy.**[45]

Alternatively, the rule of law frame generally purports that undocumented immigrants should not be legalized because society should not reward people who break the law with citizenship. Rather, this frame would contend, the undocumented should follow current legal channels if they want to gain entry into and citizenship in the United States. In this example, notice how Representative Steve King (R-IA) emphasizes the violation of the rule of law in answering Fox News host Sean Hannity's question about King's confidence in the border security provisions of immigration reform:

I only have confidence that we're not going to get border security out of these people. They were never serious about it. No, these promises are not going to be followed through. . . . That's really the only way we get this done. They are not serious, **they want to undermine the rule of law and anything that legalizes is a path to citizenship,** which is, of course, **amnesty.**[46]

We then coded for the criminal frame, which associates undocumented immigrants with crimes (DUIs, drugs, theft, murder), the proliferation of gangs, and the violent activities associated with gangs. This excerpt from a *Fox Special Report* in 2013 illustrates the criminal frame:

DOUG MCKELWAY, FOX NEWS CORRESPONDENT: Good evening, Bret. Today's was the first hearing on the Hill on comprehensive immigration reform since a bipartisan group of senators, four Republicans and four Democrats, reported progress in crafting comprehensive immigration reform. That package appears to be gaining pretty much broad support, and not a moment too soon. The Senate Judiciary Committee got an earful from panelists today describing the dysfunction of the present immigration policy. DHS secretary Janet Napolitano came under special criticism. Senator Chuck Grassley cited internal DHS documents showing the **ICE agents delayed the arrest of a child rapist** by the name of Abraham Sanchez Zabileda, apparently after learning such an arrest would garner unwanted media and congressional scrutiny.

SENATOR CHUCK GRASSLEY (R-IA): Isn't that a shocking assertion, that a U.S. citizenship and immigration service would have the discretion to grant a **child rapist** application to stay in the country. **Today, this person is free in the United States.**[47]

Finally, the familial frame often argues that creating a path to citizenship will allow families comprising both citizens and noncitizens to remain intact instead of being broken apart. In this 2013 CNN segment, the response of an undocumented immigrant named Luis to Shannon Travis's question vividly illustrates this frame:

SHANNON TRAVIS: And sir, why are you out here today?

LUIS: Because I came to support immigration. And I'm working all night last night, and also I came to Washington. **And I want to [stay] because my daughter,** she born here in New Mexico, and I no have papers, and so I don't know what—**what I can say when immigration touch me. I no have papers.**

SHANNON TRAVIS: Thank you, Luis, for talking with us.[48]

In keeping with our overall expectation that ideology drives the media framing of immigration news coverage, we expect our quantitative content analysis to reveal relatively more stories with the legal and crime frames in the more conservative outlets compared to the mainstream and liberal outlets, and more stories with the family frame arguments in the mainstream and liberal outlets compared to the conservative outlets. Given that this search does not tell us if economic arguments are positive or negative, we do not have expectations across outlets. The results of the quantitative content analysis on the percentage of all immigration stories including the different frames are presented in table 3.9. Overall, we find that immigration news stories most often included the economic frame. Specifically, 32 percent of all immigration stories contained the economic frame. The familial and crime frames were present in only 22 percent and 21 percent of news stories, respectively. Somewhat surprisingly, the rule of law frame turned up in only 6 percent of all legalization stories.

Second, we separate these numbers by news source and present the three cable news sources first. For CNN, we observe results similar to the general finding that the economic frame (50 percent) is most prevalent, followed by the familial (35 percent), crime (30 percent), and rule of law frame (9 percent). For Fox News, we find that the economic (35 percent) and crime (34 percent) frames are virtually tied for the most frequently appearing frame in Fox News stories about legalization, while the family (20 percent) frame comes in third. Again, the rule of law frame was present in relatively few Fox News legalization stories (8 percent). Finally,

Table 3.9 Immigrant Legalization Stories in Seven News Sources Including Various Frames, 2007–2013

	CNN	Fox News	MSNBC	Washington Post	Washington Times	New York Times	New York Post	All
Rule of law	9%	8%	9%	2%	11%	6%	3%	6%
Economic effects	50	35	58	18	34	43	29	32
Crime	30	34	34	10	28	28	19	21
Familial	35	20	20	14	26	35	10	22

Source: Authors' quantitative content analysis of news data.
Note: Totals may add up to more than 100 percent since stories can contain more than one frame.

MSNBC revealed very similar trends. The most frequent frame to appear in MSNBC legalization stories was the economic frame (58 percent), followed by the crime (34 percent), familial (20 percent), and rule of law frames (9 percent). The findings for the familial frame are expected, with the frame being more prominent on MSNBC and CNN than on Fox News, but the crime frame is more prominent only on Fox News compared to CNN; the use of the legal frame is similar across networks.

Turning to the print media, for both the *Washington Post* (18 percent) and the *Washington Times* (34 percent), the economic frame was the most prevalent. The only difference in the order of prevalence is that the familial frame replaced the criminal frame as the second most frequently used frame in the *Washington Post*. This is in line with expectations for differences between the two outlets. As with the cable sources, the rule of law frame was the least likely to appear in legalization stories in both the *Washington Post* and the *Times*.

While the prior findings on the inclusion of the economic frame are interesting, they are unable to distinguish the pro-economic argument (undocumented immigrants add economic value and contribute to our economy and government coffers) from the con-economic argument (undocumented immigrants impose an economic cost on our government and society). To address this issue and to develop a richer data set, we conducted a qualitative content analysis that is the basis of the results for the remainder of this section. We coded stories as including the pro-economic frame if they included mention of any type of economic benefit (such as more tax revenue, increased economic activity, or providing necessary labor) that might accrue to the federal government, state or local governments, or other American entities or persons from the presence of undocumented immigrants in the United States. Alternatively, we coded stories as including the con-economic frame if they mentioned the economic cost (such as burdening the health care, education, and criminal justice systems) accruing to the same from the presence of undocumented immigrants. Once we make this distinction, we find a clear ideological divide in each news organization's use of the pro- and con-economic frames (see table 3.10).

First, as expected, the liberal MSNBC (30.9 percent) and mainstream CNN (21.3 percent) were most likely to include the pro-economic frame in their legalization coverage, while the conservative *New York Post* was the least likely (6.9 percent). Next, Fox News (32.1 percent) and the *Washington Times* (27.7 percent) were much more likely to include con-economic frames than the more mainstream and liberal news outlets, although the *New York Post* was the least likely to make references to con-economic arguments (8.3 percent).

When examining the results for the pro–rule of law frame, we saw few differences between sources in the quantitative data. While we classified

Table 3.10 Immigrant Legalization Stories in Seven News Sources with Pro- and Con-Economic Frames, 2007, 2010, 2012, and 2013

	CNN		Fox News		MSNBC		Washington Post		Washington Times		New York Times		New York Post		All	
	Pro	Con	Pro	Con	Pro	Con	Pro	Con	Pro	Con	Pro	Con	Pro	Con	Pro	Con
2007	20.4%	20.4%	9.7%	32.3%	45.5%	54.5%	25.0%	10.7%	4.8%	33.3%	20.0%	32.7%	8.3%	8.3%	16.8%	26.7%
2010	18.9	17.0	14.3	26.2	23.1	15.4	4.8	0.0	16.1	29.0	22.7	9.1	20.0	0.0	15.6	19.4
2012	14.3	0.0	0.0	16.7	50.0	25.0	33.3	0.0	12.5	20.8%	19.4	6.5	16.7	0.0	17.5	12.3
2013	25.9	19.0	21.3	37.7	28.8	16.7	11.1	13.3	11.4	25.0	22.0	16.0	4.1	10.2	20.8	22.6
All	21.3	17.2	15.7	32.1	30.9	21.3	15.5	8.7	10.6	27.7	20.9	19.0	6.9	8.3	17.8	20.3
N	174		140		94		103		141		158		72		882	

Source: Authors' qualitative content analysis of news data.
Note: Totals may add up to more than 100 percent since stories can contain more than one frame.

the rule of law frame as more restrictive, it could also cut both ways. A pro–rule of law argument suggests that undocumented immigrants are otherwise law-abiding people, while a con–rule of law argument points out that undocumented immigrants do not respect the rule of law and in fact contribute to lawlessness and crime. Thus, to check the validity of the quantitative results, we coded for both the pro– and con–rule of law frames in the qualitative content analysis. Similar to the economic frame results, the findings regarding the inclusion of the pro– and con–rule of law frame are also consistent with the ideological news hypothesis (see table 3.11).

First, the liberal outlet, MSNBC (13.8 percent), and the mainstream outlets, the *New York Times* (28.1 percent) and CNN (12.6 percent), were most likely to include the pro–rule of law frame in their legalization coverage over the four years sampled, while the conservative *Washington Times* (4.3 percent) and *New York Post* (5.6 percent) were the least likely. Fox News (40.7 percent) coverage was by far the most likely to include the con–rule of law frame. By contrast, the con–rule of law frame appeared in only 13.6 percent and 24.5 percent of the legalization coverage of the mainstream *Washington Post* and liberal MSNBC, respectively. Thus, when we look at a finer-grained qualitative content analysis of the legal frame, the findings are in line with our expectations.

Turning to qualitative content analysis findings for the pro-familial frame, somewhat similar findings abound. We coded stories as including the familial frame if they contained language that either explicitly stated or suggested that either legalization would help keep families together or the lack of a legalization process was weakening families.[49] There is therefore no con-familial frame, primarily because of its extremely rare occurrence. Although the differences are not as stark, cable news sources' legalization coverage includes more use of the familial frame than the print media do. Again, CNN and MSNBC lead all sources with 35 percent and 34 percent of their legalization stories, respectively, including the familial frame (results not shown). However, for this frame, it is CNN, not MSNBC, that is the most frequent user. Also of note, the *Washington Post* is again the least likely to include the familial frame in its legalization stories.

The con-crime frame results from the qualitative content analysis suggest a pattern similar to that of the economic frame. We coded stories as including the con-crime frame if they contained language that either explicitly stated or suggested that legalization would either increase the amount of crime (for example, gang violence) or undermine public safety. We did not code for the pro-crime frame that "illegal" immigrants reduce crime or increase public safety owing to its extremely infrequent appearance. (Importantly, most social science research on the topic indicates that immigrants are less likely to commit violent crime than the

Table 3.11 Immigrant Legalization Stories in Seven News Sources with Pro– and Con–Rule of Law Frames, 2007, 2010, 2012, and 2013

	CNN		Fox News		MSNBC		Washington Post		Washington Times		New York Times		New York Post		All	
	Pro	Con	Pro	Con	Pro	Con	Pro	Con	Pro	Con	Pro	Con	Pro	Con	Pro	Con
2007	10.2%	46.9%	9.7%	45.2%	0.0%	72.7%	7.1%	25.0%	2.4%	35.7%	21.1%	10.9%	0.0%	8.3%	6.8%	41.6%
2010	13.2	11.3	4.8	35.7	30.8	30.8	14.3	14.3	3.2	22.6	31.8	0.0	0.0	0.0	10.6	21.9
2012	0.0	28.6	16.7	16.7	25.0	25.0	11.1	0.0	4.2	29.2	32.3	3.2	16.7	0.0	7.0	22.8
2013	17.2	19.0	11.5	44.3	12.1	15.2	11.1	8.9	6.8	18.2	32.0	6.0	6.1	0.0	12.0	21.9
All	12.6	25.3	9.3	40.7	13.8	24.5	10.7	13.6	4.3	26.2	28.1	6.3	5.6	1.4	7.4	21.1
N	174		140		94		103		141		103		141		882	

Source: Authors' qualitative content analysis of news data.
Note: Stories may contain more than one frame.

Table 3.12   **Immigrant Legalization Stories Including Various Frames, 2007, 2010, 2012, and 2013**

	All Four Years Combined	2007	2010	2012	2013
Pro–rule of law	12.9%	10.0%	12.8%	15.9%	13.9%
Con–rule of law	26.8	41.6	21.9	22.8	21.9
Pro-economic	18.3	16.8	15.6	17.5	20.8
Con-economic	21.9	26.7	19.4	12.3	22.6
Crime	19.6	20.5	21.3	5.3	21.2
Familial	6.1	5.6	5.0	0.0	8.4

Source: Authors' qualitative content analysis of news data.
Note: Stories may contain more than one frame.

native-born population, and that immigration tends to reduce crime, but we find very little instance of this kind of positive framing on immigration associated with crime in our content analysis.)[50] Finally, we find that cable news organizations use the crime frame more frequently than print sources. For example, CNN, Fox News, and MSNBC included the crime frame in 32 percent, 34 percent, and 38 percent of their legalization stories, respectively (see table 3.9). In contrast, the *Washington Post* and the *Washington Times* did so in only 10 percent and 28 percent of their stories, respectively. Another interesting finding is that the crime frame is the only frame for which FOX News does not come in a distant third among cable news sources. However, this finding is consistent with a more ideological read of the data, since the crime frame is almost always restrictive in its content and negative in its tone.

Finally, an examination of the frequency with which the four frames (economic, familial, rule of law, crime) appear over time in legalization coverage reveals a number of interesting findings. In the interest of simplicity, and given the richer coding of the qualitative analysis, we present only the qualitative results here, noting any differences in patterns from the quantitative coding analysis (see table 3.12). First, we find a substantial degree of stability in frame frequency over time. At least in the aggregate, the annual frequencies for all issue frames (pro– and con–rule of law, pro- and con-economic, crime, familial) remain relatively stable across the six-year period. For only two frames (con–rule of law and crime) is there even one year when the difference between that year's percentage and the overall overtime mean for that particular frame is greater than ten percentage points. By contrast, we find much more volatility in the quantitative analysis for nearly all of the frames considered.[51]

Another glaring inconsistency between the quantitative and qualitative results is the fact that quantitative percentages are often significantly higher than qualitative percentages. Given the thorough nature of our qualitative content analyses, we think that the quantitative searches may be picking up a large number of false positives. This finding underscores an important point about the accuracy of quantitative search term coding of issue frames: quantitative search terms identify only key words or sets of words and are often unable to pick up the nuances of news coverage in which the same words mentioned together in a sentence or paragraph can carry very different meanings. Thus, taken together with our previous finding of significant intermedia outlet variation in issue framing, it appears instead that media organizations, not year-to-year changes in context, are driving the variation in legalization framing.

To sum up, though a few time- or source-specific nuances do emerge from the data, the dominant and most consistent findings from both the quantitative content analyses and the qualitative content analyses support our assertion that the ideology of the news organization seems to be driving the framing of legalization. Conservative news outlets such as Fox News and the *Washington Times* more frequently mention con-legalization frames, while the more mainstream or liberal news outlets, such as MSNBC, CNN, and the *Washington Post*, more frequently mention pro-legalization frames. Importantly, while the contrast in framing between conservative and liberal news outlets is in line with our expectations, we find that the framing of immigrant legalization in mainstream sources such as CNN and the *Washington Post* is much closer to the framing at left-leaning MSNBC than to a midpoint between, say, Fox News and CNN.

The Effect of Frames on Public Opinion

Now that we have looked extensively at variations in news framing of comprehensive immigration reform, across time and sources and along key dimensions such as tone, type of news story, and pro and con arguments, we now examine the possible effects of some of these frames on public opinion on CIR. To explore the effect of different frames on support for CIR, we conducted a series of survey experiments in which we focused on several frames explored in the content analysis, including the amnesty versus opportunity frame, episodic versus thematic frames, and how much time immigrants have spent in the United States, along with different frames for and against CIR. We also look at how source cues affect opinions related to some of these frames.

We embedded survey experiments in the 2007 and 2010 Cooperative Congressional Election Studies (CCES), which were conducted online through YouGov. In addition to the CCES data sets, we were able to place questions on two original online experimental studies in 2011 and 2012, also conducted by YouGov.[52] Finally, to test some additional frames and source cues, we placed questions on a 2013 study on Mechanical Turk and a 2014 study with Survey Sampling International (SSI) panelists. Given the wide range of frames that we test in this chapter, we discuss our expectations as we turn to each frame.

Amnesty Versus Opportunity

We begin by looking at the general issue frames surrounding legalization, as we did with the content analysis. As we noted earlier, restrictionists typically refer to legalization attempts as "amnesty," while pro-immigrant advocates typically refer to such attempts as "opportunities" or "pathways to citizenship." To examine the effects of these different issue frames, we designed a simple survey experiment in which we varied just a few terms. More specifically, respondents in the 2007 and 2010 CCES were asked their level of agreement or disagreement with the following statement: "If we can seal our borders and enforce existing immigration laws, [*randomize:* illegal/undocumented/unauthorized] immigrants should be given [*randomize:* the opportunity to eventually become legal citizens/amnesty]." Individuals were randomly assigned to one of the three terms used to describe immigrants without legal status as well as to the amnesty or opportunity frame. We used the same amnesty or opportunity frame in our 2011, 2012, and 2014 studies.[53] Since amnesty has become a highly charged term often used by those on the right who oppose legalization, we expect that it will decrease support for legalization relative to support from those who read only "an opportunity to eventually become legal citizens." The latter statement is also ambiguous with respect to what needs to be done for an individual to become a legal citizen. We analyze the effects for the terms used to describe immigrants in a later chapter.

To explore whether attributing the amnesty or opportunity frame to a political source matters, in our 2012 YouGov study we provided information linking the frames to a source. We focus on comparing a baseline neutral source against a partisan source as well as against Fox News, in part given the high coverage of the amnesty frame on that outlet. More specifically, respondents were randomly assigned to receive one of the following prompts: "some say," "some Republicans say," "some Democrats say," or "some commentators on Fox News say." This was followed with the same question used in all of the other studies: "If we can seal our borders and enforce existing immigration laws, illegal immigrants should be given [*randomize:* amnesty/an opportunity to eventually become citizens]."

Since the messages coming from the source are supportive of comprehensive immigration reform, individuals should in general move in the direction of the message. That being said, the effectiveness of the different source cues may vary according to two characteristics. First, most

Figure 3.1   Mean Support for Legalization by Amnesty Versus Opportunity Wording, 2007, 2010, 2011, 2012, and 2014

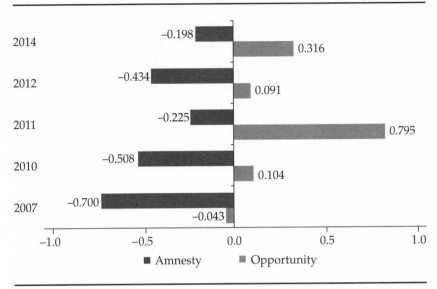

Source: Authors' analysis of YouGov and SSI 2014 data.

individuals would expect to see a Democratic source supporting CIR, so they might not be affected very much by that source cue compared to a neutral source cue. However, a statement supporting legalization coming from the Republican Party or Fox News would be more novel and might therefore be more persuasive.[54] Therefore, these latter two cues may be more effective in increasing support for legalization compared to a neutral frame. Second, whether individuals move in the direction of the source may be moderated by their partisan identification. That is, Democrats may be more persuaded by the Democratic cue and react against the Republican cue, and vice versa.[55]

Individuals were asked for their level of agreement or disagreement on a five-point Likert scale. We recode the dependent variable to run on a scale from –2 to 2, where –2 is "strongly disagree," –1 is "disagree," 0 is "neither agree nor disagree," 1 is "agree," and 2 is "strongly agree." (One exception is 2011, which runs from –3 to 3.) Therefore, higher values are more supportive of legalization. We first present mean support for legalization across the studies by the amnesty and opportunity frames in figure 3.1.

As is clear from the figure, mean support for legalization is generally to the right of the neutral point when the opportunity frame is used, which is moderately supportive of legalization, with the exception of

2007, where the mean is just left of the neutral point, toward opposition. The introduction of the amnesty frame, on the other hand, always moves opinion toward net opposition to legalization. All of these differences between the amnesty and opportunity frames are statistically significant according to difference in means tests ($p < 0.00$ in each case). Furthermore, the substantive effects are quite meaningful. The smallest difference between the two frames, in 2012, is still more than half a unit, which is impressive for a five-point scale. The largest difference is in 2011, where we find a full unit difference (1.02) between the two treatments. However, the scale for that year runs from –3 to 3. These findings suggest that the particular frames employed in media discourse on legalization can be very consequential for public opinion. Recall from the content analysis that the amnesty frame is more prominent than the opportunity frame across all media outlets, particularly the more conservative media outlets. These results hold up if we run regressions controlling for variables that are unevenly distributed across experimental conditions (see tables A3.1 to A3.5 in the appendix).[56]

In additional to the general effects of issue frames, we are also interested in exploring whether certain individuals are more or less affected by them. In this chapter, we look at whether individual reactions vary depending on partisanship, Fox News viewership (when this measure is available), education, and family immigration history, as well as whether the respondent is Latino. To do this we run an ordinary least squares (OLS) regression analysis with a dummy for the amnesty condition (and the opportunity condition serving as the baseline), a measure for the relevant subgroup, and interactions between the amnesty condition and the subgroup measure.[57] For 2007, we find that the amnesty frame is moderated by family immigration history. In figure 3.2, we plot the effect of the amnesty frame (relative to the opportunity frame) by family immigration history (see table A3.1 for full regression results).

The amnesty frame is significantly different from the opportunity frame for each generation, and it serves to reduce support for legalization. However, the effect of the amnesty frame becomes more pronounced with each generation. Therefore, individuals who have been in the United States for more generations are more affected by the amnesty frame relative to the opportunity frame. However, we find this moderating effect only in 2007. That this study came on the heels of the 2006 immigration marches may partly explain the weaker effects among those who were born outside of the United States and those in the first generation. In 2010, we find, the amnesty frame is moderated by partisanship.[58] More specifically, the amnesty frame is significant and negative for Democrats, independents, and Republicans, but the effects get stronger as we move from being a Democrat to being a Republican. Democrats in the amnesty frame are almost half a unit less supportive of legalization com-

Figure 3.2   Change in Support for Legalization Given Exposure to the Amnesty Frame Relative to the Opportunity Frame, by Family Immigration History, 2007

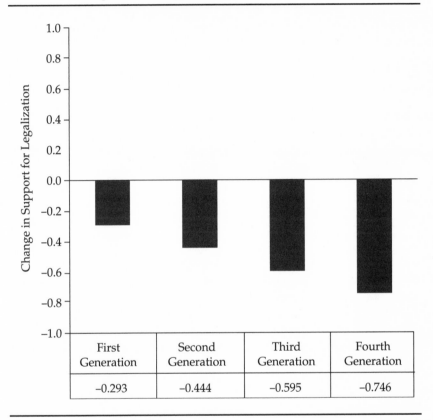

	First Generation	Second Generation	Third Generation	Fourth Generation
	−0.293	−0.444	−0.595	−0.746

Source: Authors' analysis of 2007 CCES survey data.

pared to their counterparts in the opportunity frame. The comparable effect for independents is −0.630, and for Republicans −0.790 (see table A3.2 for full regression results).

These results are even more interesting given that Republicans who watch Fox News are probably already exposed to the amnesty frame. At the same time, the frame may have resonated more with their existing predispositions on the issue. For 2007, we find similar effects for ideology, with the amnesty frame becoming more effective moving from a liberal to a conservative respondent (see table A3.1). However, in 2011 and 2012 we do not find evidence of any moderating effects, and in 2014 we find only that the effect is moderated by education (see note 59). Therefore, in two out of the five studies we find some evidence of the

Figure 3.3   Mean Support for Legalization by Source Cue, 2012

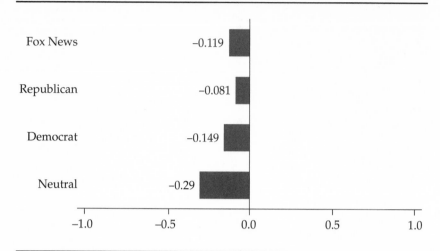

Source: Authors' analysis of 2012 YouGov survey data.

amnesty frame being more effective among those on the right. Part of the reason for the lack of moderating effects for partisanship in the later years may be that amnesty mentions in the conservative outlets decrease over time, such that the coverage begins to look similar to that in the mainstream media outlets. Since the news outlets start looking more alike, it could be that different partisan groups react similarly to the treatment. The shifts over time may also reflect the relative salience of immigration, which, according to Gallup polls, was lower in 2011, 2012, and 2013 compared to 2007 and 2010.[59] When immigration was more salient in the environment, individuals may have been better able to link the frames to their partisan dispositions.

We next turn to the source cue manipulation that we used in 2012; see figure 3.3 for mean support for legalization plotted by source cue. Recall that about half of the people in each source cue condition received the amnesty frame while about half received the opportunity frame.[60] Mean support is toward net opposition across all of the experimental conditions. However, net opposition is most pronounced in the neutral frame; stances soften with the introduction of the three source cues. The difference between the neutral cue and the Republican cue is significant according to a difference-in-means test ($p = 0.04$, two-tailed), as is the difference between the Fox News cue and the neutral cue ($p = 0.096$, two-tailed). However, there are no significant differences between the Democratic cue and the neutral cue ($p = 0.195$, two-tailed).

It therefore appears that the more unexpected positive cues coming from sources on the right are more effective relative to a neutral cue and compared to an expected cue from the left. When we test for moderating effects between the experimental conditions and education, Latino, partisanship, family immigration history, and Fox News viewership, we find evidence of such moderating effects only between the Democratic source cue and partisanship, on the one hand, and between the Democratic source cue and Latinos, on the other (see table A3.4 for full results). The effects are such that Democrats become more supportive of legalization when exposed to the Democratic source cue compared to their counterparts in the neutral cue ($\beta = 0.284$, $p = 0.062$). However, independents and Republicans are unaffected by the Democratic cue. We find a similar effect for Latinos. Latinos who receive the Democratic source cue become more supportive of legalization compared to their counterparts in the neutral cue ($\beta = 0.536$, $p = 0.014$), while the treatment has no effect on non-Latinos. This suggests that an expected source cue may be effective, but only among those who share some affinities with the source.[61]

Years Spent in the United States

We next turn to another general frame: whether the amount of time the undocumented immigrant has been in the United States matters for opinions. The amount of time the undocumented have spent in the United States did not receive very much coverage in print media—less than 2 percent coverage in all stories from 2007 to 2013. This type of information may be very important to the public's willingness to support comprehensive immigration reform, however, so we wanted to explore in what ways length of stay matters, even though such information has been limited in media coverage. For closer examination, we selected two shorter time periods, two and five years, and two longer ones, ten and twenty years. Our general expectation is that individuals will be more supportive of legalization the more time an undocumented immigrant has spent in the United States. However, the effect of this frame could vary by the source delivering the message, as it has for some of our other dependent variables, so we use the same sources that we used in looking at the amnesty and opportunity frames.

In our 2013 Mechanical Turk study, respondents were asked the following question:

[*randomize:* Some say/Some Republicans say/Some Democrats say/Some commentators on Fox News say] the U.S. government should give special consideration to [*randomize:* illegal immigrants/undocumented immigrants/illegal aliens] who have spent more than [*randomize:* two years/

Figure 3.4   Mean Support for Legalization by the Years in the United States Frame, 2013

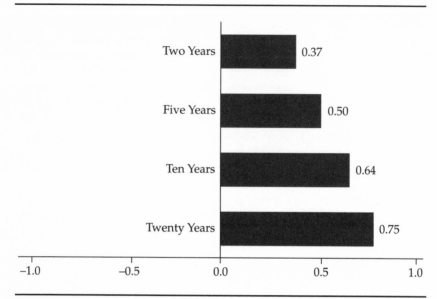

Source: Authors' analysis of 2013 Mechanical Turk survey data.

five years/ten years/twenty years] in the United States and have no criminal record. They say that such people should be allowed the opportunity to stay in this country and eventually become U.S. citizens. To what extent do you disagree or agree?[62]

We again code this measure to run from −2 to 2, with higher values being more supportive of legalization. We first present the results for the years in the United States manipulation (see figure 3.4). As expected, we see that support for legalization increases with the number of years the undocumented have been in the United States. Support is closer to the neutral point when individuals are treated with two years (mean = 0.37) and moves between neutral and "agree" for those treated with five years (mean = 0.50); support starts to move closer to the "agree" end of the scale for those who read about immigrants being in the United States ten years (mean = 0.64) and twenty years (mean = 0.75). The differences across conditions are also statistically meaningful (ANOVA: $p = 0.004$).[63] In this case, it does not appear that the source of the frame matters. There is no statistically significant difference across any of the source frames. Furthermore, the treatments are not moderated by partisanship, education, family immigration history, or Fox News viewership. The lack of many moderating relationships may also be partly related to how very novel this frame is to respondents; as such, it should be fairly effective across all groups.

The only case where we do find a moderating effect is for the Democratic source cue and Latinos.[64] Latinos in the Democratic source cue condition become almost a full unit more supportive of legalization (β = 0.92; p = 0.076) relative to their counterparts in the neutral cue condition (see table A3.6 for full regression results). It could be that hearing this cue from the Democratic Party further mobilizes support for legalization among Latinos. Overall, the results suggest that the number of years the undocumented have spent in the United States plays an important role in the extent to which immigrant legalization is supported by the public, who are much more willing to support legalization the more rooted immigrants are in the country.

More Specific Issue Frames For and Against Legalization

In our next set of survey experiments, we begin to test two issue frames surrounding legalization that are more specific: legal-based and economic-based arguments. The former receives very little coverage in the media, while the latter is the most prominent.

We first look at the legal argument framed in a more negative than positive way. In the 2010 CCES, respondents were randomly asked for their level of agreement with one of the following statements:

Allowing any [*randomize:* illegal/undocumented/unauthorized] to become citizens sets a bad precedent by rewarding people for breaking the law.

Allowing some [*randomize:* illegal/undocumented/unauthorized] to eventually become citizens recognizes that most of them are otherwise law-abiding neighbors.[65]

We recoded responses to range from −2 to 2, with 2 reflecting more favorable attitudes toward the undocumented. Again, we focus only on the legal frames, since we discuss the results for the terms used to describe those without legal status in chapter 6. Given the difference in tone between the two questions, our expectation is that opinions will be more favorable in the positive frame (law-abiding neighbors) compared to the negative frame (rewarding bad behavior), and this is exactly what we find. Opinion is right at the neutral point (mean = −0.01) among individuals exposed to the law-abiding frame and net negative among those exposed to the lawbreaking frame (mean = −0.92; p = 0.00). The shift in wording from "law-abiding" to "lawbreaking" is also substantively quite meaningful, as opinions shift almost a full unit on the five-point scale.[66] Furthermore, the findings are similar across many sub-

**Figure 3.5   Change in Support for Legalization Given Exposure to the
Lawbreaking Frame Relative to the Law-Abiding Frame, by
Family Immigration History, 2010**

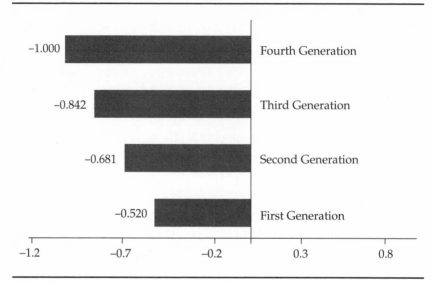

Source: Authors' analysis of 2010 CCES data (OLS regression).

groups. The only differential reaction we find is based on a person's
family immigration history (see table A3.7 for full results). As shown in
figure 3.5, the lawbreaking frame leads to more negative attitudes relative to the law-abiding frame for each generation, but the size of the effect becomes more substantial in later generations. Therefore, we see
some resistance to these frames from newer immigrants and the children of immigrants.

These results suggest that media coverage that focuses more on the
lawbreaking frame can lead to very large shifts in public opinion on immigrant legalization. These findings support arguments in the literature
for the strength of norms related to legality in the immigration debate.[67]

We next turn to a survey experiment conducted using Mechanical
Turk participants in 2013 in which we considered different economic
frames tied to different sources and their effects on a congressional bill
being considered. Individuals in the control group were asked:

> Congress is considering a bill that would give [*randomize:* illegal immi-
> grants/undocumented immigrants/illegal aliens] the opportunity to stay
> in this country, work legally, and eventually become U.S. citizens. How
> about you? To what extent do you disagree or agree that we should allow

[*randomize:* illegal immigrants/undocumented immigrants/illegal aliens]
the opportunity to eventually become legal citizens?

Individuals in the treated groups were given an additional statement
after the first sentence. They were randomly assigned to one of the following four statements and then asked for their level of agreement or
disagreement with legalization:

1. The conservative Heritage Foundation says that immigrant legalization will cost the United States over $1 trillion.

2. The conservative Cato Institute says that immigrant legalization will
   add over $1 trillion to the U.S. economy.

3. The liberal Center for American Progress says that immigrant legalization will add over $1 trillion to the U.S. economy.

4. The nonpartisan Congressional Budget Office says that immigrant
   legalization will add over $1 trillion to the U.S. economy.[68]

We expect the negative economic frame from the Heritage Foundation
to reduce support for legalization relative to the control group. The other
three conditions present the positive economic frame of immigrant legalization adding $1 trillion to the U.S. economy, though the source varies
from a liberal think tank to a conservative think tank to a nonpartisan
government entity. We can therefore see whether the effectiveness of the
positive economic frame varies depending on the source. In general, we
expect support for legalization to be higher in these conditions compared
to the control group and compared to the Heritage Foundation frame. As
with the amnesty versus opportunity analyses, the positive frame from
the CATO Institute may be particularly effective since it is from an unexpected source. Furthermore, the effects of the source frames may be moderated by partisanship. The dependent variable is again on a five-point
scale, ranging from −2 to 2, with higher values more supportive of legalization. In figure 3.6, we show mean support for legalization across the
five experimental conditions.

As expected, support for legalization is significantly lower with the
negative economic frame by the Heritage Foundation compared to the
control group ($p = 0.09$, two-tailed).[69] Meanwhile, support for legalization is higher with the positive economic frames compared to the control
group, but none of the differences are statistically meaningful. Therefore,
the negative frame is more effective in shifting opinions relative to no
frame, while the positive economic frame is ineffective. This finding is
consistent with expectations that negative messages are more effective
than positive messages.[70]

Figure 3.6   Mean Support for Legalization by Economic Frame Condition, 2013

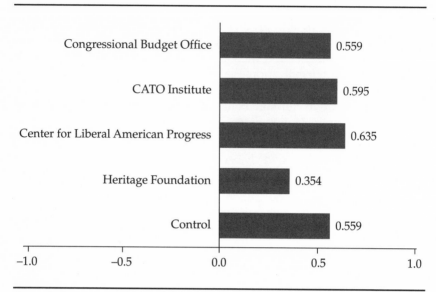

Source: Authors' analysis of 2013 Mechanical Turk survey data.

At the same time, we do see that partisans react differently to some of the frames, especially the ones coming from the Heritage Foundation and the Center for American Progress. We display these effects in figure 3.7 (see table A3.8 for regression results with and without controls). The Heritage Foundation condition reduces support for legalization across all partisan groups, as expected, but the effect is significant only for independents and Republicans, not for Democrats. Therefore, Democrats resist the message coming from an organization on the right, while it is very effective among Republicans, leading to over a half-unit decline in support for legalization. Meanwhile, Democrats become even more supportive of legalization relative to their counterparts in the control group when they are exposed to the "Center for American Progress" condition, while this treatment has no effect on independents and Republicans react against the treatment and move in the opposite direction. These findings show that individuals may react against framing effects when they are provided with the contextual information necessary to challenge information that runs counter to their dispositions (Bullock 2011; Druckman, Peterson, and Slothuus 2013; Zaller 1992).[71]

In sum, we find that the negative economic frame is quite effective, particularly among independents, Republicans, and those lower in education, while the positive economic frame resonates only with Demo-

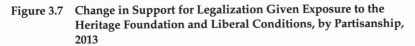

Figure 3.7 Change in Support for Legalization Given Exposure to the Heritage Foundation and Liberal Conditions, by Partisanship, 2013

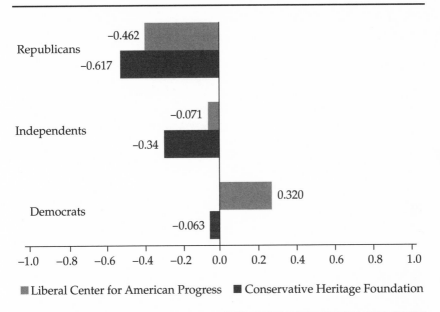

■ Liberal Center for American Progress ■ Conservative Heritage Foundation

Source: Authors' analysis of 2013 Mechanical Turk survey data (OLS regression).
Note: The effect is relative to the control group. We show only the two conditions for which we find moderating effects.

crats. Providing more positive information about the economic benefits of legalization does little to move opinions beyond the control group. This finding suggests that positive frames face more of an uphill battle in persuading the public.

The Style of the Frames

In our 2014 SSI study, we also designed an experiment to look at the style of the presentation of news information. After filling in a basic pretreatment survey, individuals were randomly assigned to a control condition or a condition in which they read a short newspaper blurb, such as one might see from the Associated Press, in which we used one of two styles, episodic or thematic, and in which we either included empathetic language or did not. The story in each case was a positively toned article on immigration and was drawn from real newspaper stories.

For the episodic human-interest frames, participants read the following story. One group assigned to this frame read the paragraph with non-empathetic language, while the other read the paragraph with empathetic language:

Immigration Reform Changes Little for Many

Steve Hendrix and Luz Lazo

For thousands of undocumented immigrants who rushed to apply for new protections from deportations, Wednesday was the life-changing day many had dreamed of for years. Advocates hailed President Obama's offer of temporary residency and work status to some young immigrants as the most significant reform in a generation. But, as some have learned as the details became clear, it is a narrowly tailored one.

Fewer than 2 million of the estimated 11 million undocumented immigrants in the country are eligible for the program, known as deferred action, which began accepting applications Wednesday, June 15th. That leaves life in the shadows to continue unchanged for the rest.

Next came the non-empathetically or empathetically phrased paragraph:

[*Non-empathetic language*] For many who have been waiting to learn the final details of the program, its launch brought disappointment. "I will be working today, that's all, if I can get work," said Ricardo Cruz, 22, a Salvadoran day laborer gathered with other job seekers in a parking lot on New Hampshire Avenue in Langley Park. "I have heard of this program, but they said it was not for me." He only learned while gathering documents to apply that he was too old when he arrived from El Salvador to be eligible.

[*Empathetic language*] For many who have been waiting to learn the final details of the program, its launch brought crushing disappointment. "It was devastating to hear I didn't qualify," said a disappointed Eliseo Hernandez after his visit to Carecen of Columbia Heights. Hernandez, 25, came to the United States when he was 17 and graduated from high school in 2008. He only learned while gathering documents to apply that he was too old when he arrived from El Salvador to be eligible. "I just want to study and be a good example to my daughters," he said.

The final paragraph was the same in the two stories:

The program targets those who were brought here as children. It is open to immigrants now ages 15 to 31, who arrived before they were 16, and have lived here continuously for the past five years or more. Among other restrictions, they must be free of serious criminal convictions and be in school or have a high school diploma or equivalent. That amounts to about

1.7 million immigrants, about 15 percent of the illegal immigrant population, although no one knows how many of those will actually apply.

In the thematic general-news conditions, the first, second, and fourth paragraphs were the same, but we changed the third paragraph to be a quote from a general specialist, with one quote being more empathetic than the other:

[*Non-empathetic language*] "It's a lot of people, but it does leave the vast majority of the undocumented population still undocumented," said Jeffrey Passel, senior demographer of the Pew Research Center. "Most of the undocumented immigrants in the country now are people who came here as adults on their own."

[*Empathetic language*] "These young people have the potential to be future doctors, nurses, teachers, and entrepreneurs," said Walter Ewing from the Immigration Policy Center. "Through no fault of their own, they didn't have legal status when they were brought to the United States as children, and this policy can help those youth overcome those hurdles and become successful."

Following exposure to the news story, respondents answered an array of immigration policy attitude questions, including the one on comprehensive immigration reform in which we varied the amnesty and opportunity wording.

Given that the frame is positively toned, we would expect any of the treatment groups to show higher support for legalization compared to those in the control group. If we compare across frames, we would expect thematic frames, as well as those that are empathetic, to be the most effective in increasing support for progressive immigration attitudes, as we noted in chapter 2. If we combine the two types of frames, we might expect the thematic empathetic frame to lead to the highest level of support for CIR and the episodic non-empathetic frame to be the least effective. Since we do not know if the style of the frame or the empathetic language is more effective, it is unclear if the thematic non-empathetic frame or the episodic empathetic frame will be more effective.

In figure 3.8, we plot mean support for CIR by experimental condition. Surprisingly, mean support is slightly higher in the control group relative to all four conditions, though none of the differences between experimental conditions is statistically significant. We also do not find any effects for the style of the frame or for empathetic language when we test whether the effects are different depending on one's family immigration history, partisanship, education, being Latino, or levels of trait empathy.

Figure 3.8   Mean Support for Legalization by Framing Style and Empathetic Language, 2014

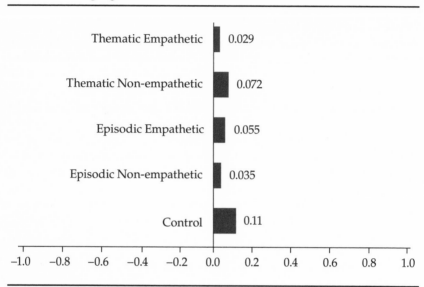

Thematic Empathetic	0.029
Thematic Non-empathetic	0.072
Episodic Empathetic	0.055
Episodic Non-empathetic	0.035
Control	0.11

−1.0   −0.8   −0.6   −0.4   −0.2   0.0   0.2   0.4   0.6   0.8   1.0

Source: Authors' analysis of 2014 SSI survey data.

Discussion and Conclusion

A few key findings stand out in our analysis of how immigrant legalization is framed in the news and what effects, if any, such frames have on public opinion. As we expected, the tone of the news coverage of immigrant legalization varies by the ideology of the news outlet, with the *Washington Times* and Fox News having the most negative coverage, MSNBC having the most positive coverage, and mainstream sources falling somewhere in between. We also, however, have some unexpected findings; the *New York Post*, for instance, is fairly neutral in its coverage of immigration reform. We also find that news coverage of immigrant legalization is more likely to include economic, family, and crime frames, with the legality frame receiving considerably less coverage. Finally, we find that mentions of amnesty decline over time, although they remain fairly high in conservative news sources such as Fox News.

We find that issue frames can have large effects on opinion, sometimes with the manipulation of just a few words. This is particularly true with respect to mentions of amnesty as compared to mentions of a pathway to citizenship. Thus, in line with recommendations by conservative strategists like Frank Luntz and rhetorical strategies employed by conservative elected officials and restrictionist interest groups and think tanks like

NumbersUSA and the Center for Immigration Studies, mentions of amnesty reduce support for immigrant legalization relative to a more positive frame.[72] Furthermore, the amnesty frame has particularly strong effects among those individuals who are more than two generations removed from the immigrant experience, as well as among independents and Republicans (in some years). Given the power of the amnesty frame, it is little surprise, then, that conservative news outlets continue to employ the term and that elected officials and interest groups opposed to immigration also continue to use the term when speaking with journalists.

However, the amnesty (versus pathway to citizenship) frame is not the only one that matters when it comes to public opinion on legalization. We also find that length of stay in the United States has a strong effect on support for immigrant legalization, with respondents much more likely to favor legalization when it involves people who are long-term residents (living in the United States for ten years or twenty years), as opposed to more recent residents (two years or five years). Importantly, however, we do not find much news mention of duration of stay in the United States, either in terms of actual years or through the use of terms like "long-term residents" or "recent arrivals." Thus, our findings suggest that pro-immigration advocates could increase public support for legalization if they consistently emphasize more novel frames like the long-term nature of the settled population of undocumented immigrants.

Third, while negative frames are often more effective than positive frames in shifting opinion on legalization, positive cues from unexpected sources can be effective in shifting opinions in a permissive direction. We find this to be the case, for example, when Fox News and the Republican Party are presented as promoting a positive frame on legalization. These results suggest that the Republican Party becoming more supportive of legalization might lead to shifts in public opinion. However, given the experiences of the 2016 Republican primary season, a shift in the party's stance in favor of legalization seems unlikely.

Finally, and surprisingly, we do not find that the style of the frames matters. That is, there are no meaningful differences in opinions toward legalization when respondents are presented with episodic compared to thematic coverage, regardless of whether we include empathetic language.

In the next chapter, we turn to the DREAM Act and Deferred Action for Childhood Arrivals, policies that gained more coverage and traction in the wake of the failure to pass comprehensive immigration reform.

4

The DREAM Act and DREAMers

WHILE CONGRESS has made several major efforts at comprehensive immigration reform, most notably in 2006, 2007, and 2013, CIR has not been the only federal policy solution aimed at immigrant integration. In this chapter, we pay specific attention to the Development, Relief, and Education for Alien Minors (or DREAM) Act. First, we introduce the historical context for the DREAM Act, from its origins in 2001 to its changing fate in 2007, 2010, and today. We also discuss the Obama administration's response to Congress's failure to pass the DREAM Act: an executive action establishing the Deferred Action for Childhood Arrivals (DACA) program.

Next, we provide a content analysis of how the DREAM Act was covered in the news. In particular, we pay attention to the relative prominence in news stories of frames that emphasize the consideration of beneficiaries as those who came to the United States as young children and those who had no choice in the matter of having a legal way to enter and stay in the United States. We also consider the extent to which the term "amnesty" is invoked in news coverage of the DREAM Act. In both cases, we again explore whether the use of these frames varies by the ideology of news source. We expect the use of the former frame to be more prevalent in liberal and mainstream outlets compared to conservative outlets, and the opposite for the amnesty frame.

After detailing coverage in print and cable media, we examine whether these issue frames make any difference for public opinion on the DREAM Act, using experimental data collected over several years. In general, we expect to find that individuals become more supportive of the DREAM Act given exposure to the child frame, and less supportive given exposure to the amnesty frame. However, we consider whether partisanship moderates reaction to these frames. Finally, we also consider how the amnesty frame affects support for DACA.

A Historical Overview of the DREAM Act

The Development, Relief, and Education for Alien Minors Act was first introduced in the U.S. Senate by Dick Durbin (D-IL) and Orrin Hatch (R-UT) on August 1, 2001, mirroring legislation introduced in the U.S. House of Representatives on May 21 of that year by Howard Berman (D-CA) and Chris Cannon (R-UT) titled Student Adjustment Act of 2001.[1] Later in 2007 and 2010, it was considered as a potential stand-alone piece of legislation that might pass in lieu of a more comprehensive effort to reform the nation's immigration laws. The primary provisions of the DREAM Act were to cancel deportation proceedings and "adjust to the status of an alien lawfully admitted for permanent residence" those who were of "good moral character," had not yet attained the age of twenty-one, and were enrolled in higher education.

Although prospects for the DREAM Act (and all other immigration reform legislation) faltered after the September 11, 2001, attacks, Durbin reintroduced the bill in each subsequent Congress. Since 2005, the bill has also included provisions for two years of military service in the United States, and it was included in the text of the Comprehensive Immigration Reform Act of 2006 and 2007.[2] When comprehensive immigration reform failed in the U.S. Senate in 2007, Senator Durbin reintroduced the DREAM Act as a stand-alone piece of legislation. The legislation had widespread popular support, with net positive support even among Republican voters.[3] However, that effort also failed to garner sufficient votes for cloture, as did a subsequent high-profile effort to pass the DREAM Act during the lame-duck session of Congress in 2010—even though Democrats held a filibuster-proof majority in the Senate and Majority Leader Harry Reid (D-NV) had just won a closely fought reelection campaign on the heels of massive outreach and mobilization efforts among Latino voters.[4]

These two stand-alone efforts in 2007 and 2010 received fairly high levels of media attention and are the focus of much of our content analysis and survey experiment findings.[5] Finally, the DREAM Act received renewed attention in the summer of 2012 as Senator Marco Rubio (R-FL) introduced a proposal that would legalize those who became undocumented as minors, but would not provide a pathway to citizenship for those individuals.[6] Soon thereafter, undocumented youth activists began to occupy President Obama's reelection campaign offices.[7] Within a week, the Obama administration replied by issuing an administrative directive creating the Deferred Action for Childhood Arrivals (DACA) program, which would exempt from deportation those who became undocumented as minors and who had no criminal record; it would also allow them to work in the United States.[8] Importantly, DACA was a temporary exemption that required potential beneficiaries to apply for the program and did not confer legal status on this class of individuals—only Congress could do that.

Our analysis in this chapter examines both aspects of policies toward undocumented children, with a primary focus on the DREAM Act but also some consideration of DACA after 2012.

Framing the DREAM Act in the News

The DREAM Act differs from what we looked at in the last chapter in being a much more targeted policy. We might therefore expect to see slightly fewer frames employed on this issue compared to legalization. In our content analysis, we look at the tone of coverage as well as the use of episodic and thematic frames, as we did in the prior chapter. Given that the issue concerns children, we also consider the additional dimension of whether there is empathetic language in the coverage. Finally, we consider a wide range of permissive and restrictive frames that are linked to the issue, focusing closely on the use of the child and amnesty frames.

As we noted in chapter 3, the advent of Fox News in 1996 has had some significant consequences for the presentation of immigration policies such as the DREAM Act.[9] The presence of Fox News has intensified the ideological presentation of a number of issues, including immigration. Thus, we expect Fox News to present the DREAM Act more negatively compared to other outlets and to highlight more restrictive frames, such as amnesty. We also expect conservative print outlets (the *New York Post* and the *Washington Times*) to have more restrictive news coverage than more mainstream outlets (the *New York Times* and the *Washington Post*).

Again similar to our case in chapter 3, we do not expect these general expectations to hold for all cable outlets. In particular, the pre-2010 tenure of restrictionist hosts Lou Dobbs and Glenn Beck should make CNN's DREAM Act coverage more restrictive than we might ordinarily expect. Similarly, we might also expect some ideological deviation for MSNBC prior to the 2009 election, when it regularly featured well-known conservatives, including Tucker Carlson and Patrick Buchanan. Thus, for CNN and MSNBC, we would expect to see changes in DREAM Act coverage before and after 2009–2010: coverage that is more permissive at MSNBC after 2009 and more balanced prior to 2009, and coverage that is split at CNN after 2010 and more conservative prior to 2010. Finally, we expect Fox News to have the most restrictive coverage throughout this period.

To explore the framing of the DREAM Act, we analyzed the content of news stories on the DREAM Act in mainstream (the *Washington Post* and the *New York Times*) and conservative (the *Washington Times* and *the New*

Table 4.1   Raw Counts of DREAM Act Stories, 2007–2013

	2007	2008	2009	2010	2011	2012	2013	All
CNN	53	17	11	132	83	265	35	596
Fox News	7	0	1	97	38	114	58	315
MSNBC	0	0	0	85	34	171	72	362
Washington Post	8	4	2	46	51	151	45	307
Washington Times	23	8	1	33	66	88	25	244
New York Times	11	2	9	45	67	159	34	327
New York Post	0	1	0	4	7	8	4	24

Source: Authors' quantitative content analysis of news data.

York Post) daily newspapers from 2007 through 2013.[10] Additionally, we analyzed DREAM Act stories from each of the three major cable networks (CNN on the mainstream side, Fox News on the conservative side, and MSNBC, which transitioned from mainstream to liberal during this time period). We retrieved a total of 596 DREAM Act stories from CNN, 315 from Fox News, 362 from MSNBC, 307 from the *Washington Post,* 244 from the *Washington Times,* 327 from the *New York Times,* and 24 from the *New York Post* (see table 4.1). To analyze these stories we employed a quantitative content analysis (child mentions, amnesty mentions) and a qualitative content analysis (tone of coverage, empathetic language, permissiveness, episodic or thematic framing).

The Tone of Coverage

We find systematic differences in the overall tone of news coverage of the DREAM Act across sources.[11] Story tone is the extent to which a news story casts "illegal" immigrants in a favorable (positive) or unfavorable (negative) light. As expected, we find that mainstream and liberal news outlets such as MSNBC and the *Washington Post* present the DREAM Act much more positively than do conservative media outlets such as Fox News and the *Washington Times.* Using a three-point measure of tone (−1 to 1), we find the average tone of DREAM Act coverage from CNN, MSNBC, the *Washington Post,* and the *New York Times* from the years 2007, 2010, 2012, and 2013 to be positive on balance (see table 4.2).[12] By contrast, the tone of similar coverage from Fox News, the *Washington Times,* and the *New York Post* is decidedly negative.

Differences in tone were related to a few key factors: (1) the presence or absence of empathetic language, (2) the use of permissive versus restrictive language, (3) the use of episodic versus thematic frames, and (4) the inclusion of policy-relevant frames such as mentions of "young children" and "amnesty." We explore each of these in greater detail.

Table 4.2   The Tone of DREAM Act Coverage in Seven News Sources, 2007, 2010, 2012, and 2013

	All Four Years Combined	2007	2010	2012	2013
Washington Times	−0.40	−0.74	−0.48	−0.06	−0.25
Washington Post	0.27	0.75	0.24	0.23	0.38
New York Times	0.17	0.30	0.05	0.23	0.20
New York Post	−0.47	—	−0.75	−0.43	−0.25
Fox News	−0.40	−0.57	−0.58	−0.20	−0.26
CNN	0.22	−0.36	0.27	0.50	0.56
MSNBC	0.65	—	0.65	0.64	0.57

Source: Authors' qualitative content analysis of news data.
Note: There were no stories on the DREAM Act in 2007 in the *New York Post* or on MSNBC.

Presence or Absence of Empathetic Language   Empathetic language is certainly used more frequently in many of the positively toned stories on the DREAM Act. Empathetic framing involves the use of phrases, objects, or concepts that evoke empathy: children, child, babies, separating families, stopping dreams, hunger, death, crossing the desert, discrimination, living in the shadows, just wanting to support families, pursuing the American Dream, being taken advantage of by employers, second-class people, suffering, poverty, working multiple jobs, and poor work conditions.[13] The following excerpt from the MSNBC show *The Last Word with Lawrence O'Donnell* is typical of left-leaning news stories that include empathetic language. Host Lawrence O'Donnell had this to say as Congress considered the DREAM Act during the 2010 lame-duck session:

Ezra, the story of those kids who would be affected by the DREAM Act is, for many, the moving kind of story that we saw told about the 9/11 responders, the kind of—there's a kind of emotionalism that can be brought to this political argument that may be able to get some traction this year. Do you expect the president to push on that one in the next session?[14]

By contrast, a segment on *Your World with Neil Cavuto* on Fox News from the same period presents a decidedly non-empathetic message; instead, the speaker seeks to invoke a sense of anger and outrage among viewers over undeserving beneficiaries.

Well, the DREAM Act were [sic] shot down, but more illegal immigrants may have a shot at in-state college tuition perks. Maryland would be the latest state to consider the move. . . . But Marylanders are frustrated like everybody else. They feel they're being—they're paying a lot of money in

Table 4.3   Empathy in DREAM Act Coverage in Seven News Sources, 2007, 2010, 2012, and 2013

	All Four Years Combined	2007	2010	2012	2013
Washington Times	34.5%	17.4%	18.2%	64.5%	14.3%
Washington Post	51.4	75.0	73.9	28.3	25.0
New York Times	86.4	90.0	72.7	91.7	96.7
New York Post	80.0	—	50.0	100.0	57.0
Fox News	12.4	28.6	12.5	11.0	22.2
CNN	38.4	32.1	30.5	54.3	41.7
MSNBC	49.6	—	38.6	65.5	51.4

Source: Authors' qualitative content analysis of news data.
Note: There were no stories on the DREAM Act in 2007 in the *New York Post* or on MSNBC.

taxes for all services and the economies everywhere are still continuing to struggle. Now, aren't you asking them to pick up an extra tab for people that may not have paid fully into the system so their kids can get a tax break?[15]

We use data from our qualitative content analysis to evaluate expectations on empathetic language. More specifically, we code each article on the extent to which it contains empathetic language. Each story is assigned one of three codes: no empathy, some empathy (one to two empathetic words or phrases), or significant empathy (three or more empathetic words or phrases). Examples of empathetic words and phrases include: "children," "hunger," "pursuing the American Dream," "supporting families," "experiencing discrimination," "living in the shadows," and "being exploited by employers." Our results indicate that empathetic language stands out as a key difference between the DREAM Act coverage of right-leaning and more mainstream media (see table 4.3).

During the DREAM Act's most salient years of news coverage (2007, 2010, 2012, and 2013), only 12.4 percent of Fox News and 34.5 percent of *Washington Times* DREAM Act stories included empathetic language (talk of dashing the hopes of immigrant children or of immigrants achieving the American Dream).[16] By contrast, among the more mainstream and liberal media—CNN (38.4 percent), MSNBC (49.6 percent), the *Washington Post* (51.4 percent), and the *New York Times* (86.4 percent)—the proportion of empathetic stories was much higher. We attribute some of these differences to mainstream media more often mentioning children, which could prompt empathy. Additionally, the more frequent mentions of amnesty in the more conservative news sources, by

Table 4.4   Restrictiveness of the Language of DREAM Act Coverage in
Seven News Sources, 2007, 2010, 2012, and 2013

	All Four Years Combined	2007	2010	2012	2013
Washington Times	−0.72	−1.22	−0.85	−0.23	−0.43
Washington Post	0.40	1.25	0.50	0.26	0.46
New York Times	0.00	−0.10	−0.25	−0.15	0.63
New York Post	−0.67	—	−0.25	−0.71	−1.00
Fox News	−0.49	−0.57	−0.72	−0.25	−0.07
CNN	0.34	−0.51	0.48	0.70	0.83
MSNBC	0.93	—	0.99	0.84	0.83

Source: Authors' qualitative content analysis of news data.
Note: Mean values, with (−2) as mostly restrictive and (2) as mostly permissive.

possibly obviating empathy, could also account for these stark differences.[17]

Permissive Versus Restrictive Language   The use of neutral, permissive, or restrictive terms was another source of variation between stories that we coded in our qualitative content analysis. Stories were coded as mostly permissive (2), slightly permissive (1), even (0), slightly restrictive (−1), and mostly restrictive (−2). Overall, the restrictiveness of the language used in DREAM Act stories maps onto the ideological divide between sources (see table 4.4).[18] More conservative outlets like the *Washington Times*, the *New York Post*, and Fox News used more restrictive language, while liberal and mainstream sources such as MSNBC, CNN, and the *Washington Post* used more permissive language. By comparison, the *New York Times* had neutral coverage, with a mean score of 0.

In the following excerpt, guest host Bill Tucker on a 2007 segment of *Lou Dobbs Tonight* voices several restrictive terms while introducing the DREAM Act (restrictive terms in bold):

> The Development, Relief and Education for Alien Minors Act, or DREAM Act, as it's better known, has been around since 2002. It's never passed Congress. But the bill, which would allow states to offer **illegal aliens** in-state tuition, create **amnesty** and a path to citizenship, has been reintroduced to the House by Representative Lincoln Diaz-Balart of Florida. The opposition is already on the move.

Then, the segment's guest, the prominent restrictionist advocate Kris Kobach, continues in the same rhetorical vein, using nearly identical terms:

The DREAM Act is a nightmare when it comes to the rule of law. First of all, it gives in-state tuition to **illegal aliens** who are violating the law. Meanwhile, U.S. citizens who follow the law from out of state, they have to pay full tuition. Secondly, it's part of a **massive amnesty** for **illegal aliens** who happen to attend college.[19]

By contrast, liberal media were less likely to use restrictive terms such as "amnesty," opting instead for more neutral terms, such as the bill's name (DREAM Act), or terms used by proponents of immigration reform, such as "pathway to citizenship." The following is an example from *The Countdown with Keith Olbermann* on MSNBC in December 2010 (neutral or permissive terms in bold):

I think the **DREAM Act** is a real—is a tragedy that it didn't pass. You are talking about providing a **pathway to citizenship** for high—often high-producing students who want to go to higher—want to go to a higher—to acquire higher education or be part of the military. I mean, you know, I heard a story of Dr. Quinonez (ph) at John Hopkins, who came over the border illegally when he was nineteen, and now is a neurosurgeon and is saving American lives every single day. And by the way, those same hands that picked the produce fifteen years ago are now the ones that are performing the surgery. So that, I think, is what Americans are about. They want to know that this country's going to be as good as it was ten years ago, even better. And the answer isn't whether **these individuals** are going to come or go. The answer is whether they're going to know the rule of law, have access to accurate information, participate in this democracy, and be **good neighbors.**[20]

Conversely, Fox News used phrases like "the so-called DREAM Act" and "stealth amnesty," which essentially questioned the legitimacy and sincerity of this legislation, as this segment from Neil Cavuto indicates:

Well, a vote to extend the Bush tax cuts [is] not priority number one for outgoing Speaker Nancy Pelosi. What is? Fox News confirming she wants a vote on the so-called DREAM Act as early as next [week]. Now, critics claim it will mean amnesty for thousands and eventually millions of illegals.[21]

Episodic Human-Interest Accounts Versus Thematic General Accounts   The contrasting tone between liberal, mainstream, and conservative news sources is also reflected in the more frequent use of concrete, episodically framed stories in the former as opposed to thematically framed stories in the latter (see table 4.5). As we noted in chapter 2, episodically framed stories present real-life examples of people whose lives are affected by

Table 4.5   Episodic Human-Interest Framing of DREAM Act Stories in Seven News Sources in 2007, 2010, 2012, and 2013

	All Four Years Combined	2007	2010	2012	2013
Washington Times	5.9%	4.3%	3.0%	9.7%	7.1%
Washington Post	23.4	12.5	17.4	30.2	20.8
New York Times	28.8	60.0	22.7	22.9	36.6
New York Post	6.7	—	0.0	14.3	0.0
Fox News	7.2	14.3	3.1	11.0	40.7
CNN	23.9	30.2	14.8	35.1	39.6
MSNBC	12.1	—	10.8	13.8	45.7

Source: Authors' qualitative content analysis of news data.

current policy, while thematically framed stories provide general and relatively impersonal accounts of the policy area, with greater attention to broader strokes than to specific cases.[22]

Comparing the DREAM Act coverage of the more ideologically defined media sources, we find that while the *Washington Times* (5.9 percent), the *New York Post* (6.7 percent), and Fox News (7.2 percent) engage in almost no episodic framing, this is not the case for the more mainstream outlets CNN (23.9 percent), the *New York Times* (28.8 percent), and the *Washington Post* (23.4 percent) and the more liberal MSNBC (12.1 percent). And while we observe a higher proportion of episodically framed stories in the mainstream media, their appearance is somewhat infrequent. The following excerpt is an episodically framed editorial from the *Washington Post* (episodic terms in bold):

> In many ways, **Eric Balderas's story** is the typical American dream. **He** came to the U.S. with his parents at age 4. **He** was the valedictorian of Highlands High School in San Antonio and was admitted to Harvard's class of 2013. There, **he studies molecular and cellular biology** and is about to begin **his** sophomore year. **He** dreams of helping to find a cure for cancer. But there is one problem: **He** is not in the country legally. On June 7, boarding an airplane back to Boston after visiting **his** mother in San Antonio, **he was arrested and threatened with deportation**. There was an outcry—on Facebook, in newspapers, even from members of Congress. Finally, [ICE] said it would not pursue **his** deportation, allowing **him** to remain in the country. . . . Congress should pass the **DREAM Act**.[23]

We present another episodically framed story, from MSNBC, in which Celso, an undocumented immigrant, tells his story to an immigration panel at the University of San Diego (episodic terms in bold):

Yes, I mean, I think both sides of the argument have fear. And **I think** fear is what is keeping us from solving the issues that affect us, this issue of immigration. I think that if both of us—both of the sides of this story can sort of come together and overcome that fear. For example, right now, I can say I am undocumented and unafraid. I say that so I can share **my story** and let you know that **my values** are the American values that I grew up with. **I grew up in this country wanting to serve after high school.** And I couldn't. **But I continued with my education.**[24]

This rich episodic segment on MSNBC stands in stark contrast to the relatively impersonal portrayal of the DREAM Act in many conservative outlets, particularly Fox News. In this Fox News example of thematic framing, notice the use of typical thematic markers such as generalities, hypotheticals, and a lack of individual accounts (thematic terms in bold):

There's **something** called "deferral of action." If you get down to the bottom line of all those, what they mean is you would bureaucratically wave **people** in and say, "Even though **you** are here illegally, we are going to give **you** a semi-official amnesty." Now, **if they pursued a robust version of all of these options,** it **could** affect millions of people. Just to give you one example, this "deferred action," **they** talk about how it could apply to the children of illegal immigrants who are eligible, **potentially,** for amnesty **if something** called the DREAM Act ever passes. It hasn't actually passed Congress. . . . There are very reputable estimates the DREAM Act **could apply to 2.1 million people.**[25]

Of course, there is no a priori reason to believe that episodic human-interest framing is impossible for conservative stories on immigration policies such as the DREAM Act—for example, networks like Fox News and print outlets like the *Washington Times* could conduct in-depth reporting on native-born young adults who have lost their jobs to competition from immigrants. As the labor market research by Giovanni Peri and others suggests, however, it may be difficult to pin job losses on the arrival of immigrants or even to the legalization of undocumented immigrants.[26] Still, there may be other opportunities for conservative news outlets to use episodic human-interest framing to advance a restrictive agenda on immigration, as revealed by the extensive coverage of the recent shooting of Kathryn Steinle, a white woman killed by a stray bullet in San Francisco from the gun of Juan Francisco Lopez-Sanchez, an unauthorized immigrant. At the same time, this kind of coverage may be more difficult to achieve for DREAM Act news coverage than for coverage on immigrant legalization more generally.

Table 4.6   DREAM Act Stories in Seven News Sources Mentioning Children or Amnesty, 2007–2015

	All	2007	2008	2009	2010	2011	2012	2013
Child mentions								
Washington Times	59%	57%	75%	0%[a]	55%	50%	68%	52%
Washington Post	74	100	100[a]	50[a]	70	71	74	78
New York Post	71	—[a]	0	—[a]	50	71	75	100
New York Times	81	91	100	89	82	76	78	94
Fox News	79	86	—[a]	100[a]	71	87	88	69
CNN	99	98	100	100	100	100	98	97
MSNBC	93	—[a]	—[a]	—[a]	91	88	95	94
Amnesty mentions								
Washington Times	30	61	75	0[a]	33	18	22	44
Washington Post	15	25	0[a]	50[a]	22	20	15	4
New York Post	21	—[a]	0	—[a]	25	0	38	25
New York Times	21	55	0	0	13	18	25	12
Fox News	35	71[a]	—[a]	100[a]	39	45	30	24
CNN	24	64	12	36	23	23	20	11
MSNBC	16	—[a]	—[a]	—[a]	5	12	17	28

Source: Authors' quantitative content analysis of news data.
[a]*Fewer* than eight DREAM Act stories in this population.

Considerations of "Children" and "Amnesty"   The tone of news coverage is also related to particular issue frames. As we saw in chapter 3, conservative commentators and news outlets have used the word "amnesty" to cast a negative light on comprehensive immigration reform. Accordingly, we can expect conservative news outlets to be much more likely to include "amnesty" in their DREAM Act stories than more mainstream and liberal outlets. Our qualitative content analysis of DREAM Act stories from this period bears out this expectation. We find that "amnesty" appears far less frequently in mainstream sources such as the *Washington Post* (15 percent) than in the right-leaning *Washington Times* (30 percent) (see table 4.6). Similarly, Fox News (35 percent) is substantially more likely to refer to the DREAM Act using the word "amnesty" than the more progressive MSNBC (16 percent). Surprisingly, the *New York Post* (21 percent), a relatively conservative newspaper owned by Rupert Murdoch, was more similar to mainstream media like the *New York Times* (21 percent) than fellow conservative outlets like the *Washington Times* (30 percent) and Fox News (35 percent).

Use of the word "amnesty" might cast the DREAM Act in a negative light, but references to "children" may have the opposite effect. In fact, previous research finds that policies known to benefit children are more likely to be viewed positively and to gain support than those specifically for older adults or for people in general. For example, previous work shows that public support for incarceration is significantly related to whether young offenders are viewed as children or as quasi-adults.[27] Issue framing effects, particularly those affecting children, have also been found in debates over obesity and gay rights.[28]

Consistent with our expectation of an ideological divide, we expect that progressive and mainstream news outlets will more often mention "children" in their DREAM Act coverage than conservative outlets. Indeed, we do find that some version of the word "children" was much more likely to appear in DREAM Act stories by mainstream newspapers such as the *Washington Post* (74 percent) than in more conservative outlets such as the *Washington Times* (59 percent). Similarly with cable news coverage, we find that a smaller proportion of Fox News stories (79 percent) include child references compared to CNN (99 percent) and MSNBC (93 percent) (see table 4.6).

The following excerpt from a CNN story in December 2010 provides a more concrete example of the use of the child frame:

> Well, today, Congress could vote on the DREAM Act, giving almost a million illegal immigrants a path to citizenship by going to college or for serving in the military for two years. But critics are calling it reckless and call it mass amnesty in some cases. We are joined now by two people, both illegal immigrants who would be directly impacted by the bill. Cesar Vargas's parents brought him to Brooklyn from Mexico when he was just five years old, and Gaby Pacheco's parents came from Ecuador when she was seven.[29]

By contrast, the amnesty frame is much more prevalent in conservative sources. This next excerpt, a letter to the editor of the *Washington Times* from a leader of a restrictionist group in the Midwest, exemplifies how the media use the amnesty frame in DREAM Act coverage:

> Why do the media always stop short in their description of the DREAM Act? It is not just about allowing students here illegally to go to college and then earn citizenship. The DREAM Act is a rolling amnesty because these students would also be permitted to sponsor their parents for legalization.[30]

Like this writer's reference to the DREAM Act as a "rolling amnesty," stories from conservative media often use other negative terms, such as "stealth amnesty" and "backdoor amnesty."

To sum up, we see that differences in cable news coverage in mentions of amnesty with respect to the DREAM Act were also strongly related to other differences in framing, such as the use of empathetic appeals and episodic or thematic framing. Having demonstrated ideological divergence in the content of media coverage across outlets, in the next section we look at whether the child and amnesty frames, along with the episodic versus thematic frames, are consequential for public opinion on the DREAM Act.

The Effects of Frames on Public Opinion

As in the last chapter, we used survey experiments to test how different frames affect support for immigration policies, this time for the provisions of the DREAM Act as well as DACA. We focus on testing two different frames: the frame that the policy involves children who did not choose to come to the United States, and the frame that the DREAM Act and DACA are just another form of amnesty. We expect the former frame to increase support for both policies and the latter to decrease support for them. In addition, we look at how episodic versus thematic framing and the use of empathetic frames influence support for both policies.

We embedded survey experiments related to these policies and frames in the 2007 and 2010 Cooperative Congressional Election Studies, which were conducted online through YouGov during the fall elections. In addition, we were able to place questions about the DREAM Act in our YouGov 2011 and 2012 studies, as well as questions about support for DACA in the latter study. Finally, to look at episodic versus thematic frames and empathetic language, we rely on our 2014 SSI study.[31]

The DREAM Act and the Child Frame

We turn first to our survey experiment on using a child frame in relation to the DREAM Act. In the 2007 and 2010 studies, respondents were asked for their level of agreement on a five-point scale with the following statement:

> Some say [*randomized:* illegal/undocumented/unauthorized] immigrants [*randomized: (no additional wording)*/who came to the United States as young children] should be able to earn legal status if they graduated from a U.S. high school, have stayed out of trouble, and have enrolled in college or the military.

As can be seen in this question, subjects were randomly assigned to a control wording or one in which we highlighted that immigrants came to the United States as young children. In addition, they were randomly assigned to the term used to describe immigrants ("illegal," "undocumented," or "unauthorized"). In our 2014 SSI study, we used the same wording but did not vary the term used to describe those without legal status.[32] We used a similar question in our 2012 study, though we used slightly different terms there to describe those without legal status, and we also added an amnesty frame manipulation:

> Some say [*randomized:* illegal immigrants/illegal aliens/undocumented immigrants] [*randomized: (no additional wording)*/who came to the United States as young children] should be able to earn legal status if they graduated from a U.S. high school, have stayed out of trouble, and have enrolled in college or the military. [*randomized: (no additional wording)*/Others argue that this just constitutes another form of amnesty]. To what extent do you support providing legal status to [*randomized:* illegal immigrants/illegal aliens/undocumented immigrants] if they meet the conditions above?

All of the measures are coded on a scale of −2 to 2 that runs from strong opposition to strong support for the DREAM Act. Therefore, 0 is the neutral point, and anything to the left is net opposition, while anything to the right is net support. Our general expectation is that individuals who receive the additional statement "who came to the United States as young children" will be more supportive of the DREAM Act. As we noted earlier, numerous examples from the policy arena suggest that voters are sensitive to appeals that refer to the effects of policies on children.[33] We focus on the amnesty condition used in 2012 in the next section of the chapter and on the terms used to describe those without legal status in chapter 6.

In figure 4.1, we present mean levels of support for the DREAM Act between those who were exposed to the child frame across the four surveys and those in the control group.[34] We find that, when asking about opinions on the DREAM Act in 2007 and 2010, the mere mention of the fact that it would benefit those illegal immigrants "who came to the United States as young children" makes support stronger than it would have been otherwise. In 2007 mean support among those in the control group, who did not read the child frame, is 0.069, or very close to the neutral point. By comparison, those who read the child frame are mildly supportive of the policy (mean = 0.412), and this difference is statistically significant (according to a difference-in-means test: $p = 0.00$). We observe a similar pattern in 2010, where mean support among those who did not read the child frame is close to the neutral point (mean = 0.208) but becomes more supportive (mean = 0.445) among those who read the frame, and this difference is again statistically meaningful ($p = 0.001$).

We do not show the results for 2011 in the figure because we asked the dependent variable on a different scale, ranging from −3 to 3. We find that the effects of the child frame disappear in 2011, with mean support statistically indistinguishable between those who did not read the child frame (mean = 0.891) and those who did (mean = 0.885; $p = 0.969$). The

Figure 4.1   Mean Support for the DREAM Act by Child Wording Condition, 2007, 2010, 2012, and 2014

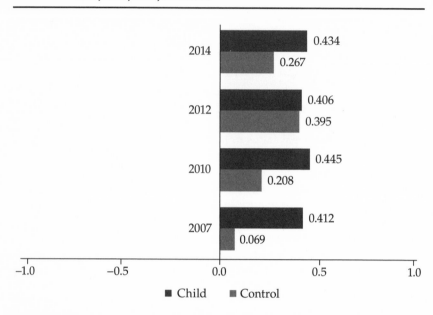

Source: Authors' analysis of CCES (2007, 2010), YouGov (2012), and SSI (2014) survey data.

higher support levels in both the control and child frame conditions in this study probably reflect the larger sample of Latinos, who constituted half of the sample. It may be that the child frame is less effective among this group since they are already quite supportive of the policy; however, the same null results obtain in our 2012 study. Mean support in the control group is 0.395 and is statistically indistinguishable from support among those exposed to the child frame (0.406, $p = 0.930$).[35] However, the findings for the 2014 study show that the frame is again effective. Mean support is somewhat supportive in the control group (mean = 0.267) and increases even further among those exposed to the child frame (mean = 0.434; $p = 0.022$). Therefore, in three out of the five studies, we find that the mere mention of coming to the United States as young children increases support for the DREAM Act, though the size of the effect gets smaller in later years.[36]

This pattern of findings suggests that the child frame is most effective in increasing support when the public knows little about the policy. As the policy becomes better known over time, the child wording has weaker effects as baseline support for the measure (even without the mention of children) increases over time and as more members of the

Figure 4.2   Change in Mean Support for the DREAM Act Moving from the Control Wording to the Child Wording, 2007, 2010, and 2012

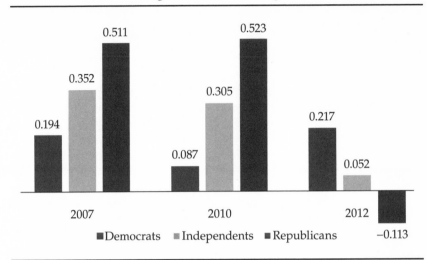

Source: Authors' analysis of CCES (2007, 2010) and YouGov (2010) survey data (OLS regression).

public are likely to have been already exposed to the frame.[37] This may have particularly been the case in 2012 since DACA was implemented in that year, making the issue highly salient.

Of course, it may be the case that responses to the child frame are not the same across all individuals. Some individuals may be more susceptible and some less susceptible to framing effects, while others may even reject framing effects.[38] In this chapter, we focus on whether partisans react differently to frames surrounding the DREAM Act.[39] Prior studies have found differential reactions to immigration frames depending on an individual's party identification.[40] For the analyses, we used a three-point party identification scale in which 1 is Democrat, 2 is independent, and 3 is Republican. To test for moderating effects by partisanship, we ran an OLS regression analysis including dummy variables for the experimental conditions, the party identification scale, and interactions between the two.[41]

For three out of the five data sets (2007, 2010, and 2012), we find evidence of partisans reacting differently to the child frame (see tables A4.1–A4.3 for OLS results).[42] Illustrating how the effects of the child frame vary by partisanship, figure 4.2 shows the shift in mean support for the Dream Act for those in the child frame relative to the control group broken down by partisanship. In 2007 the wording "came as young children" has a similar effect in boosting support for the DREAM Act across all partisan groups, but the effect is stronger on increasing support among Republicans. Republicans in this condition are about half a unit more supportive of the DREAM Act relative to their counterparts in the control group.[43] In 2010 we find the same pattern, though the effect of the child frame is not significant for Democrats.

We find that by 2012 the child wording again increases support among Democrats, but it no longer exerts an effect among independents or Republicans.[44] These latter findings suggest that during the 2012 time period Republicans were able to counterargue the otherwise effective child frame. Part of this may have been due to Republican elites taking very strong stands against immigration, especially during the party primaries. However, in 2011 and 2014, we find no moderating effects for partisanship. The differential moderating effects by partisanship across years could be the result of different samples or the different characteristics of the two years. The DREAM Act was not widely covered in the news in either year, which may partly explain why partisanship did not moderate the relationship. In their work on frames related to the DREAM Act, Druckman, Peterson, and Slothuus find that partisans do not pay attention to the strength of a frame in a polarized political environment, but do pay attention in a nonpolarized political environment.[45] This might explain why the child frame did not work for Republicans in the highly salient and polarized environment of 2012 but did work in 2014, when immigration was less salient.

The DREAM Act and the Amnesty Frame

We now turn to the effect of the amnesty frame, introduced in our 2012 study on the DREAM Act. To refresh, after the basic description of the DREAM Act (provided earlier), subjects were randomly assigned either to no additional wording or to the following additional statement: "Others argue that this just constitutes another form of amnesty." Individuals in both conditions were then asked for their level of support or opposition to the policy.[46] In the same study, we also introduced a question about Obama's DACA plan:

> Obama recently issued an executive order to defer deportations of [*randomized:* illegal immigrants/illegal aliens/undocumented immigrants] under the age of thirty who came to the United States before the age of sixteen, have lived here at least five years, and are in school, are high school graduates, or are military veterans. Such individuals will be allowed to apply for a two-year work visa and will need to renew every two years. [*randomized: (no additional wording)*/Some argue that this will only lead to amnesty.] To what extent do you support or oppose this policy?

Figure 4.3   Mean Support for the DREAM Act and DACA by Amnesty
Frame, 2012

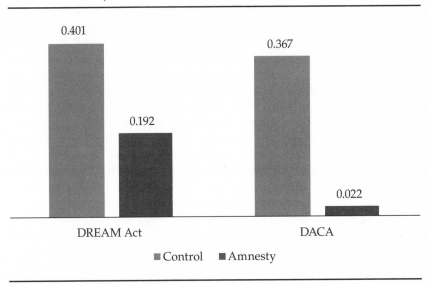

Source: Authors' analysis of 2012 YouGov survey data.

As with the other measure, the variable is recoded to run from −2 to 2, with higher values indicating more support for the policy. Since "amnesty" has become a highly charged term often used by those on the right who oppose legalization, we expect that tying it to the DREAM Act and DACA will reduce support for both policies. This effect is consistent with past framing research by the conservative pollster Frank Luntz on the use of the "amnesty" term.[47]

In figure 4.3, we present mean support for both policies among those in the control group compared to those who received the additional statement about amnesty.[48] We find very strong evidence that the amnesty condition reduces support for both policies. On the DREAM Act, mean support among those in the control group is moderately supportive (mean = 0.401) and drops to close to neutral (mean = 0.192) among those in the amnesty group, a difference that is statistically significant (according to a difference in means test: $p = 0.016$). The difference is even more pronounced with respect to DACA. Mean support for DACA is again moderately supportive (mean = 0.367) in the control group and drops to the neutral point (mean = 0.022) in the amnesty condition, a difference that is statistically meaningful ($p = 0.00$).[49] These main experimental effects are similar to those found by Druckman and his colleagues, who use a somewhat similar frame related to the DREAM Act leading to more illegal immigration.[50]

As in the previous analysis, we also test whether reaction to the amnesty frame is different depending on the respondent's partisan stripes (see tables A4.4 and A4.7).[51] We find clear evidence that this is the case for the DREAM Act (the interaction term is statistically significant: $p = 0.032$), and more suggestive evidence that this is the case for DACA.[52]

For the DREAM Act, Democrats are not significantly affected by the amnesty wording ($p = 0.898$), while independents and Republicans are ($p = 0.010$ and 0.002, respectively). Independents exposed to the amnesty wording are about 0.21 units less supportive of the DREAM Act relative to their counterparts in the control group, while the effect among Republicans is a 0.45-unit drop in support for the DREAM Act. For DACA, the amnesty condition has a negative effect on support for the policy for all partisan groups, but the effects are slightly more pronounced among independents and Republicans compared to Democrats. For example, while exposure to the amnesty condition (relative to the control group) drops support for DACA by 0.27 units among Democrats, the effect among independents and Republicans is a drop of 0.29 units and 0.31 units, respectively. It makes sense that Republicans would be more responsive to the amnesty frame across the two questions, since the frame is more consistent with their predispositions about immigration policy, and it is one they would have heard more often if they tune in to conservative media outlets.

Finally, for the DREAM Act question, we look at the intersection of the child frame and the amnesty frame. In figure 4.4, we plot mean support for the DREAM Act for those in the control group, those exposed only to the child frame, those exposed only to the amnesty frame, and those exposed to both frames. As we saw before, the child frame is not effective relative to the control group. Mean support for the DREAM Act dips to 0.180 for those exposed only to the amnesty frame, and this effect is significantly different relative to the control group ($p = 0.07$). Mean support is also lower among those exposed to both the child and amnesty frames (0.205) compared to the control group, and this difference is just outside of conventional significance levels ($p = 0.12$). These results suggest that the amnesty frame is effective, even in the presence of a counterframe. However, this analysis does not yet take partisanship into account.

If we look at whether the effects are moderated by partisanship, we find that Democrats become more supportive of the DREAM Act when exposed to the child frame regardless of whether they also receive the amnesty frame, and that they are unaffected when they receive only the amnesty frame. We find the exact opposite pattern among Republicans, who are unaffected by the child frame but become less supportive of the DREAM Act given the amnesty frame, with or without exposure to the child frame. Therefore, it seems that both partisan groups are able to counterargue the frame that runs against their predispositions. Again,

Figure 4.4   **Mean Support for the DREAM Act by Child and Amnesty Frame,**
2012

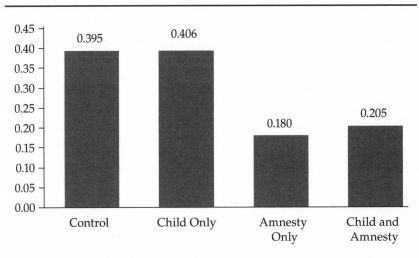

Source: Authors' analysis of 2012 YouGov survey data.

part of the reason they could do this may have had to do with the fact that immigration policies were highly salient and polarized in 2012. Finally, independents are not affected by any of the experimental conditions (see tables A4.4 and A4.5 for full results).[53]

The Style of the Frames

Recall from the last chapter that in our 2014 SSI study we varied the style of the presentation of news information after respondents filled out a basic pretest survey. Individuals were randomly assigned to a control condition or a condition in which they read a short newspaper article that had a positive tone on immigration but differed with respect to the style: whether it included episodic human-interest elements and empathetic framing (see chapter 3). The five experimental conditions were control, episodic no-empathy, episodic-empathy, thematic no-empathy, and thematic empathy.

Following exposure to the stories, individuals answered a battery of post-treatment survey questions. One of the questions was the DREAM Act question, reviewed earlier in this chapter, in which we manipulated the child wording. We also asked another question related to DACA in this survey. Respondents were randomly assigned to one of the versions of the following question:

As you may know, [*randomize: (no additional wording)*/Congress was un-able to pass the so-called DREAM Act, which would provide legal status to those who were illegal or undocumented immigrants as children.] President Obama issued an executive order last year that provided similar legal protections against deportation for those who were illegal or undocumented immigrants as children. He did this without seeking congressional approval. To what extent do you support or oppose the president's decision?

Both dependent variables are coded from −2 to 2, with higher values indicating more support for the DREAM Act and DACA, respectively. Given that the news stories are positively toned, we would expect any of the treatment groups to have higher support for the DREAM Act and DACA compared to those in the control group. If we compare across the style of the frames, the literature would lead us to expect that thematic frames, as well as those that are empathetic, are the most effective in increasing support for progressive immigration attitudes, as we noted in chapter 2. If we combine the two types of frames, we might expect the thematic empathetic frame to lead to the highest level of support for these policies and the episodic non-empathetic frame to be the least effective. Since we do not know whether the style of the frame or empathetic language is more effective, it is unclear whether the episodic non-empathetic or thematic empathetic condition will be more effective. We might expect higher levels of support when respondents read that Congress was unable to pass the DACA bill, since individuals may be less supportive of the president acting without congressional approval.

We first plot mean support for both policies by the style of the frame (see figure 4.5). Turning first to the DREAM Act, mean support is slightly right of the neutral point (0.376) among those in the control group, which signifies very modest support for the policy. Contrary to expectations, mean support is lower for the episodic non-empathetic (mean = 0.273), episodic empathetic (mean = 0.362), and thematic non-empathetic (mean = 0.306) frames, though none of these effects are statistically different from the control group. The only frame that appears to increase support for the DREAM Act beyond the mean in the control group is the thematic empathetic frame (mean = 0.462); however, this effect is not statistically significant either.

When we look at support for DACA, mean support among those in the control group is slightly left of the neutral point, at −0.131, which represents modest opposition to the policy. One reason for the lower support in this study compared to the 2012 study may be that we highlighted in the question that Obama acted without congressional approval. If we

Figure 4.5   Mean Support for the DREAM Act and DACA by Frame Style, 2014

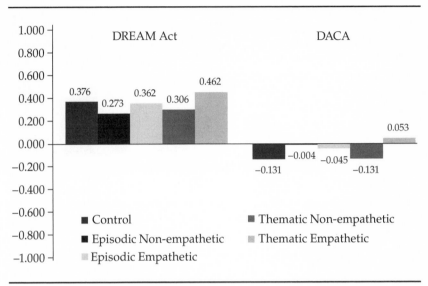

Source: Authors' analysis of 2014 SSI survey data.

look at mean support across those who read the treatment stories, we again find null effects for the episodic non-empathetic, episodic thematic, and thematic non-empathetic frames. However, mean support is marginally higher among those exposed to the thematic empathetic frame (mean = 0.053; p = 0.07, one-tailed) and pushes respondents just to the right of the neutral point, making them more supportive of the policy.[54] Across the two sets of the results, there is some modest evidence that the thematic empathetic frame may be most effective in shifting opinions, as expected.

For both policies, we do not find any evidence that the style of the frames is moderated by partisanship, Fox News viewership, family immigration history, education, or being Latino. However, we do find differential reactions to the conditions depending on the respondent's level of trait empathy.[55] We measured trait empathy from a battery of three questions: (1) "I often have tender, concerned feelings for people less fortunate than me"; (2) I sometimes find it difficult to see things from the 'other person's' point of view"; and (3) "I believe that there are two sides to every question and try to look at them both." In a principal components factor analysis, all three questions loaded highly onto one factor, and we split this factor at the median so that we have individuals low

Figure 4.6   Change in Mean Support for the DREAM Act and DACA Moving from the Control Group to the Given Experimental Condition, by Trait Empathy, 2014

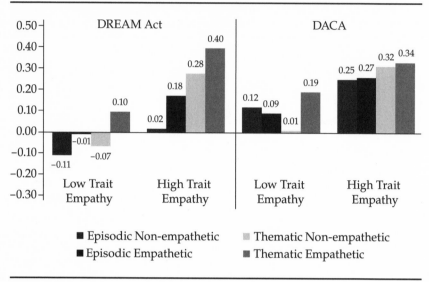

Source: Authors' analysis of 2014 SSI survey data (OLS regression).

and high in trait empathy. In figure 4.6, we plot the change in support for each policy moving from the control group to the given treatment group for those low and high in trait empathy.

Among those low in trait empathy, we find only a close to significant effect for the thematic empathetic frame on DACA ($p = 0.12$). Overall then, individuals low in trait empathy are not affected by reading an article sympathetic to undocumented immigrants, regardless of the style of the frame. If we turn to those high in trait empathy, a different picture emerges. Those high in trait empathy become more supportive of both policies relative to the control group for all of the treatment conditions; however, for the DREAM Act the only significant differences are for the two thematic general news conditions, while for DACA all four conditions increase support for the policy. The thematic non-empathetic condition increases support for the DREAM Act by 0.28 units ($p = 0.059$), while the increase is higher for the thematic empathetic condition at 0.40 units ($p = 0.008$).

We also find a stronger effect for the thematic general news conditions, particularly the thematic empathetic condition, when we turn to support for DACA. The change in support for DACA moving from the control group to each condition among those high in trait empathy is as follows: episodic non-empathetic, 0.25 (p = 0.096); episodic empathetic, 0.27 (p = 0.095); thematic non-empathetic, 0.32 (p = 0.052); and thematic empathetic, 0.34 (p = 0.042). In sum, even among those who are high in trait empathy and may be more inclined to empathize with the plight of the undocumented, the thematic frame that contains empathetic language is most effective in increasing support for the policies, though the episodic frames are significant for one of the policies.[56]

For the manipulation on the DACA question where we varied whether respondents read that Congress was unable to pass the DREAM Act, we find no significant differences between the two versions of the question (p = 0.52). Mean support hovers around the neutral point whether respondents read that Congress failed to pass the DREAM Act or not.

Discussion and Conclusion

When we examine the framing of the DREAM Act in the news media and its effects on public opinion, a few key findings stand out. With respect to the style of coverage, our findings suggest that positive thematic coverage that contains empathetic appeals is likely to be most effective in increasing support for the policy, for those both low and high in trait empathy. Although the use of thematic coverage was high across all media outlets, empathetic appeals were more common in the mainstream and liberal outlets.

Looking next at the effects of issue frames on opinion, our findings echo the results in chapter 3, where the manipulation of a few words, such as "amnesty," can have large effects. Even if the term "amnesty" is not entirely apt to depict various versions of the DREAM Act or DACA, it continues to be used in news stories, particularly those in conservative outlets, and in statements by immigration restrictionists. In our survey experiments, we find that using the term consistently produces a drop in voter support. By contrast, the child frame increases voter support for the DREAM Act, but this effect diminished over time as baseline support for the DREAM Act (that is, support among those in the control condition) increased from 2007 to 2014. Our newspaper content analysis suggests that this increase in the control group may be due to a pretreatment effect, as coverage of the DREAM Act was high in 2010, it remained high in subsequent years, and young children were consistently and frequently mentioned in conservative and mainstream media outlets alike. At the same time, the fact that voters were less subject to the countervailing amnesty frame in news stories probably also played a role in raising baseline levels of support for the DREAM Act among Democrats and Republicans alike.

It remains to be seen how effective the amnesty frame will be moving forward. As we noted in chapter 3, the 2012 elections prompted a significant round of soul-searching among Republican leaders, with the Republican National Committee's *Growth and Opportunity Project* signaling a friendlier approach on immigration, particularly vis-à-vis Latino and Asian American voters. Coinciding with the report's publication, a range of prominent Republicans such as Rand Paul (R-KY), Marco Rubio (R-FL), and Paul Ryan (R-WI), signaled their support for immigrant legalization, and in particular the DREAM Act. For example, House Majority Leader Eric Cantor (R-VA) noted, in a widely publicized speech at the American Enterprise Institute in February 2013, that "one of the great founding principles of our country was that children would not be punished for the mistakes of their parents. . . . It is time to provide an opportunity for legal residence and citizenship for those who were brought to this country as children and who know no other home."[57]

The legislative and electoral dynamics among House Republicans, however, pushed in the opposite direction. House incumbents, who by the summer of 2013 were more worried about midterm primary challenges than the party's 2016 presidential prospects, began resisting leadership attempts to pass any immigration reform measure that included "amnesty" provisions. As early as May 2013, Tea Party activists created super PACs to challenge Republican moderates on immigration.[58] The following spring they captured their biggest prize by defeating House Majority Leader Cantor—an outcome based in large part on his support for the DREAM Act "amnesty."[59] Indeed, when we extend our news content analysis to 2014 and 2015, we find that mentions of amnesty rose sharply in Fox News stories related to the DREAM Act, from 24 percent in 2013 to 50 and 60 percent in 2014 and 2015, respectively.

Finally, as the 2016 presidential primaries amply demonstrated, moderate rhetoric on immigration was still a losing formula for Republican nominees; Donald Trump and Ted Cruz effectively used incendiary rhetoric on immigration to win early support, while more moderate Republicans like Jeb Bush and Marco Rubio were forced to disavow their prior support for immigrant legalization. Thus, it is likely that the electoral logic of presidential and congressional primaries will continue to make viable the market for restrictive rhetoric among the Republican Party faithful, even if such rhetoric may ultimately prove costly to the party's attempts to regain the White House.

5

Framing Deportations in the News Media and Public Opinion

THE FIRST federal legislation authorizing the deportation, or removal, of noncitizens was passed in 1798 as the United States was preparing for potential war with France over what it perceived to be that country's incitement of unrest in the United States. Thus, the Federalists pushed legislation, signed by John Adams in 1798, that was broadly referred to as the Alien and Sedition Acts.[1] The Alien Act in particular allowed the president "to *order* all such *aliens* as he shall judge dangerous to the peace and safety of the United States, or shall have reasonable grounds to suspect are concerned in any treasonable or secret machinations against the government thereof, to depart out of the territory of the United States" (emphasis in the original).[2] However, the Act was never enforced, and it would take nearly another century, after the United States passed the Chinese Exclusion Act of 1882, before any significant number of deportations began.[3] Even so, the annual number of deportations, or "removals," of immigrants in the United States remained relatively small for another few decades before increasing during periods of wartime and social upheaval during the 1910s and during the Great Depression, when tens of thousands of Mexican immigrants (and even their native-born children) were encouraged to leave the United States, and during Operation Wetback in the 1950s.[4]

Even these spurts in deportations, however, pale in comparison to the last two decades in U.S. immigration enforcement. As historical data from the Department of Homeland Security show (figure 5.1), the annual number of deportations in the United States rose steadily after the passage of the Immigration Reform and Control Act (IRCA) in 1986, which granted legalization to most unauthorized immigrants but also put into place a set of employer sanctions and a 50 percent increase in staffing for border enforcement.[5] However, there was a big jump in deportations following the passage by the 104th Congress of the Illegal Immigration Re-

Figure 5.1   Annual Number of Deportations in the United States, 1892 to 2012

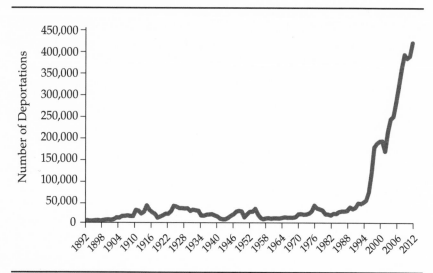

Source: U.S. Department of Homeland Security 2013.

form and Immigrant Responsibility Act (IIRAIRA) of 1996. IIRAIRA had several provisions that increased enforcement actions against unauthorized immigrants, including substantial increases in border enforcement and interior enforcement, provisions allowing for cooperation between the federal government and local law enforcement on identifying and removing unauthorized immigrants, and exclusion of unauthorized immigrants from reentering the United States for ten years.[6] The number of deportations soared, more than doubling between 1996 and 1999 (from about 70,000 to 183,000) and subsequently rocketing even higher, to over 300,000 annual removals by 2007 and over 400,000 by 2012. Indeed, more immigrants have been deported in the last ten years than during the prior 112 years (figure 5.1), and the Obama administration has overseen the largest number of deportations of any president, building on the prior record of over 2 million set by the George W. Bush administration.[7]

Given the prominence of immigrant deportations in contemporary immigration policy in the United States, it is important for us to understand how deportation policy is depicted and framed in news coverage and how framing on certain key aspects of deportations affects American public opinion on the issue. As we have indicated elsewhere in the book, much existing work on public opinion and immigration uses fairly rough proxies for attitudes on subjects like support for levels of immigration, and these attitude measures do not delve into particular policies or the associated complexities of opinion.

In this chapter, we expect to find variation in how different media sources cover deportation. More specifically, we expect the tone of media coverage on deportation to be most negative in conservative media outlets, most positive in liberal outlets, and somewhere in between in mainstream outlets. We expect to find similar patterns when we look at the balance of pro-deportation arguments. With respect to frames against deportation, we expect to find more of these covered in liberal media outlets than in mainstream or conservative outlets. We also expect to find that framing deportation policy in different ways is consequential for public opinion. That is, not only will individuals be influenced by the direction of the frames, but the content of particular frames may be more or less effective in swaying public opinion on deportation policies.

As in previous chapters, we conduct a systematic content analysis across three cable networks (Fox News, CNN, and MSNBC) and four print media outlets (the *Washington Times,* the *Washington Post,* the *New York Times,* and the *New York Post*) from the years 2007 to 2013. We examine the tone associated with news coverage of deportation and whether news coverage was largely thematic in nature (focusing on numbers and trends in deportations) or episodic (focusing on stories of particular immigrants being deported or others affected personally by deportation). We also look at the specific arguments that were prevalent in news coverage of deportation and the public discourse, including the rule of law, civil liberties, and effects on families and local economies.

After showing our findings on how deportation is covered across different media outlets, we explore the effect of some of the different issue frames on public opinion. We examine both frames that have received much play across media outlets, to test whether they actually matter to public opinion, and frames that have received less coverage, to see how such frames may influence opinions. As in prior chapters, we rely on a series of survey experiments, often conducted with nationally representative samples, to test the effects of different frames on support for deportation policies.

Framing Deportation in the News

The media's coverage of deportation has been relatively uniform, with conservative media outlets favoring some version of a deportation policy that enforces the rule of law and protects our borders and liberal media, while not rejecting the policy outright, certainly pointing out its many problems. As was the case with the DREAM Act and legalization, however, interesting nuances have surfaced over time and divergent frames have emerged. We demonstrate how significant differences in issue frames have accompanied these different deportation frames.

As we noted in earlier chapters, the advent of Fox News in 1996 injected a significant amount of ideological polarization into the presentation of immigration policies such as deportation.[8] As before, we would expect the deportation news coverage of "illegal" immigrants to vary according to the ideological leanings of the news source. We would expect more conservative print outlets (such as the *Washington Times*) to have more restrictive news coverage compared to more mainstream and liberal print outlets (such as the *Washington Post*).

Also, as in chapters 3 and 4, we do not expect these expectations to hold for all cable coverage. In particular, the pre-2010 tenure of restrictionist hosts Lou Dobbs and Glenn Beck should make CNN's deportation coverage more restrictive than we might ordinarily expect. Similarly, we might also expect some ideological deviation from MSNBC prior to the 2009 election, a period when it regularly featured Tucker Carlson and Patrick Buchanan. Thus, for CNN and MSNBC, we would expect to see changes in deportation coverage before and after 2009–2010: more permissive coverage at MSNBC after 2009 and more balanced prior to 2009, and coverage that was split at CNN after 2010 and more conservative prior. Finally, we expect Fox News to have the most restrictive coverage throughout this period.

So how do these different deportation frames correspond to news coverage? We qualitatively and quantitatively analyzed the content of news stories on deportation in mainstream and conservative daily newspapers (the *Washington Post* and the *New York Times* on the mainstream side and the *Washington Times* and the *New York Post* on the conservative side) from 2007 to 2013.[9] Additionally, we analyzed deportation stories from each of the three major cable news networks (CNN on the mainstream side, Fox News on the conservative side, and MSNBC, which transitioned from mainstream to liberal during this time period). We retrieved 344 deportation stories from CNN, 109 from Fox News, 395 from MSNBC, 516 from the *Washington Post*, 235 from the *Washington Times*, 874 from the *New York Times*, and 128 from the *New York Post*. We employed a qualitative content analysis (tone of coverage, empathetic language, permissiveness, episodic or thematic framing, pro or con issue frames) and a quantitative content analysis (volume of coverage) to analyze these stories.

The Volume of Coverage

It is first useful to get a sense of the volume of deportation coverage. Drawing from the quantitative content analysis of deportation stories from the five news organizations from January 1, 2007, through Decem-

Table 5.1   Raw Counts of Deportation Stories, 2007–2013

	2007	2008	2009	2010	2011	2012	2013	All Years Combined
CNN	29	32	46	47	50	122	20	346
Fox News	40	11	4	13	15	17	9	109
MSNBC	27	7	6	45	32	164	114	395
Washington Post	114	85	48	82	48	86	53	516
Washington Times	50	29	14	21	35	47	39	235
New York Times	133	96	107	141	128	161	108	874
New York Post	17	17	20	19	15	35	5	128

Source: Authors' qualitative content analysis of news data.

ber 31, 2013, we find some interesting differences in the volume of coverage across outlets (see table 5.1). First, while the volume of coverage in mainstream and liberal news organizations remained somewhat constant from 2007 through 2012 and increased thereafter, coverage among conservative sources spiked earlier, in 2007. For example, while CNN ran 50 or fewer deportation stories each year from 2007 to 2011, in 2012 the network increased its coverage to 122 stories. Similarly, MSNBC ran fewer than 50 stories prior to 2012, but 2012 saw a spike to 164 stories. The volume of deportation coverage for Fox News and the *Washington Times* was very different. Fox News ran 40 stories on deportation compared to 17 or fewer per year from 2008 through the end of 2012. Similarly, the *Washington Times* ran the most stories on deportation in 2007, with 50.

Many of these differences in volume can be attributed to differences in the immigration debate of the time. While the immigration debate was dominated throughout 2007 by a broadly negative tone, after the 2012 presidential elections the conversation among elites and the media became much more positive. Particularly notable was the movement of the conversation among conservative news media away from the amnesty and "out of control" frame so prevalent in 2007 and toward the frame of immigration reform being imminent and politically necessary in late 2012 and early 2013. Thus, it should not be surprising that mentions of deportations declined in these outlets between 2007 and 2013. On the other hand, more progressive and mainstream news outlets started to focus on the record levels of deportations that were continuing under the Obama administration and discussed immigration reform in the context of these continued deportations. Thus, we see divergent trajectories in the mention of immigration deportations in conservative, mainstream, and progressive media for reasons that were related to the broader policy and political context of immigration reform, the 2012 elections, and the deportation actions by the Obama administration.

Table 5.2   The Tone of Deportation Coverage in Seven News Sources, 2007, 2010, 2012, and 2013

	All Four Years Combined	2007	2010	2012	2013
Washington Times	−0.37	−0.56	−0.62	−0.16	0.11
Washington Post	0.18	0.07	0.00	0.44	0.11
New York Times	0.01	0.09	−0.18	0.04	0.16
New York Post	−0.01	−0.06	−0.11	0.06	0.00
Fox News	−0.58	−0.59	−0.77	−0.53	−0.20
CNN	0.42	0.07	0.42	0.53	0.09
MSNBC	0.47	0.46	0.40	0.51	0.44

Source: Authors' qualitative content analysis of news data.

The Tone of Coverage

We also find systematic differences in the overall tone of news coverage across sources (see table 5.2). By tone, we mean the extent to which a news story on deportation casts undocumented immigrants in a favorable or unfavorable light. As in prior chapters, we expect deportation stories in conservative media to be more negatively toned, liberal outlets to be more positively toned, and mainstream outlets to fall somewhere in between. Using a three-point measure of tone (−1 to 1), we find the average tone of deportation coverage from 2007, 2010, 2012, and 2013 to be most positive on MSNBC (0.47) and CNN (0.42), with the *Washington Post* net positive as well (0.18).[10] The *New York Times* and the *New York Post* are right around the neutral point (0.01 and −0.01, respectively), while Fox News and the *Washington Times* have more negative coverage (−0.58 and −0.37, respectively). This general pattern certainly comports with our expectations, with the exception of the *New York Post*.

If we look at the trends over time, there are some notable shifts in tone. Specifically, we find that 2012 was the most positive (0.35) and permissive (0.49) year in terms of deportation coverage across all seven news organizations.[11] By contrast, 2007 and 2010 were the most negative and restrictive years. This pattern is consistent with what we see for the volume of coverage and tracks well with the more general immigration debate. Much of this shift over time is attributable to the conservative news outlets, which became much less negative in their coverage over time, while the mainstream and liberal outlets did not change as much (with the exception of CNN, where coverage became less negative, as expected, after the departures of Lou Dobbs and Glenn Beck). It also comports with the agenda-setting effects of President Obama's DACA announcement and the Supreme Court decision striking down most aspects of Arizona's pro-deportation law.[12] Finally, running counter to our expectations, the tone of MSNBC's coverage did not get much more positive over time.

Differences in tone across organizations and over time were related to a few key factors: (1) the presence or absence of empathetic language; (2) the use of episodic versus thematic frames, and (3) the invocation of different pro and con frames on the issue.

The Presence or Absence of Empathetic Language   One factor shaping the tone of deportation coverage was the presence or absence of empathetic language. Empathetic language is defined as phrases, objects, and concepts that evoke empathy: children, child, babies, separating families, stopping dreams, hunger, death, crossing the desert, discrimination, living in the shadows, just wanting to support families, pursuing the American Dream, being taken advantage of by employers, second-class people, suffering, poverty, working multiple jobs, and having poor work conditions.[13] The following excerpt is typical of a deportation story containing empathetic language (relevant sections in bold):

MALVEAUX: Our Rafael Romo is taking a look at how current immigration is affecting many, many **families**.

ROMO: **A tearful hug made incomplete by a wall.** This is no ordinary wall. These metal bars separate Mexico and the United States at Nogales, Arizona.

EVELYN RIVERA, COLOMBIAN IMMIGRANT: Love has no border. The **love of a mother and her daughter can't be separated by borders,** can't be separated by anything, and for them to remember that they have families as well.

ROMO: Twenty-four-year-old Evelyn Rivera is an undocumented immigrant. Her mother, Yolanda Ravi, was deported to their native Colombia. They're meeting for the first time since she was expelled from the U.S. Rivera has been able to stay in the country thanks to an executive order issued last June by President Obama. It allows immigrants who are in the United States illegally, after being brought here by the parents as children, to stay in the U.S. until June of 2014.

OBAMA: This is **about incredible young people who understand themselves to be Americans, who have done everything right** but have still been hampered in achieving their **American Dream**.

ROMO: Back at the border, Gorte Teodoro meeting her twenty-five-year-old daughter Renata **for the first time since the Brazilian woman was deported**.

GORTE TEODORO, DEPORTED MOTHER: **I just asked why. I just want to be with my kids. I live in America ... fifty years, fifty years.** Why deport me?

RENATA TEODORO, BRAZILIAN IMMIGRANT: **I just want to be with my**

mom. I want her to be there at my graduation. I want to go to movie nights again with her.[14]

Alternatively, deportation stories that did not include any of the aforementioned words or phrases were coded as empathy-absent. For example, consider the following deportation story:

> Eight law enforcement agencies in Virginia and Maryland have recently joined a sweeping federal program that aims to identify and deport illegal immigrants who commit serious crimes. The agencies join about 150 other jurisdictions in 19 states as part of a program the Obama administration hopes will be in all 3,100 local jails nationwide by 2013.
>
> The Secure Communities program, part of a U.S. Immigration and Customs Enforcement effort to streamline how it identifies and removes criminal illegal immigrants, allows local law enforcement officers to check fingerprints against the FBI criminal database and the Department of Homeland Security's biometric database. Officials hope that the system will more efficiently prevent serious criminals from being released back onto the streets.
>
> Arlington, Fauquier, Loudoun and Stafford counties, along with the City of Alexandria, are the most recent additions to the program, ICE officials announced last week. They join Prince William and Fairfax counties in Virginia. A week earlier, officials announced that Frederick, St. Mary's and Queen Anne's counties in Maryland had joined the effort, which was underway in Prince George's County. ICE officials said this week that they are working with the District to deploy the program as well.[15]

As the empathy-present example illustrates, deportation stories that include empathetic language can give a positive hue to a story's tone. Relatedly, we find that over 73 percent of the deportation stories we coded as positive included empathetic language. Conversely, only 15 percent of stories that were negatively toned contained empathetic language. Empathy-present stories can motivate readers and viewers to take the perspective of deported immigrants and their families or to experience emotions that are likely to heighten their support for policies that help these immigrants.[16] Given previous research finding that empathy can improve audience attitudes toward and policy support for the subject group, we would expect liberal media outlets (MSNBC) to include empathetic language more often than conservative outlets (Fox News).[17] As expected, we find that differences in empathetic language largely track this ideological divide.[18]

During the years in which the deportation issue was most salient (2007, 2010, 2012, and 2013), only 38 percent of Fox News stories, 34 percent of *Washington Times* stories, and 22 percent of *New York Post* stories included empathetic language (table 5.3). In contrast, the more liberal

Table 5.3   The Presence of Empathetic Language in Deportation Coverage by Seven News Sources, 2007, 2010, 2012, and 2013

	All Four Years Combined	2007	2010	2012	2013
Washington Times	34%	34%	46%	42%	53%
Washington Post	42	74	58	63	59
New York Times	32	30	36	40	20
New York Post	22	12	11	31	40
Fox News	38	41	15	41	60
CNN	56	68	67	54	18
MSNBC	49	33	35	51	57
All deportation stories	46	43	41	49	48

Source: Authors' qualitative content analysis of news data.

and mainstream outlets CNN (56 percent), MSNBC (49 percent), the *Washington Post* (42 percent), and the *New York Times* (32 percent) included empathetic language more frequently. These figures suggest, however, that a significant proportion of deportation stories did not include empathetic language (50 percent overall). Many of these stories were short two- to three-sentence process-oriented blurbs reporting the status of deportation-related legislation. If we look at trends over time, we find, as expected, that MSNBC's coverage became more empathetic over time. However, we did not see any increase in empathetic language at CNN after the departure of Lou Dobbs.

Episodic Human-Interest Accounts Versus Thematic General News Accounts   One slight departure in the ideological theme of deportation coverage is the extent to which these stories are episodically versus thematically framed. As we noted in chapter 2, episodically framed stories present real-life examples of people whose lives are affected by current policy, while thematically framed stories use broader strokes to provide generic and relatively impersonal accounts of the policy area rather than details of specific cases.[19]

In prior chapters, we found that liberal outlets (MSNBC) were more likely to include episodic framing than conservative outlets (Fox News). We do not find this to be the case, however, for deportation coverage (table 5.4): 62 percent of deportation stories on Fox News were episodic, compared to 44 percent in the *Washington Post*, 35 percent in the *New York Times*, 38 percent on CNN, 28 percent in the *Washington Times*, 14 percent in the *New York Post*, and 17 percent on MSNBC.[20]

While these results demonstrate little relationship between episodic/human interest coverage and the ideological leaning of the news organi-

Table 5.4   Episodic Human-Interest Framing of Deportation Stories in Seven
News Sources, 2007, 2010, 2012, and 2013

	All Four Years Combined	2007	2010	2012	2013
Washington Times	28%	37%	38%	7%	39%
Washington Post	44	67	49	30	39
New York Times	35	62	30	26	20
New York Post	14	6	26	11	20
Fox News	62	85	54	20	20
CNN	38	96	85	13	36
MSNBC	17	54	32	9	14

Source: Authors' qualitative content analysis of news data.

zation, there is a subtler story that one can take from the data that is more
source and issue-specific. For example, while previous findings suggest
that heavy episodic coverage on Fox News would add to the empathetic
and positive nature of their coverage, instead we find that the *episodic
framing* on the network focused primarily on negative stories about undocumented immigrants, dealing with drugs, gangs, crime, and illegal
border crossing. In particular, two stories drove a large portion of this
coverage especially for Fox News' and Lou Dobb's CNN coverage: the
Elvira Arellano church holdup story and the Ignacio Ramos and Jose
Compean border shooting incident. Below are examples of both of these
stories, the Arellano story from CNN and the Ramos and Compean story
from Fox News:

HAYES: We don't think she's a martyr. **We think again that she's a
criminal fugitive alien who was in violation of the U.S. law.** Certainly, most criminal aliens and most **fugitives** do not hold press conferences. I think [that] certainly gave her an added vulnerability by
advising the government of where she was.

WIAN: **Arellano was caught sneaking across the Mexican border in
1997.** She was deported, reentered the country, and was rearrested in
2002. After being convicted of using someone else's Social Security
number to obtain a job cleaning airplanes at Chicago's O'Hare Air-
port, she was again [ordered] deported. Instead, Arellano sought sanc-
tuary and publicity, almost **daring authorities to arrest her,** while
pleading to remain in the United States.[21]

NAUERT: A big development now on the jailing of two border agents
for shooting an illegal immigrant who was smuggling drugs into the

country along with himself. Dozens of U.S. lawmakers have been trying for months to get the government to free Jose Compean and Ignacio Ramos who say they were wrongly imprisoned for simply doing
their jobs.

GIBSON: Their pleas have fallen on deaf ears but they're not giving up.
In fact, they are more fired up than ever because of how the pair are
being treated behind bars. Allegedly, worse than some terror suspects.
BIG STORY correspondent Douglas Kennedy spoke to the lawmaker
leading the charge to get those border agents freed. Douglas?[22]

Alternatively, given our previous finding of an episodic-heavy
MSNBC coverage, one might infer that the same is the case for its deportation coverage. To the contrary, we find that MSNBC coverage is the
least episodic (17 percent), likely because MSNBC's deportation coverage tends to highlight empathy, less from individual stories of immigrants than from broader characterizations of immigrants as a class. The
following example showcases the empathy frame in an otherwise thematically framed MSNBC story that portrays deportation as socially disruptive to families and children:

VILLARAIGOSA: Well, as I said, I believe that there needs to be a path to
earn legalization, to earn citizenship, for the 11 million people who are
here. We don't want to divide—

SCHULTZ: Regardless of their skills, correct?

VILLARAIGOSA: Right. We don't want to divide the parents from the
kids. **We don't want to deport the parents and leave the kids here.
Remember, those 11 million undocumented have 5 million citizen
children and a couple of million DREAMers.**[23]

More specifically, the empathetic and positive nature of MSNBC's deportation coverage is due more to the network's use of thematic general
news coverage and the use of con-deportation considerations in particular. Thus, while prior work suggests that empathetic framing is more
likely to occur with episodic news stories than with thematic ones, we
find that this relationship holds true only in print sources, not in cable
news sources, and that the extent to which this is the case is probably
conditional on the particular policies being considered.[24]

Pro and Con Considerations on Deportations   In addition to variations in
empathy and tone, the deportation debate comprises a plethora of issue
frames both in support of and opposed to the deportation of "illegal"
immigrants. In this section, using a qualitative content analysis, we identify those pro and con arguments and report the extent to which they

appear in deportation stories across news organizations and time. Using an initial exploratory search of deportation news stories, we identified the following pro-deportation frames: public safety, rule of law (legality), national security, economic cost, cultural change, and unfairness.[25] The public safety frame is that "illegal" immigrants should be deported because they increase crime and put our safety at risk, as illustrated by the following excerpt of a Tom Tancredo presidential campaign ad from *Tucker* on MSNBC in December 2007:

> REP. TOM TANCREDO: Hi, I'm Tom Tancredo, and I approve this message because someone needs to say it.
>
> UNIDENTIFIED MALE: **Mothers killed, children executed, the tactics of vicious Central American gangs now on U.S. soil. Pushing drugs, raping kids, destroying lives. Thanks to gutless politicians who refuse to defend our borders.** One man dares say it must be done. **Secure the borders, deport those who don't belong, make sure they never come back.**
>
> CARLSON: Let's be honest. This ad is very offensive to every good government liberal in America, but there's nothing in this ad that's inaccurate. It's inarguably true.[26]

The rule of law frame is that "illegal" immigrants should be deported because they broke the law. Pay attention to how Fox News anchor Neil Cavuto and his guest, the restaurant owner Joseph Vento, respond with the legality argument to undocumented immigrant Elvira Arellano's claim that it is the U.S. government that broke the law by letting people come over without documents:

> VENTO: Well, technically, she is right. **But refusing to enforce the law is one thing. She broke the law.** There's a big difference there.
>
> CAVUTO: But, essentially, we opened the door for her, in a way.
>
> VENTO: Yes.
>
> CAVUTO: And she—she ran through it.
>
> VENTO: Well, yes, that is okay. But it would be like me leaving the back door of my house open. Because I left it open for whatever reason, it doesn't give anybody the right to come into it. **She broke the law. She is where she should have been. And she should have been there a year or so ago there.**[27]

Another pro-deportation frame is the national security frame: undocumented immigrants should be deported because they may be terrorists, putting our national security at risk. In another excerpt addressing the

2007 Elvira Arellano deportation controversy, Fox News commentator Bill O'Reilly invokes the national security frame in his lead-in: "Now the Feds say Elvira actively broke the law. And **allowing illegal aliens to work at airports under fake Social Security credentials** would make it easy for **terrorists to plant bombs on planes to do other damage.**"[28]

Another common issue frame is the economic cost frame: undocumented immigrants should be deported because they place an undue economic burden on American citizens by taking American jobs and using public services without paying taxes. The following excerpt from a 2012 *Washington Times* op-ed by Rep. Lamar Smith (R-TX) illustrates the economic cost frame:

> It's disappointing that the Obama administration continues to put illegal immigrants ahead of the interests of American citizens. **Twenty-three million Americans are unemployed or looking for full-time work. Meanwhile, 7 million illegal immigrants have jobs in the U.S. We could free up millions of those jobs for citizens and legal immigrants if we simply enforced our immigration laws.**[29]

The cultural change frame reasons that "illegal" immigrants should be deported because they are changing America's language, cultural values and norms, and ethno-racial makeup, as well as the appearance of American communities. In the following excerpt, Bill O'Reilly makes this cultural case on his Fox News show by invoking ethnicity and race, implying that undocumented immigrants such as Armendariz are importing a culture of crime and lawlessness:

> Okay. I don't have a problem with before and after. But a federal judge has to order the **deportation**. All right. So I mean, unless you don't think the federal system is fair, because a judge has to go over, has to order the deportation. It's not like they just put you on a bus and kick you out. Let's think this **Armendariz, whatever his name is.** Before the cocaine beef, he had two DUIs. Now you're telling me, why should this guy be allowed to stay in the United States? **He's a Mexican alien. He's a scofflaw.** He's got three convictions on his sheet. I mean, you've got to get rid of him. You have to get rid of him, Ms. Parker. It's just—we have enough of our own criminals to deal with here.[30]

Finally, the unfairness frame is that "illegal" immigrants should be deported because they are cutting in line. Thus, if legal citizens have to "wait in line," it is not fair to allow "illegal" immigrants to circumvent this waiting period. This excerpt from the *Washington Times* in 2013 illustrates the unfairness frame: "Mr. Goodlatte again appeared to oppose giving what he called **"a special pathway to citizenship"** to illegal immigrants, saying that **gives them an advantage over others who waited in line to enter the country the right way.**"[31]

Additionally, we coded for the following frames that are typically used against deportation policies: family or social disruption, impracticality, morality, economic cost, educational disruptions, violations of civil liberties or rights, and unfairness.[32] First, the social disruption frame is that "illegal" immigrants should not be deported because deportation tears apart families and separates mothers from children and American-born children from their undocumented parents. The report from the CNN senior Latin affairs editor Rafael Romo from which we quoted earlier is a good example of this frame. Recall that Romo reports that twenty-four-year-old Evelyn Rivera, an undocumented immigrant, was meeting up with her mother, Yolanda Ravi, for the first time since she was deported to their native Colombia, and that the Brazilian Gorte Teodoro was seeing her twenty-five-year-old daughter Renata for the first time since she was deported. "I just want to be with my kids," Teodoro said. "I live in America fifty years, fifty years. Why deport me?" Her daughter added: "I just want to be with my mom. I want her to be there at my graduation. I want to go to movie nights again with her."[33]

Second, the impracticality frame is that "illegal" immigrants should not be deported because there is no clear-cut way to deport all 12 million of them. In this 2010 response to a flurry of state and local laws, the *Washington Post* editorial board published the following editorial that included this frame:

> In fact, **deportation on such a scale would be impractical and economically self-defeating.** According to polling data, it would also be broadly unpopular. Even among Americans who don't depend directly on illegal immigrants as a source of unskilled labor—which many do—**there is little appetite for wrenching millions of undocumented families, including many with roots, relatives and children in America, from their communities and shoving them across the border.**[34]

The morality frame is that "illegal" immigrants should not be deported because doing so is not right. More specifically, its negative effects on families and communities are not morally justifiable. The following exchange from Fox News in June 2012 illustrates this frame:

CHRIS WALLACE, HOST: Bill, what do you think of the policy [DACA]?

BILL KRISTOL, *WEEKLY STANDARD:* I think it's a sensible policy. I think it would be much better if that were the law of the land. And I think the president is pushing the edges of the limits of prosecutorial discretion and say we're not going to enforce a law in order to leave these people in the country, but I think **it's the right thing to do** actually. . . .

Joe Trippi, Democratic strategist: **I think the policy is the right one.** It's about—I mean, I think he articulated it the right way, this is about what—who we are going after? They deported 400,000 people last year. So you're looking at, **let's go after criminals, people who are violent in the community, people who are a threat to the American community, and not put so much focus, any focus on students, people seeking an education who are here because their parents brought them here and who see themselves as Americans.**[35]

The economic cost frame is that "illegal" immigrants should not be deported because doing so would bring about negative economic consequences. Specifically, deportation would negatively affect our local communities, businesses, consumer prices, public school systems, and overall economy. The following is an excerpt in which *Politics Nation* host Al Sharpton runs a video clip of former president George W. Bush addressing the economic contribution of immigrants:

Al Sharpton: Isn't that incredible? Well, listen to George Bush on immigration today.

President George W. Bush: Not only do **immigrants help build our economy,** they invigorate our soul. As our nation debates the proper course of action relating with regard to immigration, I hope we do so with a benevolent spirit and keep in mind the **contribution of immigrants.**[36]

A narrower version of the social disruption frame is the educational disruption frame, which claims that "illegal" immigrants should not be deported because their removal would severely disrupt not only our public education systems but also the lives of all public school children, both legal and illegal immigrant and non-immigrant. The following exemplifies this frame:

A Virginia teenager who was scheduled to be deported a few days after her high school graduation earned a last-minute reprieve Monday afternoon. Heydi Mejia, 18, and her mother, Dora Aldana, 40, were granted a one-year deferral by the Department of Homeland Security. Mejia and Aldana, the subjects of a story in The Washington Post on Monday, were prepared to leave for Guatemala this week. Mejia was 4 when her mother brought her to the United States across the Rio Grande, and she graduated with honors from Meadowbrook High School in Richmond on Friday. She had planned to go to college, until immigration officials came to her family's two-bedroom apartment in December, turning her senior year into a countdown to deportation.[37]

The civil liberties frame is that "illegal" immigrants should not be deported because such action is a violation of our Constitution, including the Equal Protection and Due Process Clauses. The following is a typical example:

> A coalition of immigrant-rights advocates filed a lawsuit Thursday seeking to overturn an order by Arizona Gov. Jan Brewer that denies driver's licenses to illegal immigrants who avoided deportation under a new Obama administration policy. . . . **The lawsuit claims that the Arizona policy violates the Supremacy Clause of the U.S. Constitution by interfering with federal immigration law, and also violates the Fourteenth Amendment's Equal Protection Clause by discriminating against certain noncitizens.** Arizona's motor vehicle division implemented Ms. Brewer's Sept. 18 order.[38]

Finally, in the unfairness frame, "illegal" immigrants should not be deported because of their important contributions to the growth and vibrancy of local communities and economies, often under difficult working conditions. The frame against unfair deportations also includes keeping families intact. The following excerpt from the *Washington Post* illustrates this issue frame:

> Who deserves to be a U.S. citizen? It's a question President Obama and Congress are trying to answer. But it's also one we've been grappling with since our country's earliest days. The founders had a clear answer: **People who immigrated and spent years building lives in this country deserved citizenship.** They were also keenly aware that making new immigrants wait a long time for citizenship denied them the very rights that Americans had just fought to claim for themselves.[39]

Having presented examples of the different types of pro- and con-deportation issue frames, we now show the number of pro and con frames used per story by news organization (see table 5.5).[40] In general, we expect to see more pro-deportation frames from the more conservative outlets and more con-deportation frames from the mainstream and liberal outlets. While we observe the same ideological divide for pro-deportation frames, the same cannot be said for con-deportation frames.

As expected, conservative news outlets such as Fox News (2.04 arguments per article) and the *Washington Times* (1.39) employed pro-deportation frames more frequently than more mainstream and liberal outlets such as CNN (0.81), MSNBC (0.67), the *Washington Post* (0.85),

Table 5.5   Mean Number of Pro- or Con-Deportation Arguments per
Deportation Story in Seven News Sources, 2007–2013

	All Four Years Combined	2007	2010	2012	2013
Pro-deportation arguments					
Washington Post	0.85	1.02	1.08	0.62	0.78
Washington Times	1.39	1.46	2.15	1.26	1.18
New York Times	0.65	0.88	0.82	0.58	0.30
New York Post	0.34	0.18	0.84	0.17	0.20
Fox News	2.04	2.23	1.77	1.82	2.00
MSNBC	0.67	1.71	1.19	0.44	0.58
CNN	0.81	2.14	1.21	0.42	0.64
Con-deportation arguments					
Washington Post	0.54	0.69	0.85	0.31	0.41
Washington Times	0.46	0.22	0.23	0.37	0.89
New York Times	0.62	0.90	0.48	0.70	0.40
New York Post	0.28	0.18	0.21	0.40	0.00
Fox News	0.65	1.00	0.31	0.29	0.00
MSNBC	0.28	0.58	0.42	0.23	0.24
CNN	0.52	1.21	1.12	0.23	0.36

Source: Authors' qualitative content analysis of news data.

and the *New York Times* (0.65); the liberal MSNBC was among the least likely to employ such frames. However, when we look at the prevalence of con-deportation frames, we observe no apparent pattern: the *Washington Post* had 0.54 con arguments per article, the *Washington Times* 0.46, the *New York Times* 0.62, the *New York Post* 0.28, Fox News 0.65, MSNBC 0.28, and CNN 0.52.

Moreover, the ideological divide in the pro-deportation angle can be seen even more clearly in terms of the percentage of stories that included at least one pro-deportation frame (see table 5.6). For example, over 77 percent and 95 percent of the *Washington Times* and Fox News stories included at least one pro-deportation frame, respectively.[41] By contrast, this was the case for only 56, 37, 41, and 42 percent of *Washington Post*, *New York Times*, MSNBC, and CNN deportation stories, respectively.

While the number of frames per article can give readers a window into the restrictiveness of the coverage, it sheds little light on its content. To do so, we examine the frequency with which each news organization used the various pro-deportation frames. In general, we expect conservative media to rely more on restrictive issue frames, liberal media to rely more on permissive issue frames, and the mainstream media to fall somewhere in between.

Table 5.6   Deportation Stories Including One or More Pro-Deportation Arguments, by News Organization, 2007, 2010, 2012, and 2013

	All Four Years Combined	2007	2010	2012	2013
Washington Post	56%	71%	70%	37%	57%
Washington Times	77	85	92	67	74%
New York Times	37	48	42	36	20%
New York Post	20	12	42	11	20%
Fox News	95	97	85	94	100%
MSNBC	41	83	58	31	40%
CNN	42	75	64	29	36%

Source: Authors' qualitative content analysis of news data.

Table 5.7   Deportation Stories Including Specific Pro-Deportation Arguments, by News Organization, 2007, 2010, 2012, and 2013

	Washington Post	Washington Times	Fox News	MSNBC	CNN	New York Times	New York Post
Public safety	35%	37%	53%	7%	12%	24%	9%
Rule of law	30	58	85	21	30	30	18
National security	10	24	24	9	9	9	4
Economic costs	9	16	27	24	19	1	3
Cultural change	0	0	9	5	10	0	0
Unfairness	0	2	5	1	2	0	0

Source: Authors' qualitative content analysis of news data.

First, to give an impression of the overall coverage, we find that the most frequently used pro-deportation frame was the legality frame. The legality, or rule of law, frame appeared in 33.3 percent of all deportation stories in the seven-source, four-year sample. In second was the public safety frame (21.8 percent), followed by the economic cost frame (14.9 percent) and the national security frame (11.5 percent). Surprisingly, the cultural change frame and unfairness to legal immigrants frame appeared in fewer than 4 percent of deportation stories.

Next, we present data on the appearance of particular frames by news organization, starting with a discussion of the most frequently appearing frame, the legality frame (see table 5.7). The legality frame appears most often in Fox News (85 percent of deportation stories), followed by the *Washington Times* (58 percent). Conversely, this same frame turns up in fewer than 30 percent of deportation stories in the rest of our news sources.

Similarly, the public safety frame shows up most frequently in two of the conservative-leaning news organizations: in 53 and 37 percent of Fox News and *Washington Times* deportation stories, respectively. The pattern for these frames generally falls in line with our expectations.

Finally, the data reveal slightly different and unexpected results for the third most frequently used frame, the economic cost frame. This frame appears most often in Fox News (27 percent), followed closely by MSNBC (24 percent). In this case, the *Washington Times* included the economic cost frame in only 16 percent of its coverage, ranking it fourth behind CNN (19 percent) and in front of the *Washington Post* (9 percent).

We now turn to the appearance of frames opposing deportation (see table 5.8). First, in terms of overall frequency, the most frequently included frames were the economic costs and social disruptions of deporting immigrants, each averaging 9 percent of all deportation stories in the four-year period. These were followed closely by the violation of civil liberties (7.3 percent), moral consideration, and unfairness frames (6.4 percent each). The other con-deportation frames appeared in about 4 percent of deportation stories (see table 5.8). Of note, con-deportation frames appeared much less frequently than pro-deportation frames.

With respect to the evidence regarding particular frames by news organization, we find that the economic cost (con) deportation frame was consistently employed across news organizations, with the exception of Fox News and the two New York–based news organizations. Specifically, the economic cost frame was in 11, 10, 11, and 11 percent of deportation stories in the *Washington Post*, the *Washington Times*, MSNBC, and CNN, respectively. By contrast, this same frame turned up in only 4, 5, and 4 percent of the deportation stories of Fox News, the *New York Times*, and the *New York Post*.

A different pattern emerges for the civil liberties frame. Here, Fox News (12 percent) led the way, followed closely by the *Washington Post* (11 percent), the *Washington Times* (9 percent), CNN (8 percent), and MSNBC (5 percent). With respect to the disrupting families (social disruption) frame, again Fox News and the *New York Times* (16 percent) are most likely to include this frame, followed by the *Washington Post* at 11 percent, the *Washington Times* at 10 percent, CNN at 7 percent, and finally, MSNBC at 3 percent. Later we address the somewhat surprising finding that Fox leads the way with con-deportation frames.

Overall, a few interesting findings emerge from the data. First, Fox News deportation coverage is the most saturated with pro-deportation issue frames at more than two pro-deportation frames per story. Strikingly, this is more than two times as many pro-deportation frames as the *Washington Post* and CNN use, and over three times as many as appear in MSNBC coverage. Second, the paucity of appearances of the con-

Table 5.8 Deportation Stories Including Specific Con-Deportation Arguments, by News Organization, 2007, 2010, 2012, and 2013

	Washington Post	Washington Times	Fox News	MSNBC	CNN	New York Times	New York Post	All
Social disruption	11%	10%	16%	3%	7%	16%	5%	9.0%
Impracticality	4	4	12	2	9	0	0	4.0
Moral considerations	7	8	12	0	1	14	3	6.4
Economic costs	11	10	4	11	11	5	4	9.0
Educational disruptions	5	1	4	6	4	4	5	4.4
Violation of civil liberties	11	9	12	5	8	6	0	7.3
Unfairness	5	4	3	2	7	17	11	6.4

Source: Authors' qualitative content analysis of news data.

deportation frames is also very striking. While media sources over the entire time period used 0.95 pro-deportation frames per story, this number was only 0.45 for con-deportation frames. This difference is exacerbated when we focus on Fox News and *Washington Times* coverage, which used over three times as many pro- as con-deportation frames. Therefore, even though Fox News used some con-deportation frames, the number is dwarfed in comparison to the number of pro-deportation frames used. Finally, we should note the dominance of the legality, public safety, and economic cost (pro-deportation) frames, which appeared in 35, 22.5, and 18.9 percent of all deportation stories, respectively. These are the most salient frames driving the national conversation on deportation.

If we look at patterns over time, an interesting finding is the robustness of 2007's deportation coverage compared to 2010, 2012, and 2013, particularly with respect to the inclusion of pro-deportation frames. Specifically, 2007 was the year with the highest percentage of deportation stories that included each of the top four frames (legality, public safety, economic cost, and national security). For example, in 2007 the legality frame appeared in 55 percent of all deportation stories, compared to 45 percent in 2010, 21 percent in 2012, and 27 percent in 2013. We might attribute this pattern to the high priority given to immigration reform in 2007 by the Bush administration and congressional leaders; the mobilization of conservative voters through talk radio and other conservative news media that year was the only remaining bulwark against the passage of comprehensive immigration reform.[42] By contrast, in 2012 immigration reform reappeared on the political radar after President Obama won reelection with an overwhelming percentage of Latino votes. Many commentators, including conservative Fox News personalities such as Sean Hannity and Bill O'Reilly, began to signal that their opinions on immigration reform were evolving and that they might support policies they had previously decried as amnesty. Pro-deportation frames thus found much less resonance and receptiveness in conservative media in late 2012 and early 2013 than they did in 2007.

Years in the United States

Finally, the policy debate on deportations features another issue frame that is not inherently for or against deportations—years spent in the United States. This frame is typically invoked by immigration advocates to highlight the plight of long-term residents, whose deportation, they argue, is far more difficult to justify than the deportation of more recent arrivals. Indeed, as Elizabeth Cohen contends, the argument for time as a basis for political membership (and relief from deportation) was a central component of early Anglo and American conceptions of citizenship.[43]

This frame may be an important part of advocates' argument against the deportation of long-term residents, but we found very few stories that mentioned how long deportees or potential deportees had spent in the United States; few stories cited the specific number of years or even used more qualitative terms such as "long-term residents," "recent arrivals," or "recently arrived." In none of the news sources we examined did length of stay appear in more than 5 percent of all news stories on deportation, with one notable exception: the *New York Times*, where "decades" or "years" was mentioned in about 7 and 8.5 percent, respectively, of news passages related to deportations. Overall, we find slightly higher mentions of years in the United States in deportation stories that appeared in print sources (ranging from 2.1 to 8.5 percent) than in those appearing in cable news sources (ranging from 0 to 2.4 percent).

The Effect of Frames on Public Opinion

Now that we have looked extensively at variations in news framing of deportation—across time and across sources and along key dimensions such as tone, empathy, episodic versus thematic frames, and pro and con issue frames—we now examine the possible effects of some of these frames on public opinion on deportation. We were interested in exploring both frames that were very prevalent in the media and those that received less play, such as several of the con-deportation arguments and years in the United States. We also explore the effects of episodic compared to thematic frames. As in previous chapters, we used survey experiments to test how different frames affect support for policies involving deportation and enforcement. We begin by looking at how the different issue frames used for and against deportation affect public opinion. We then examine how the number of years an immigrant has been in the United States affects support for deportation. Finally, we examine how episodic compared to thematic framing affects support for deportation policy.

Pro- and Con-Deportation Frames

We tested different pro- and con-deportation arguments in the 2007 and 2010 studies. In the 2007 study, respondents were randomly assigned to read a survey question with no argument in favor of deportation, with a legal argument, or with a security argument; and a survey question with no argument opposed to deportation, with a disrupting families argument, or with an economic costs argument.[44] The pro-deportation frames were as follows:

Legal frame: "Some people say that we cannot just allow people to ignore our immigration laws."

Security frame: "Some people say that we cannot risk having millions of potential terrorists in our country."[45]

The con-deportation frames were as follows:

Families frame: "Some people say that mass deportation would break up families and cause social disruption."

Economic cost frame: "Some people say that deporting 12 million people would be very expensive and cause economic disruption."[46]

We chose these arguments for several reasons. With respect to the pro-deportation arguments, the legal argument was the most prominent in media coverage, and the security argument also received a fair amount of coverage. In general, we expect that both frames may increase support for deportations given that they are pro arguments. However, we expect that the legal argument may be more effective than the security argument. First, the legal argument taps into norms that the public is expected to obey.[47] Pointing out that individuals are violating societal norms, especially those related to law, may be particularly effective in influencing public opinion. Second, individuals may be less persuaded that undocumented immigrants pose a national security risk to the country since most people think of undocumented immigrants as coming from Mexico, which is not a hotbed of international terrorist activity.[48] In that sense, the national security argument may be a weaker frame. In fact, in a survey in which we tested the perceived effectiveness of the arguments, the security argument was perceived as weaker than the legal argument.[49]

Recall that the con-deportation arguments received very little coverage in the media: the con argument that deportation disrupts families is often raised by immigrant rights advocates, but it did not receive as much media coverage as pro-deportation frames. The economic cost argument against deportation is also used by immigrant rights advocates, if not as prominently as the families argument, but it also received little coverage in the media. Given that these are con-arguments, we expect to find that they decrease support for deportations. In exploring whether one is more effective than the other, we note that some research finds that social and symbolic frames related to immigration are more effective than economic frames.[50] On the other hand, the economic cost con frame may be more novel than the family frame and may therefore be more effective.[51] We therefore have no clear expectations about which of these two frames will be more effective in shifting opinion on deportation.

Following these arguments—or not in the no-argument condition—respondents were asked if they would vote for or against a proposal to deport all illegal immigrants and how strongly they supported or op-

Figure 5.2   Mean Support for Deportations by Arguments in Favor, 2007

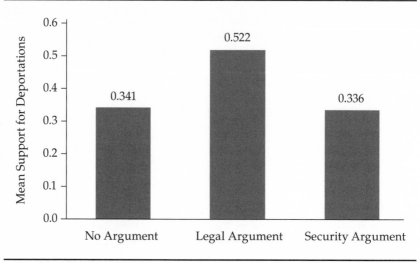

Source: Authors' analysis of 2007 CCES survey data.

posed the proposal. We coded responses on a seven-point scale ranging from −3 (strongly opposed to deportations) to 3 (strongly supportive of deportations).

We first present mean support broken down by whether respondents received no argument in favor of deportations, the legal argument, or the security argument in figure 5.2. Among those in the control group, mean support for deportations is 0.341, which is very close to neutral but on the side of supporting deportations. Turning to those exposed to the legal argument, mean support is 0.522, which is marginally more supportive of deportations compared to the control group (according to a difference in means test: $p = 0.08$, one-tailed). Among those exposed to the security argument, mean support, at 0.336, is statistically indistinguishable from the control group ($p = 0.967$, two-tailed). Therefore, only the legal frame, which we expected to be more effective, is indeed effective in increasing support for deportations.

We next present the results broken down by whether respondents received no argument opposed to deportations, the families argument, or the cost argument. Mean support for deportations among those in the control group is 0.539, which is somewhat supportive of deportations (see figure 5.3). Exposure to the families argument decreases support for deportations, as expected (mean = 0.389), but the mean is just outside of statistical significance in relation to the control group ($p = 0.129$, one-tailed). Turning to the cost-based argument, we again find that support

Figure 5.3   Mean Support for Deportations by Arguments Opposed, 2007

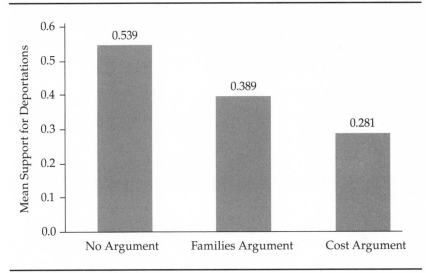

Source: Authors' analysis of 2007 CCES survey data.

for deportation is lower given exposure to this rationale (mean = 0.281); this mean is significantly different from the control group ($p = 0.024$, one-tailed).

Therefore, arguments about the costs of deporting undocumented immigrants are more effective than those that talk about breaking up families, suggesting that the novel frame is more effective.[52] We also find that people react similarly to these frames. That is, we do not find that the effects are moderated by partisanship, Fox News viewership, family immigration history, or being Latino. The one moderating effect that we find is that the cost rationale is effective in decreasing support for deportations only among those low in education.[53]

In 2010 we replicated the legal and security arguments in favor of deportations and added two more in favor of deportations—economic arguments, which were prevalent in news coverage, and cultural arguments, which received less news coverage:[54]

Cultural arguments: "Some people say that illegal immigrants are threatening our country's language and culture and we should deport anyone who is in the country illegally."

Economic arguments: "Some people say that illegal immigrants are taking away jobs from Americans and we should deport anyone who is in the country illegally."[55]

Figure 5.4   Mean Support for Deportations by Arguments in Favor, 2010

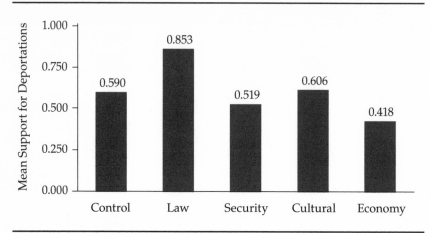

Source: Authors' analysis of 2010 CCES survey data.

Respondents were randomly assigned to no argument or to one of these arguments in favor of deportation. Given that these are all pro-deportation statements, we expected that they would increase support for deportations. Following the prompt, participants were asked for their level of support for deportation on a scale ranging from –2 to 2. In figure 5.4, we show mean support for deportations across the frames presented to respondents.

Mean support among those who did not read any argument (the control group) is 0.59, which is similar to mean support in our 2007 study. Turning to the arguments we tested in prior studies, legal and security, only the legal argument significantly boosts support for deportations relative to the control group (mean = 0.85; p = 0.014, one-tailed), which is similar to the findings from the 2007 study. With respect to the economic and cultural arguments, neither is significantly different from the control group.[56]

We tested whether respondents with different characteristics reacted differently to the frames. The only effect we find is that individuals in the first, second, and third generations react against the economic frame, becoming less supportive of deportation (see figure 5.5; see table A5.4 for full results). As expected, the strongest negative reaction comes from those in the first generation, who become over a full unit less supportive of deportations given exposure to the economic frame. This is a very large effect for a scale that ranges from only –2 to 2. They reacted against claims that immigrants take jobs away from Americans and became even less supportive of deportations.

Figure 5.5   Change in Mean Support for Deportations Moving from the
Control Group to the Economy Condition, by Family
Immigration History, 2010

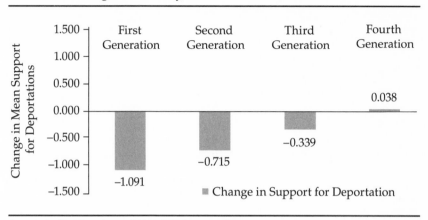

Source: Authors' analysis of 2010 CCES survey data.

Across these studies, we find a consistent pattern: legal arguments
that point out that undocumented individuals ignored immigration laws
when coming to the United States are most effective in increasing support for deportations. Recall that this was the most prevalent pro-
deportation frame in our media content analysis across all news outlets;
use of the frame exceeded 90 percent of deportation stories for Fox News.
While the national security frame received a fair amount of coverage, we
did not find any effects for this frame. Among the counterframes to deportations, it is a bit surprising that the argument focusing on families
was not effective; however, individuals might already have these considerations in mind, so exposure to the frame would not move opinion very
much.[57] However, highlighting the costs of increased deportations was a
very effective frame in lowering support for deportations, and this frame
was likely more novel to respondents as well.

Years in the United States

One frame in our media content analysis that did not receive much coverage was the length of time those without legal status had spent in the
United States. Nevertheless, we know that immigrant advocates often
invoke the frame of deportees as long-term community residents when
they argue against the disruption to families and communities caused by
immigration raids and arrests.[58] We wanted to explore to what extent
individuals would be less supportive of deportations the longer those

without legal status have been in the United States. We also wanted to look at how the partisan source of such a message influenced opinions.

We used a years manipulation in four of our survey experiments: 2008 pre-election (YouGov), 2010 (YouGov), 2012 (YouGov), and 2014 (SSI). Following is a sample of the question wording and years manipulation for the 2008 pre-election study:

> The government should give special consideration to illegal immigrants who have spent more than [*randomize:* five/ten/twenty] years in the United States and have no criminal record. Such people should not be automatically deported. To what extent do you agree or disagree?

In each study, we presented slightly different years, though there was overlap in the years presented. In 2010, we had no year mention, ten years, fifteen years, and twenty years. In 2012 and 2014, we used five years, ten years, and twenty years.[59] We coded responses from −2 to 2, with higher values being less supportive of special considerations (or more supportive of deportations). We present the results from all four years in figure 5.6.

As expected, support for deportations diminishes the longer undocumented immigrants have been in the United States. In 2008 mean support for deportations is right at the neutral point for those who have been in the United States for five years (mean = −.047), drops to being slightly less supportive of deportations for those who have been in the United States for ten years (mean = −0.198), and is even lower for those who have been in the United States for twenty years (mean = −0.285). The difference between five and ten years and between five and twenty years is statistically significant according to a difference-in-means test ($p = 0.046$ and 0.004, one-tailed), though the difference between ten and twenty years is not ($p = 0.163$, one-tailed). We find a similar pattern in 2010, and the findings are also statistically meaningful. When no mention is made of the number of years an undocumented immigrant has been in the United States, mean support for deportations is neutral and leaning toward being supportive (mean = 0.089). However, support for deportations drops below the neutral point when respondents are treated with ten years (mean = −.160), fifteen years (mean = −0.263), and twenty years (mean = −0.271).[60]

We had the same manipulations in 2012 and 2014. For 2012, we do not observe significant differences between five years (mean = −0.112) and ten years (mean = −0.128), as we do for 2008. Instead, respondents in the twenty-years condition (mean = −0.375) are significantly less supportive of deportations compared to those in the five- and ten-year conditions. Finally, in 2014, we again do not observe significant differences between

Figure 5.6   Mean Support for Deportations by Years in the United States, 2008, 2010, 2012, and 2014

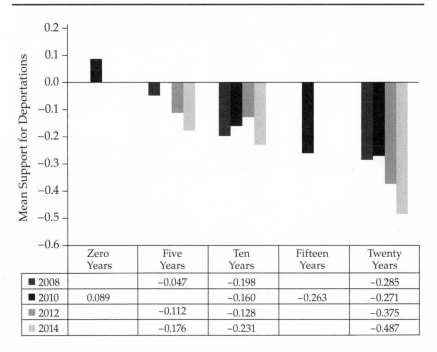

	Zero Years	Five Years	Ten Years	Fifteen Years	Twenty Years
■ 2008		−0.047	−0.198		−0.285
■ 2010	0.089		−0.160	−0.263	−0.271
■ 2012		−0.112	−0.128		−0.375
■ 2014		−0.176	−0.231		−0.487

Source: Authors' analysis of 2008 and 2010 CCES, 2012 YouGov, and 2014 SSI survey data.

five years (mean = −0.176) and ten years (mean = −0.231; p = 0.559); however, both of these conditions are significantly different from twenty years (mean = −0.487; p < 0.01 in both comparisons). Although there are slight differences across the studies, a clear pattern emerges: individuals become less supportive of deportations the longer those without legal status have been in the United States. In 2008, 2010, and 2012, none of these effects are moderated by partisanship, Fox News viewership, immigration family history, education, or being Latino.

In 2014 we find a significant moderating effect for both years manipulations by partisanship. In figure 5.7, we show the change in support for deportations moving from the five-year to the ten-year manipulation and from the five-year to the twenty-year manipulation by partisan group (see table A5.6 for full regression results). There are no differences between the ten-year and five-year manipulations in the full sample, but Democrats are significantly less supportive of deportations when treated

Figure 5.7   Change in Mean Support for Deportations Relative to the Five-Year Manipulation, by Partisanship, 2014

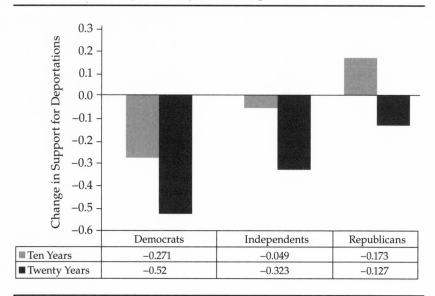

	Democrats	Independents	Republicans
■ Ten Years	−0.271	−0.049	−0.173
■ Twenty Years	−0.52	−0.323	−0.127

Source: Authors' analysis of 2014 SSI survey data (OLS regression).

with ten years compared to five years ($p = 0.047$); there are no significant differences for independents and Republicans. Meanwhile, the twenty-year manipulation does reduce support for deportations (relative to the five-year manipulation) by almost a half-unit among Democrats ($p = 0.00$) and by one-third of a unit among independents ($p = 0.00$) but has no effect on Republicans. This provides suggestive evidence that Republicans are more resistant to this frame, most likely because party elites and party activists have become more restrictive on immigration over time.

For 2012, we attached the years manipulation to a source. As we noted in chapter 2, we sometimes manipulated the partisan source of a frame to see whether it conditions the effect of the frame on immigration attitudes. Respondents were randomly assigned to the following:

[*randomize:* Some say/Some Republicans say/Some Democrats say/Some commentators at Fox News say] the U.S. government should give special consideration to illegal immigrants who have spent more than [*randomize:* five years/ten years/twenty years] in the United States and have no criminal record. Such people should not be automatically deported. To what extent do you agree or disagree?

Figure 5.8   Mean Support for Deportations by Source Cue, 2012

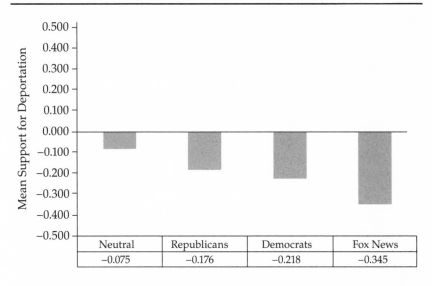

	Neutral	Republicans	Democrats	Fox News
	−0.075	−0.176	−0.218	−0.345

Source: Authors' analysis of 2012 YouGov survey data.

For the full sample, we expect that the Republican or Fox News cue may be more effective, since the more progressive frame is coming from an unexpected source, especially with respect to Fox News.[61] Indeed, in late 2012 and early 2013, after the landslide reelection of President Barack Obama, conservative Fox News anchors Sean Hannity and Bill O'Reilly surprisingly softened their support for deportation and came out in favor of amnesty. Soon thereafter, we observe survey evidence showing a significant uptick in public support for legalization, suggesting that this turnabout from conservative sources might have made the difference.[62] We might also find that the effect of the different source cues are moderated by partisanship, such that partisans move in the direction of their favored source and may react against cues coming from opposing partisans.[63]

In figure 5.8, we plot mean support for deportations by source cue. We see that support for deportations was lower for the partisan and Fox News source cues relative to the neutral cue ("Some say . . ."). However, the differences are not significant for the Republican cue; they are marginally significant for the Democratic source cue ($p = 0.09$, one-tailed) and significant for the Fox News cue ($p = 0.005$, one-tailed). The Fox News cue is even more effective than the Republican cue ($p = 0.050$). One might wonder why the Republican source cue does not lead to the same

Figure 5.9   Mean Support for Deportations by Style of Frame, 2014

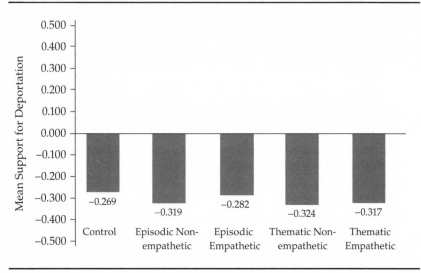

Source: Authors' analysis of 2014 SSI survey data.

effect, but some prominent Republicans have been supportive of more progressive immigration reforms, so such a frame may not have been as surprising and novel coming from the party. Somewhat surprisingly, we do not find that partisanship moderates the effect of the Democratic or Fox News cue. However, the Republican cue is significant among Republicans ($p = 0.108$; see table A5.5 for full regression results).

Episodic Human-Interest Framing Versus Thematic General Framing

Recall from previous chapters that respondents in our 2014 Survey Sampling International study were randomly assigned to either a control group or a condition in which they read a newspaper article prior to answering a battery of immigration policy questions. The treatment article was either episodic with empathetic language, episodic with non-empathetic language, thematic with empathetic language, or thematic with non-empathetic language (see chapter 3). One of the policy questions they were asked about after reading the article was the deportation question used in the previous section, scaled from −2 to 2. (The question also contained the years manipulation from the previous section.).

In figure 5.9, we plot mean support for deportations by the style of the frame. Mean support ranges from −0.269 in the control group to −0.324 in the thematic non-empathetic condition, indicating slight opposition to the policy, but none of the differences between the experimental conditions are statistically significant. These results suggest that the way in which the article is presented and the presence or absence of empathetic language makes no difference for opinions on deportation.

Although there are no main effects for the frames, we do find evidence that the style matters depending on one's family immigration history. More specifically, individuals in the first generation become just over a half-unit (−.55) less supportive of deportations when exposed to the episodic empathetic frame compared to their counterparts in the control group ($p = 0.08$; see table A5.6 for full results). The comparable effect for those in the second generation is a decline of one-third of a unit in support for deportations given exposure to this frame, though the effect is marginally significant ($p = 0.11$). Meanwhile, the frame had no effect for those in the third and fourth generations. While in previous chapters the thematic empathetic frame was most effective among the whole sample, here we find that episodic frames can be effective among the population closely linked to the policy.

Furthermore, while we find no significant moderating effects by partisanship, Fox News viewers were affected by some of the frames (see table A5.6 for full results). Fox News viewers exposed to the episodic non-empathetic condition become half a unit (−0.50) less supportive of deportations relative to their counterparts in the control group ($p = 0.03$), while those in the episodic empathetic condition become one-third of a unit less supportive, though this effect is just outside of conventional significance levels ($p = 0.14$). Those in the thematic non-empathetic condition also become less supportive of deportations relative to their counterparts in the control group ($p = 0.05$), though there is no significant effect for the thematic empathetic condition ($p = 0.38$). In sum, episodic or thematic stories with a positive presentation of undocumented immigrants but without empathetic language reduce support for deportations among Fox News viewers, while they resist the same type of coverage with empathetic language.

Finally, as in previous chapters, we look at whether reaction to these particular frames varies by trait empathy. In figure 5.10, we show the change in support for deportations moving from the control group to one of the frames in the treatment article by levels of trait empathy.

Turning first to those low in trait empathy, we find no significant differences between the treatment groups and the control group. However, we see significant effects of the treatment stories among those high in trait empathy, as we have seen for other policies. More specifically, individuals high in trait empathy in the episodic non-empathetic condition become one-quarter unit less supportive of deportations relative to their counterparts in the control group, and this effect is statistically significant ($p = 0.083$). While the episodic empathetic condition has no significant effect ($p = 0.528$), both of the thematic stories significantly reduce

Figure 5.10   Change in Mean Support for Deportations by Style of Frame (Relative to Control Group) and Trait Empathy, 2014

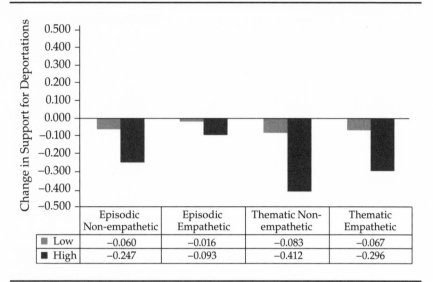

	Episodic Non-empathetic	Episodic Empathetic	Thematic Non-empathetic	Thematic Empathetic
■ Low	−0.060	−0.016	−0.083	−0.067
■ High	−0.247	−0.093	−0.412	−0.296

Source: Authors' analysis of 2014 SSI survey data (OLS regression).

support for deportations among this group. Support for deportations diminishes by one-third of a unit for the thematic empathetic frame ($p = 0.054$) and by almost a half-unit for those in the thematic non-empathetic frame ($p = 0.007$).

As we have noted in other chapters, this pattern of thematic general news frames being particularly effective is consistent with expectations from the literature, since such presentations create a context in which audiences are more likely to blame the system rather than individuals. This effect is especially likely among a population viewed as outsiders.[64] It is important to note, however, that in the controlled setting of our survey experiment, these differences in effects between thematic and episodic framing are not related to other factors such as variation in tone (which was the same across all treatments) or empathy (which was kept constant in either the empathetic or non-empathetic condition).

Discussion and Conclusions

By combining our analysis of news coverage and issue framing in the context of survey experiments, some interesting patterns and gaps emerge. First, we find that legal considerations consistently increased support for deportations, regardless of the year in which our survey experiments were conducted. To the extent that these frames are used by news media, particularly by conservative news outlets, they are likely to increase aggregate public support for deportation.

Next, we find that arguments against deportation are very sparse across all of the media that we examine. Even when con-deportation arguments are used, we find that the type of frame makes a difference. Many immigration advocates focus on the disruption that deportation causes to immigrant families, but this frame does not increase public opposition to deportation. By contrast, focusing on the economic disruption caused by massive deportations seems to produce stronger effects—we find significant effects in one of our two studies, and it is worth replicating these frames to see whether they continue to sway public opinion. It may be tempting, based on these findings, to suggest that immigrant advocates increase their emphasis on economic disruptions from deportations in their framing efforts instead of focusing primarily on disruptions to families. However, we also find that news stories emphasizing the human costs of deportation tend to provoke greater opposition to deportation among those with immigrant family histories, an effect that was particularly strong among first-generation survey respondents. Thus, while the emphasis on families may have limited effects in terms of swaying general public opinion, the evidence from this chapter and elsewhere suggests that humanizing the effects of immigration policy is likely to provoke greater support among first-generation immigrants. It is possible that this type of appeal is also important in spurring participation among first-generation immigrants.[65]

Another gap that we find when comparing our survey experiment data and our news framing data pertains to "length of stay" among undocumented immigrants in the United States. In our survey experiment data, mention of undocumented immigrants as living in the United States for ten years or twenty years significantly lowered support for deportation. Despite the seeming effectiveness of this frame, we do not find much evidence of its use in news coverage. This gap suggests that immigrant advocacy groups could increase public opposition to deportation if they were to refer more consistently to frames of undocumented immigrants as "long-term residents and community members." At the same time, it is possible that this strategy would increase public opposition to only certain types of deportations (of long-term residents) and not others.

Finally, we see that public opinion on particular aspects of deportation and other immigration enforcement action can be very malleable. We find this to be true in our survey experiments relating to the DREAM Act and comprehensive immigration reform, and we also find it here with respect to particular aspects of deportation policy. More generally, it seems that for aspects of immigration opinion for which the public has little knowledge, variations in issue framing can play a relatively strong role in shaping opinion. By contrast, for aspects of immigration opinion that are better known among the American public, variations in framing are less consequential. We saw this in chapter 4 with the diminishing effectiveness of the child frame over time with respect to public opinion on the DREAM Act. Still, framing can make a significant enough difference in the short term to prove consequential to public opinion and its mobilization for legislative ends. This was evident in 2007 when immigration restrictionists successfully deployed fears of amnesty to derail comprehensive immigration reform in the U.S. Senate. It was also evident in 2012 on the pro-immigrant side when the Obama administration framed children as bearing little responsibility for their undocumented status in an attempt to shore up public support for its "deferred action" program and other key components of immigration reform such as the DREAM Act.

Looking forward, if there are continued efforts to deploy issue frames to move public opinion on immigration, we expect that success will most likely be achieved on dimensions of immigration policy that have relatively low information. Although the effects of such frames may be short-lived, they may be sufficient to either resist policy change or put it over the top.

6

What's in a Name: Illegal, Undocumented, or Unauthorized?

negative connotation [handwritten]

I N THE fight over various policy solutions to illegal immigration, liberal and conservative advocates have sought rhetorical advantage,
not only in the ways that each policy is framed but also in the ways
that immigrants themselves are labeled: as "illegal immigrants" or as
"undocumented immigrants." Intuitively, we suspect that the semantic
differences between "illegal" and "undocumented" are important, since
the terms we use convey emotional affect and stereotypes, which in turn
can mold impressions and sway public opinion. In many ways, concerns
over the use of group labels echo the debates over the terms used to describe blacks in the late 1960s and 1970s ("Negroes," "blacks," or "African Americans"); those used to describe affirmative action in the 1980s
and 1990s ("affirmative action," "quotas," or "reverse discrimination");
and the stigma believed to be attached to the word "liberal" throughout
the 1990s. It is important to note that the belief that labels are politically
powerful is not just a matter of conjecture; a fair amount of scholarship
supports the contention that using some terms over others makes a difference, particularly on matters of race and poverty.[1]

On the liberal side of the immigration policy debate, advocates have
long argued that conservatives use the term "illegal," whether as an ad-
jective modifying "immigrant" ("illegal immigrants") or as a noun ("illegals"), to tilt policy debates in favor of immigration enforcement and
restriction. The logic underlying opposition to the term "illegal" is perhaps best expressed in a 2007 *New York Times* editorial:

semantic influencing policy support [handwritten]

Since the word [illegal] modifies not the crime but the whole person, it
goes too far. It spreads, like a stain that cannot wash out. It leaves its target
diminished as a human, a lifetime member of a presumptive criminal class.
People are often surprised to learn that illegal immigrants have rights.

147

Really? Constitutional rights? But aren't they illegal? Of course they have rights: they have the presumption of innocence and the civil liberties that the Constitution wisely bestows on all people, not just citizens.

Many people object to the alternate word "undocumented" as a politically correct euphemism, and they have a point. . . . But at least "undocumented"—and an even better word, "unauthorized"—contain the possibility of reparation and atonement, and allow for a sensible reaction proportional to the offense.[2]

While many of the reframing efforts of liberal advocacy organizations have been focused on elite-level discourse—such as the efforts of the National Association of Hispanic Journalists to get reporters to use the term "undocumented immigrants" or "undocumented workers"—more recent efforts, such as the Drop the I-Word Campaign begun in 2010, have also sought to raise awareness among the general public, in addition to enlisting commitments from media organizations.[3] As the campaign's website noted at the height of its activism, many advocates consider the term "illegal" "a damaging word that *divides* and *dehumanizes* communities and is used to *discriminate* against immigrants and people of color. The I-Word is shorthand for illegal alien, illegal immigrant and other harmful racially charged terms [emphasis in the original]."[4]

Meanwhile, advocates on the conservative side have continued to insist on using the terms "illegal alien" and "illegal immigrant," arguing that they are accurate depictions of the ways in which people have either crossed the border or maintained their presence in the United States beyond the terms set by the country's immigration laws. Indeed, one of the common phrases used by immigration conservatives—as emblazoned on T-shirts, on bumper stickers, and in many blog postings and comments—is the question: "What part of illegal don't you understand?" By framing the issue as entirely about legality, conservative groups have sought to direct attention primarily to policies of enforcement over more comprehensive solutions that include legalization. The frame of illegality also helps restrictionists deflect criticism that their movements are tinged by racial prejudice or ethnocentrism.[5] The defense and political implications of using the term "illegal" rather than "undocumented" is perhaps best articulated by the editorial board of the *Washington Times,* an influential conservative daily:

The word "illegal" accurately describes the issue at the center of the controversy. A legal alien or immigrant is someone who has gone through the legal process for entry to the United States; an illegal alien or immigrant is someone who has not. This definition is enshrined in law—for example the "Illegal Immigration Reform and Immigrant Responsibility Act of

1996"—and in terminology used by the U.S. Citizenship and Immigration Services. . . .

The term "illegal alien" is highly specific and accurately describes the problem, unlike "undocumented immigrant," which purposefully removes a stigma that should rightly remain.[6]

Finally, many demographers, research organizations, and federal government agencies have chosen to use the term "unauthorized immigrants" instead of the other terms mentioned so far. As Frank Bean and Lindsay Lowell note:

The phrase "illegal immigrant" is arguably inaccurate when applied in the U.S. case. As an alternative, the term "unauthorized migrant" is employed here to refer to persons who reside in the U.S. but whose status is not that of U.S. citizens, permanent residents, or other authorized visitors. . . . The term "undocumented" is not entirely appropriate, because many contemporary unauthorized migrants possess documents, although usually counterfeit ones. The term "illegal" does not exactly fit, because the U.S. expressly made it legal to hire such people before the Immigration Reform and Control Act (IRCA) was passed in 1986. Moreover, the federal government since then has not systematically enforced the provisions of IRCA that make it illegal to hire such workers.[7]

Framing Immigrants in the News

Given the care and attention that different actors devote to the terms used to describe immigrants without authorization, it is important to see how these terms map onto the terms utilized by news media. Our expectation, based on how the immigration debate has become polarized along party lines in the United States, is that explicitly conservative news outlets such as the *Washington Times* and the *New York Post* will use the terms "illegal immigrant" and "illegal alien" more frequently in their coverage of immigration than mainstream newspapers such as the *Washington Post* and the *New York Times*.[8] Similarly, we would expect to see considerable differences between Fox News, CNN, and MSNBC in the frequency with which these networks use the terms "illegal" and "undocumented." At the same time, we recognize that, outside of editorials, news outlets may be more constrained in their ability to use different terms to describe those without legal status. Style guidelines used by news organizations and associations provide instructions on terms to use when covering different topics and groups, including immigration. At the same time, these style guidelines cover only a small portion of the issue space (providing guidance, for example, on the use of "illegal immigrant" but having nothing to say about "amnesty"). Furthermore, advocacy groups and legislators can also play a role in shaping the terms used in news coverage by consistently using one term instead of another in the hope of being directly quoted.

We conducted a quantitative content analysis of news stories on "illegal" immigration in mainstream and conservative daily newspapers (with the *Washington Post* and the *New York Times* on the mainstream side and the *Washington Times* and the *New York Post* on the conservative side) from 2007 through 2013.[9] Additionally, we analyzed immigration stories from each of the three major cable news networks (CNN on the mainstream side, Fox News on the conservative side, and MSNBC, which transitioned from mainstream to liberal during this time period). Although we could not access all of the style manuals for our print sources, the suggestion in the manuals for the *New York Times*, the Associated Press, and the conservative *Washington Times* during the time frame of much of our content analysis that the term "illegal immigrant" be used may dampen any differences across outlets. We retrieved a total of 3,518 immigration stories from CNN, 1,893 from Fox News, 643 from MSNBC, 5,523 from the *Washington Post*, 2,752 from the *Washington Times*, 8,585 from the *New York Times*, and 1,284 from the *New York Post*. To analyze these stories we employed a quantitative content analysis.

In table 6.1, we present the incidence of these terms in these news outlets. We conducted the analysis by searching all news stories from January 1, 2007, to December 31, 2013, in which either "immigrant(s)" or "immigration" *and* "illegal," "undocumented," or "unauthorized" appeared in the headline or lead paragraph. To provide a standard measure across news outlets, we present each data point as a share of the total number of stories mentioning "immigrant(s)" or "immigration."

Overall, we find that 35 percent of all stories on immigration during this time period dealt with illegal, unauthorized, or undocumented immigrants and that this coverage was much more prevalent in conservative media compared to mainstream outlets. Among the print sources we examined, the differences were greatest between the two newspapers in Washington, D.C.: the conservative *Washington Times* was more than twice as likely to focus on illegal immigrants in its coverage of immigration as the *Washington Post* (67 percent versus 29 percent). Between the *New York Post* and the *New York Times*, the difference was significant, albeit smaller than in the case of the Washington newspapers (27 percent versus 20 percent, respectively). Among cable news sources, there was also an ideological divide: Fox News devoted the most coverage to illegal immigrants, accounting for 64 percent of all stories on immigration between 2007 and 2013. By contrast, 42 percent of immigration stories on CNN and only 37 percent of immigration stories on MSNBC dealt with illegal immigration.

Table 6.1 Terms Used to Describe Those Without Legal Status, by News Source, 2007–2013

	Total	Washington Post	Washington Times	New York Post	New York Times	CNN	Fox News	MSNBC
As proportion of all stories on immigration								
Illegal	35%	29%	67%	27%	20%	42%	64%	37%
Undocumented	2	5	0	0	1	2	1	5
Unauthorized	0	0	0	0	0	0	0	0
As proportion of all stories on those without legal status								
Illegal	94	85	99	100	92	95	99	88
Undocumented	5	14	<1	<1	6	4	1	11
Unauthorized	1	1	0	0	2	0	0	1

Source: Authors' quantitative content analysis of news data.

Interestingly, however, after taking into account differences in the frequency of attention to illegal immigration, there was less variation across news sources in the use of "illegal," "undocumented," or "unauthorized." Liberal, conservative, and mainstream sources were all very likely to use the term "illegal immigrant," with the *Washington Post* at 85 percent and all other sources at 88 percent or greater. One notable exception was the use of the term "illegal alien," which accounted for a greater proportion of stories on illegal immigration in conservative newspapers (32 percent for the *Washington Times* and 34 percent for the *New York Post*) than in the *New York Times* (1 percent) or the *Washington Post* (2 percent). The term "unauthorized" was used in fewer than 2 percent of all news stories on immigration (fifty-four times in nearly 6,600 stories), and most of these instances were in the *New York Times* (thirty-two stories) and the *Washington Post* (fifteen stories). Finally, the term "undocumented" was used in 14 percent of stories in the *Washington Post*, 6 percent of stories in the *New York Times*, 11 percent of the stories on MSNBC, and in fewer than 1 percent of stories in all of the conservative sources we analyzed.

That the *New York Times* uses terms like "undocumented" infrequently makes sense given the newspaper's style guidelines. Indeed, in response to calls to "drop the I-word," Margaret Sullivan, the public editor of the *New York Times*, insisted in October 2012 that the term "[illegal immigrant] is clear and accurate; it gets its job done in two words that are easily understood."[10] Importantly, alternative terms to "illegal" appeared much less frequently in the news sections of these newspapers than in the editorial sections, which are less subject to a newspaper's style guidelines.[11]

At the same time, we see a shift in terminology among mainstream news sources between 2012 and 2013 (table 6.2). In April 2013, the Associated Press and *USA Today* indicated that they would no longer use the word "illegal" to describe a person, although reporters could still continue to use the term to describe actions such as "illegal immigration" and "entering a country illegally."[12] The *New York Times* took a more complicated stand on the issue. First, in October 2012, Margaret Sullivan, the public editor, explained and defended the use of the term "illegal immigrant" in the *Times* in a lengthy note:

> Just as "illegal tenant" in a real estate story (another phrase you could have seen in Times stories or headlines) is brief and descriptive, so is "illegal immigrant." In neither case is there an implication that those described that way necessarily have committed a crime, although in some cases they may have. The Times rightly forbids the expressions "illegals" and "illegal aliens."
>
> This is not a judgment on immigration policy or on the various positions surrounding immigration reform, or those who hold those positions. Nor is it meant to be uncaring about the people to whom the words apply.

Table 6.2   Shift from 2010 to 2013 in the Terms Used to Describe Those Without Legal Status, by News Source

	2010	2011	2012	2013
Washington Post				
Illegal	84%	74%	78%	64%
Undocumented	12	26	21	33
Unauthorized	4	0	1	3
Washington Times				
Illegal	99	99	95	97
Undocumented	1	0	3	2
Unauthorized	0	1	2	1
New York Times				
Illegal	98	95	90	63
Undocumented	1	3	8	25
Unauthorized	1	1	2	12
New York Post				
Illegal	100	100	94	100
Undocumented	0	0	6	0
Unauthorized	0	0	0	0
CNN				
Illegal	96	97	83	54
Undocumented	3	3	17	46
Unauthorized	1	0	0	0
Fox News				
Illegal	100	99	100	94
Undocumented	0	1	0	4
Unauthorized	0	0	0	1
MSNBC				
Illegal	89	100	70	65
Undocumented	11	0	30	29
Unauthorized	0	0	0	6

Source: Authors' quantitative content analysis of news data.

It's simply a judgment about clarity and accuracy, which readers hold so dear.[13]

Within six months, however, the newspaper had adopted a more nuanced approach in its style guidelines: reporters and editors were discouraged from using the term, but still allowed to make the ultimate determination of which terms to use. As the newspaper reported in April 2013, the *New York Times* would "continue to allow the phrase ['illegal immigrant'] to be used for 'someone who enters, lives in or works in the United States without proper legal authorization.'" But it encouraged reporters and editors to "consider alternatives when appropriate to explain the specific circumstances of the person in question, or to focus on actions."[14]

This policy shift seems to have made a significant difference: we find that stories in the *New York Times* started to use the term "illegal immigrant" less frequently, declining from 90 percent in 2012 to 63 percent in 2013, and there was a corresponding increase in the use of "undocumented," from 8 percent in 2012 to 25 percent in 2013 (table 6.2). At the same time, we also see increasing use of the term "in the country illegally" in the *New York Times*, accounting for 4 percent of stories on the unauthorized immigrant population in 2013 as well as 2014. Similarly, in the *Washington Post*, news mentions of "undocumented" rose from 21 percent in 2012 to 33 percent in 2013. The growing use of "undocumented" after 2012 was even more pronounced for MSNBC and CNN. Still, it is important to note that even at the end of our content analysis period the term "illegal immigrant" was still used with relative frequency—in a majority of cases among mainstream news sources, and in an overwhelming majority of cases among the conservative outlets Fox News, the *New York Post*, and the *Washington Times*.

In both the newspaper and cable news data, a clear pattern emerges: in covering the general issue of immigration, conservative news outlets—whether on TV or in print—are more likely to focus on "illegal immigrants" and "illegal immigration" than their mainstream or liberal counterparts; they are also more likely to use the term "illegal alien." Still, all major news sources, not just conservative ones, have generally continued to use the term "illegal immigrants" when describing those without legal status. While organizations such as the Society of Professional Journalists and efforts such as the Drop the I-Word Campaign have sought to encourage journalists to use terms such as "undocumented" and "unauthorized," those terms appear only rarely in our analysis of news coverage prior to 2012, and mainstream outlets have been slow to change their style manuals. However, with prominent outlets like the *New York Times* gradually shifting their guidelines, we may see more divergence across news outlets in the future.

Framing Immigrants in Congressional Debates

Although media data may be indicative of the general discourse on immigration, we should also analyze the immigration discourse set by congressional policymakers, for three reasons. First, the media discourse patterns may help frame the public debate, but it is the U.S. Congress that is responsible for debating and setting immigration policy. If we are interested in understanding how framing relates to immigration policy, analyzing what Congress says on immigration may be more telling. Second, presenting only media data may mislead us into thinking that the media are more responsible for driving the immigration discourse than may actually be the case. Given the waxing and waning of news coverage on immigration in tandem with congressional legislative efforts (see table 3.1), it is likely that Congress plays an important role as well. Finally, members of Congress do not operate under any formal style guidelines on the use of terms, although as we find in our analysis, there may be powerful partisan constraints on what members of Congress can and cannot say with respect to undocumented immigrants.

To provide some insight into these points, we analyze U.S. Senate floor speeches from the 113th Congress using the Thomas Database from the Library of Congress. Specifically, we count the number of times a U.S. senator (Republican, independent, or Democrat) mentioned one of the four terms used to refer to immigrants without legal status ("illegal," "illegal alien," "undocumented," "unauthorized") in a floor speech over this two-year period. Republican speeches mentioned immigrants without legal status 222 times, Democrats 150 times, and independents four times.

We expect to find an ideological divide in congressional data perhaps even more pronounced than it is in the media data. Rather than being subject to media norms (for example, the *New York Times* style guide), elected officials are subject to partisan norms that are often set by the more extreme party activists, who are driving the political agenda because of their access to and role in the primary election process. Thus, we expect to find Democratic senators to be significantly more likely to use the term "undocumented," since Democratic activists have made it clear (for example, through the Drop the I-Word Campaign) that they find the "illegal" term offensive. Alternatively, we expect to find Republicans to be more likely to use the terms "illegal alien" and "illegal immigrant," since many prominent and vocal party activists continue to insist on the correctness of these terms.

Consistent with our expectations, we find strong evidence of a partisan divide among elected officials. Analyzing senatorial data from the 113th Congress, we find that Democratic senators were significantly more likely to invoke the term "undocumented immigrant" than any of the alternatives. Democrats invoked the term "undocumented" in 75 percent of the floor speeches in which they specifically referred to immigrants without legal status, and another 6 percent used the term "unauthorized" (see table 6.3). Unsurprisingly, Senate Judiciary Committee Democrats, such as Patrick Leahy (D-VT) and Dick Durbin (D-IL), led the way, using "undocumented" in 83 percent and 88 percent of their immi-

Table 6.3   Terms Used in Floor Speeches When Describing Immigrants Without Legal Status, U.S. Senate, 2013–2014

	Illegal Aliens	Illegal	Unauthorized	Undocumented	Total Mentions
Total					
No party	6.8%	43.2%	6.8%	43.2%	44
Independent	0.0	50.0	0.0	50.0	4
Republican	27.5	61.7	1.3	9.4	149
Democrat	4.3	14.5	5.8	75.4	69
Republicans					
Sessions	37.7	62.3	0.0	0.0	53
Vitter	72.7	27.3	0.0	0.0	11
Cruz	33.3	66.7	0.0	0.0	3
Lee	28.6	71.4	0.0	0.0	7
Ayotte	0.0	100.0	0.0	0.0	3
Cornyn	7.7	76.9	7.7	7.7	13
Coats	28.6	71.4	0.0	0.0	7
Grassley	5.9	23.5	5.9	64.7	17
Hatch	0.0	100.0	0.0	0.0	4
Rubio	0.0	100.0	0.0	0.0	5
McConnell	50.0	50.0	0.0	0.0	2
Other Republican	20.8	70.8	0.0	8.3	24
Democrats					
Schumer	0.0	80.0	0.0	20.0	5
Blumenthal	0.0	0.0	0.0	100.0	3
Durbin	0.0	12.5	0.0	87.5	8
Reid	0.0	0.0	0.0	100.0	9
Leahy	0.0	16.7	0.0	83.3	6
Feinstein	0.0	0.0	25.0	75.0	4
Menendez	0.0	25.0	0.0	75.0	4
Other Democrat	10.0	10.0	10.0	70.0	30
Independents					
Sanders	0.0	50.0	0.0	50.0	4

Source: Authors' quantitative content analysis of senate floor speeches.

gration speeches, respectively. However, the "I-word" was not absent from Democratic senatorial discourse: 15 percent mentioned "illegal immigrants," and another 4 percent mentioned "illegal aliens."[15]

We find that the opposite pattern holds among Republican senators. Using the same Senate floor speech data from the *Congressional Record*, we find that Republican senators generally choose to use the terms "illegal alien" and "illegal immigrant" instead. Republicans used the term "illegal alien" in 28 percent and "illegal immigrant" in 62 percent of their floor speeches on illegal immigration. In only 1 percent of cases did Republican senators use the term "unauthorized," and in only 9 percent of cases did they say "undocumented"; most of these latter mentions were by Senate Judiciary Committee chairman Chuck Grassley (R-IA). Interestingly, mentions of "illegal aliens" were primarily driven by his fellow Judiciary Committee members Jeff Sessions (R-AL) (38 percent) and David Vitter (R-LA) (73 percent), who have been among the most vocal opponents to immigrant legalization in the U.S. Senate. However, other Republicans, such as Senators Orrin Hatch (R-UT), John Cornyn (R-TX), and Marco Rubio (R-FL), who had each sponsored or supported various immigration reform measures in the past, were more likely to opt for the term "illegal immigrant."

In short, we find a strong partisan divide in the usage of terms to describe "illegal" and "undocumented" immigrants, with Republican and Democratic senators employing rhetoric very similar to that of their most vocal party activists.

Are (Illegal) Immigrant Frames Consequential?

Recent stylebook decisions indicate that we might soon see a bigger shift in news coverage in the relative use of terms such as "illegal" versus "undocumented," although our analysis of news coverage of the 2016 presidential primaries indicates an uptick in news mentions of "illegal immigrants," largely in response to statements made by Donald Trump and other Republican presidential candidates.[16] It also remains an open question whether changing labels on "illegal immigrants" would be as consequential for public opinion as advocates and critics believe they might be. As in other chapters, we use survey experiments to test for the potential importance of the frames used to describe immigrants without legal status. The vast majority of our experiments use tests in which we randomly expose individuals to survey questions about a host of immigration policies that reference either "illegal immigrants," "undocumented immigrants," or "unauthorized immigrants." A few of our studies also test the term "illegal alien."

To refresh, these frames are different from those we have tested in prior chapters. Up until this point, we have looked at how different issue frames influence public opinion on a range of immigration policies. That is, simply because we highlight some considerations rather than others, individuals might report different opinions on immigration policies.[17] In this chapter, we focus on something more akin to equivalency frames—using different terms to describe the same thing. The terms "illegal immigrant," "illegal alien," "undocumented immigrant," and "unauthorized immigrant" are all logically equivalent. However, as we indicated in chapters 1 and 2, the use of different terms for the same underlying concept can still lead to very different opinions. To date, few studies have examined how the use of different words to describe legal status can affect policy preferences. One was a survey wording experiment with a sample of Iowa voters conducted by Benjamin Knoll and his colleagues, who found null effects between using the terms "illegal" or "undocumented" on support for various legalization programs.[18] It is unclear, however, whether these results would generalize to the national electorate, to other types of immigration policies, or to the "unauthorized" label favored by many social scientists or the "illegal alien" label applied by some on the right.

How might these different terms to describe immigrants influence opinions on the range of policies we have explored in other chapters? The term "illegal" carries more negative associations and may bring to mind negative stereotypes of immigrants. More specifically, using the term "illegal" brings to mind that someone has broken the law and engaged in a criminal act.[19] We may therefore expect that attitudes on immigration policy will become more restrictive when the term "illegal" is used rather than "undocumented" or "unauthorized." This may especially be the case when the term "illegal alien" is used, since this term comprises two negative words, with "alien" bringing to mind the ultimate outsider.

At the same time, reactions to these frames may vary across subgroups in the population. For example, as we saw in the content analysis, since the term "illegal alien" is more often used by media on the right side of the political spectrum, it may be especially effective among Republicans and Fox News viewers and resisted by Democrats and those who do not watch Fox News. Natalie Masuoka and Jane Junn contend that racial minorities may resist framing immigration with terms like "illegal" given their position in the racial hierarchy.[20] Although the only sample in our study large enough to test such a claim is the Latino subgroup, we would argue that a similar process may be at work among newer immigrant groups. That is, individuals who are first- or second-generation immigrants in the United States may react against the illegal frame. In addition to these subgroups, we also look, as we did in prior chapters, at whether reaction to the frames varies by educational status: those higher in educational status may be more resistant to negative frames and more open to positive frames, given higher levels of tolerance among this group.

To test for the effect of the different terms used to describe those without legal status, we turn once again to the survey experiments conducted from 2007 to 2014 through various outlets, including YouGov, Survey Sampling International, and Mechanical Turk.[21] In many of the issue frame survey experiments reported in prior chapters, we also randomized the terms used to describe those without legal status. Since we are now taking a look across a wide range of policies, we present the findings for each policy separately.

Legalization

The first policy we return to is legalization. To refresh, in the 2007 and 2010 YouGov studies respondents were asked their level of agreement or disagreement with the following statement: "If we can seal our borders and enforce existing immigration laws, [*randomize:* illegal/undocumented/unauthorized] immigrants should be given [*randomize:* the opportunity to eventually become legal citizens/amnesty]." We asked the same question in a 2011 YouGov study, but used the term "illegal alien" instead of "unauthorized immigrant." As in prior chapters, the dependent variable was recoded to range from –2 to 2, with higher values being more supportive of legalization. Recall from chapter 3 that we found very strong effects for the amnesty issue frame across all of the years of our study: individuals exposed to that frame were much less supportive of legalization compared to those exposed to the opportunity frame. These were among the strongest issue framing effects that we have found across all of our studies. Now we look at whether we find similar effects for the terms used to describe those without legal status.

In figure 6.1, we plot mean support for legalization by experimental condition and year of study. In 2007 and 2010, we see essentially no difference in support for legalization across experimental conditions. That is, whether the term "illegal immigrant," "undocumented immigrant," or "unauthorized immigrant" is used, mean support for legalization hovers around –0.35, or mild opposition, in 2007 and –0.17 in 2010. In our 2011 study, mean support for legalization is positive across all experimental conditions; it is highest in the illegal condition and similar in the undocumented and illegal alien conditions, though again, none of these differences are statistically meaningful. We therefore find very little evidence that the terms used to describe those without legal status influence opinions on legalization.[22]

As we noted earlier, it could be that subgroups react differently to the frames. As in previous chapters, we tested whether reactions to the frames varied across partisan groups and by Fox News viewers versus non–Fox News viewers, education, among Latinos, and respondent's family immigration history. In our 2007 study, we find that reaction to the undocumented and unauthorized frames varies by one's family immigration history, and in 2011 we find the same for the undocumented frame. (That study did not include the unauthorized frame.) In figure 6.2,

Figure 6.1   Mean Support for Legalization by Term Used to Describe Immigrants, 2007, 2010, and 2011

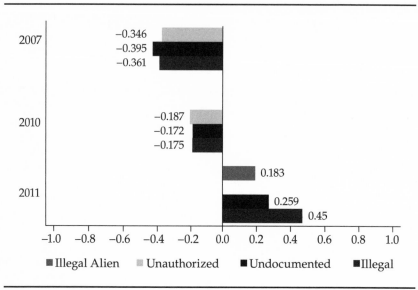

Source: Authors' analysis of YouGov survey data.

we show the change in support for legalization moving from the illegal immigrant frame to the undocumented or unauthorized frame for each generation (see table A6.1 for regression results).

To summarize the results, we find that support for legalization is significantly lower for first- and second-generation immigrants who receive the undocumented condition versus the illegal immigrant condition in both 2007 and 2011 ($p < 0.10$ in all cases). We find the same general pattern if we compare the illegal to unauthorized condition, though the significance is marginal.[23] Thus, even as immigrant rights advocates are pushing to reduce usage of the term "illegal" in news stories and public discourse, our findings suggest that usage of the term has its greatest impact on first- and second-generation immigrants, who seem to react against the "illegal" label and become even more supportive of the policy than when the terms "unauthorized" or "undocumented" are used. For example, in the 2011 study, a first-generation immigrant receiving the illegal condition is three-quarters of a unit *more* supportive of legalization than her counterpart receiving the undocumented condition. This is a pretty sizable effect for a scale that only ranges five units.

In our 2014 Mechanical Turk study, we also included a survey experiment on the terms used to describe those without legal status on another legalization question. Respondents were asked:

Figure 6.2   Change in Support for Legalization Moving from the Illegal
Condition to the Undocumented/Unauthorized Condition, by
Family Immigration History, 2007 and 2011

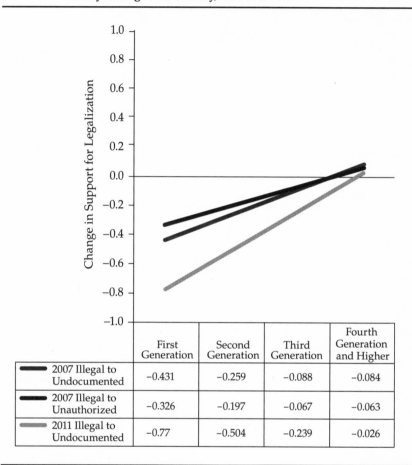

	First Generation	Second Generation	Third Generation	Fourth Generation and Higher
2007 Illegal to Undocumented	−0.431	−0.259	−0.088	−0.084
2007 Illegal to Unauthorized	−0.326	−0.197	−0.067	−0.063
2011 Illegal to Undocumented	−0.77	−0.504	−0.239	−0.026

Source: Authors' analysis of YouGov survey data.

[*randomize:* Some say/Some Republicans say/Some Democrats say/Some commentators on Fox News say] the U.S. government should give special consideration to [*randomize:* illegal immigrants/undocumented immigrants/illegal aliens] who have spent more than [*randomize:* two years/five years/ten years/twenty years] in the United States and have no criminal record. They say that such people should be allowed the opportunity to stay in this country and eventually become U.S. citizens. To what extent do you disagree or agree?

Figure 6.3   Mean Support for Legalization by Term Used to Describe Immigrants, 2013

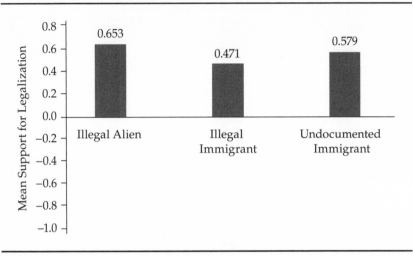

Source: Authors' analysis of 2013 Mechanical Turk survey data.

This measure is again coded from −2 to 2, with higher values being more supportive of legalization. Recall from chapter 3 that we found no effect for the source cues in this question, but did find that support varied significantly based on the number of years immigrants have been in the United States. The substantive effects were such that support for legalization increased by about 0.381 units moving from two years to twenty years spent in the United States. In figure 6.3, we show mean support for legalization across the terms used to describe those without legal status.

Somewhat surprisingly, we find that mean support is highest among those in the illegal alien condition (0.653), lowest among those in the illegal immigrant condition (0.471), and in between for those in the undocumented condition (0.579). However, the only significant difference is between the illegal alien and illegal immigrant conditions ($p = 0.055$).[24] With respect to the substantive meaning of the results, the difference between these conditions is still smaller than what we find for the years manipulation. We had expected support to be lowest among those in the illegal alien condition, but it appears that those in the full sample react against this frame. Of course, the Mechanical Turk sample is more left-leaning and younger than the YouGov and SSI samples, so it makes more sense that they might react against the double-negative illegal alien frame. In this study, all of the subgroups we explore react similarly to the frames (partisanship, Fox News viewership, education, being Latino, and family immigration history).

Although there is some evidence of reacting against the illegal alien frame in the Mechanical Turk study, we find null effects for the terms used to describe those without legal status on two other questions related to legalization in that study.[25] Thus, overall, the picture points to largely null effects for the terms used to describe those without legal status, the only exception being that individuals, especially newer immigrants, sometimes react against the "illegal" label.

The Dream Act

Recall from chapter 5 that individuals in our 2007 and 2010 YouGov studies were asked for their level of agreement with the following statement: "[randomize: Illegal/undocumented/unauthorized] immigrants [randomize: (no additional wording)/who came to the United States as young children] should be able to earn legal status if they graduated from a U.S. high school, have stayed out of trouble, and have enrolled in college or the military." In our 2011 and 2012 YouGov studies, we asked the same question, but replaced "unauthorized immigrants" with "illegal aliens." As in chapter 5, the dependent variable is coded on a scale from −2 to 2, with higher values indicating more support for the DREAM Act. When we analyzed the effects of the child wording in chapter 5, we found that the wording increased support for the DREAM Act in three of the studies. We now assess whether support for the DREAM Act also shifts given exposure to different terms to describe those without legal status.

In figure 6.4, we show mean support for the DREAM Act across the different terms used to describe those without legal status. In 2007 we find no differences in support for the DREAM Act across the three different terms. That is, support for the DREAM Act is slightly positive whether immigrants are described as "illegal," "undocumented," or "unauthorized."[26] In 2010 we begin to see some movement in support depending on the terms used, with support higher in the conditions that described immigrants as "undocumented" and "unauthorized" compared to "illegal"; however, only the difference between the unauthorized and illegal conditions is statistically significant ($p = 0.04$).[27] Furthermore, the substantive effect is not very large, leading to only a 0.22-unit increase in support for the DREAM Act. In contrast, the effect of the child wording was about double that size. In 2011 support appears higher in the undocumented condition (1.056) relative to the illegal immigrant (0.799) or illegal alien (0.811) condition, but none of these differences are statistically significant.

Finally, in 2012 we again find no difference in support for the DREAM Act between the illegal immigrant and undocumented immigrant conditions, but we do find that exposure to the illegal alien frame reduces support for the DREAM Act relative to those exposed to the illegal immi-

Figure 6.4   Mean Support for the DREAM Act by Term Used to Describe Immigrants, 2007, 2010, 2011, and 2012

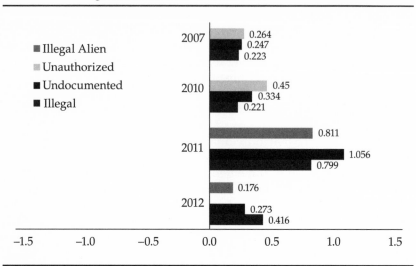

Source: Authors' analysis of YouGov survey data.

grant frame ($p = 0.02$).[28] Exposure to the double-negative illegal alien frame drops support by about one-quarter of a unit. We had expected this frame to lead to the biggest reduction in support for progressive immigration policies. In sum, we again find mostly null results for whether the terms used to describe those without legal status matters for opinions on the DREAM Act. In only one case does support increase given exposure to a more neutral description of immigrants, as expected, and that is the unauthorized condition in 2010. In addition, in only one case does the most negative frame, "illegal alien," reduce support for the DREAM Act, also as expected. We do find a similar effect for the illegal alien frame in the 2012 study when we asked about support for DACA.[29] These mostly null findings are therefore very similar to what we found for legalization.

As with legalization, we tested whether reaction to the frames would vary across different subgroups in the population. In the 2007 study, we again find that reaction to the terms varies by family immigration history. In figure 6.5, we show how mean support for the DREAM Act changes moving from the illegal immigrant frame to the undocumented and unauthorized frames by respondent's family immigration history (see table A6.3 for regression results). As we saw for legalization, those in the first and second generations actually become less supportive of the DREAM Act given the undocumented frame compared to the illegal immigrant frame (all of these effects are significant at $p < 0.10$, with the ex-

Figure 6.5   Change in Support for the DREAM Act Moving from the Illegal Condition to the Undocumented/Unauthorized Condition, by Family Immigration History, 2007 and 2011

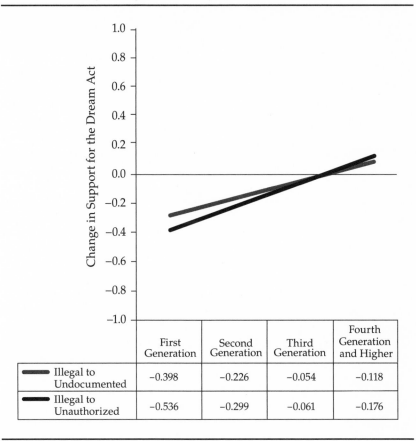

		First Generation	Second Generation	Third Generation	Fourth Generation and Higher
▬▬	Illegal to Undocumented	−0.398	−0.226	−0.054	−0.118
▬▬	Illegal to Unauthorized	−0.536	−0.299	−0.061	−0.176

Source: Authors' analysis of YouGov survey data.

ception of the undocumented frame for the second generation, where the p-value is 0.12), which suggests that they are reacting against the illegal frame. That is, exposure to the illegal frame further reinforces their support for the DREAM Act. Furthermore, we find that the unauthorized frame increases support for the DREAM Act by about 0.17 units among those in the fourth generation and higher ($p = 0.04$) relative to their counterparts exposed to the illegal immigrant frame. We do not, however, see any moderating effects for family immigration history in 2010 (there are no moderating effects at all in the 2010 study) or 2011 (we did not have this measure in the 2012 study). Therefore, groups may react against frames at some points in time, but that will not necessarily always be the case. The highly charged environment in 2007 around immigration may have provided the necessary cueing information for newer immigrant groups to react against such frames.

With respect to other moderators, we find that partisanship seems to matter in how people reacted to the frames in two of the studies. In 2011 we find that the undocumented frame (relative to the illegal immigrant frame) increases support for the DREAM Act by almost half a unit (0.47) among Democrats ($p = 0.04$), but it has no effect on independents ($p = 0.258$) or Republicans ($p = 0.991$). We find a similar effect among non–Fox News viewers, who become half a unit (0.54) more supportive of the DREAM Act given exposure to the undocumented frame ($p = 0.013$).[30] In 2012 we find that partisans react differently to the illegal alien and undocumented frames compared to the illegal immigrant frame (see table A6.3 for regression results). Independents are 0.29 units less supportive of the DREAM Act in the illegal alien frame compared to the illegal immigrant frame ($p = 0.004$), while Republicans are almost half a unit less supportive ($\beta = -0.489, p = 0.005$). However, there is no difference among Democrats ($p = 0.472$).[31] Republicans also become less supportive of the DREAM Act when they are exposed to the undocumented frame compared to the illegal immigrant frame, by about 0.40 units ($p = 0.019$). It seems that they are reacting against the undocumented frame, which we generally expect to lead to more support for the DREAM Act. We find no effect for this frame relative to the illegal immigrant frame among Democrats ($p = 0.385$) or independents ($p = 0.169$).

As with legalization, we see a mixed bag with respect to the extent to which the terms used to describe those without legal status matters for policy opinions. Somewhat surprisingly, the undocumented and unauthorized frames did not increase support for the DREAM Act relative to the illegal immigrant frame in most cases. All we find is some evidence of Democrats becoming more supportive of the DREAM Act given this frame in the 2011 study, while Republicans react against it in 2012. We do see a reduction in support for the DREAM Act when the illegal alien frame is used, but only for one of the two studies, and the effect is confined to independents and Republicans. These findings show that partisans sometimes process frames through partisan filters.

Deportation

To understand how the terms used to describe immigrants affect support for deportation policies, we turn to two questions from the 2010 YouGov study and one question from the 2014 SSI study. In the 2010 study, we randomly assigned the terms used to describe those without legal status for the question on special considerations: "The U.S. government should give special consideration to [*randomize:* illegal/undocumented/unau-

Figure 6.6   Mean Support for Deportations by Term Used to Describe Immigrants, 2010 and 2014

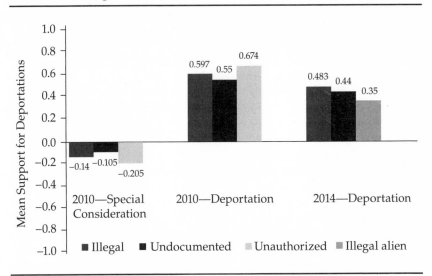

Source: Authors' analysis of 2010 CCES and 2014 SSI survey data.

thorized] immigrants who have spent more than [x number of years] in the United States and have no criminal record. Such people should not be automatically deported. To what extent do you agree or disagree?" In the same study, we also randomized the terms used to describe those without legal status for the question that asked for support for deportations given different rationales (control group, legal argument, cultural argument, economic argument, and national security argument; see chapter 5). Both questions are coded on a −2 to 2 scale, with higher values indicating more support for deportations.

In our 2014 SSI study, we asked respondents: "Thinking about the estimated 12 million [*randomize:* illegal immigrants/undocumented immigrants/illegal aliens] living in the United States, would you vote for or against a proposal to deport all [*randomize:* illegal immigrants/undocumented immigrants/illegal aliens]?" This question did not have a middle option, so we coded the scale to run from −2 to 3, with higher values again indicating more support for deportations.

In figure 6.6, we plot mean support for each question across the terms used to describe those without legal status. We can see that mean opinion is more progressive for the special consideration question across all three terms used to describe those without legal status; there are no meaningful differences between them. For the two deportation questions, individuals are slightly supportive of deportations regardless of the terms used to describe those without legal status. For this policy domain, then, the terms used to describe immigrants does not alter opinions, at least not in the full sample.[32]

As with our prior analyses, we tested whether different subgroups would react differently to the terms used to describe those without legal status. We do not find any moderating effects for the special consideration measure. For the deportation measure used in the 2010 study, we find only a moderating effect based on the respondent's family immigration history, though the effects are a bit different from what we found for the other policy issues. Individuals in the first and second generations exposed to the undocumented frame become less supportive of deportations compared to their counterparts exposed to the illegal immigrant frame (see tables A6.5 and A6.6). They therefore moved in the direction of the more neutral frame compared to the more negative frame. Recall that for legalization and the DREAM Act, those in the first and second generations had reacted against the illegal frame. Finally, for the deportation question in 2014, we find only a moderating effect for Latinos, who become more supportive of deportations given exposure to the undocumented frame relative to their counterparts who received the illegal frame ($\beta = 1.115$; $p = 0.07$). It therefore seems that Latinos may have been reacting against the illegal immigrant frame in a way similar to what we found for those in the first and second generations on legalization and the DREAM Act. Surprisingly, however, they made no distinctions between the illegal alien and illegal immigrant frame (see tables A5.5 and A5.6). As we noted earlier, differences in reactions to the frames may have been related to the information environment in different years. In a more highly charged environment, like 2007 and 2014, newer immigrants and immigrant-rooted groups may be more likely to react against the illegal frame and further increase their support for progressive immigration policies, while in less politically charged environments they may be influenced by the more positive frames.

Discussion and Conclusion

In prior chapters, we find a wide degree of variation in media frames on immigration policy across liberal, mainstream, and conservative media outlets, and we often find that these frames are consequential in terms of public support for or opposition to comprehensive immigration reform, the DREAM Act, and deportation. Given the fervor with which immigrant advocates mobilize around the usage of terms such as "illegal" and "undocumented," we might have expected equivalency frames to produce a similar pattern. However, we find that these equivalency frames are largely inconsequential, both in how news media cover the illegal/ undocumented population in the United States and in the lack of any discernible effects on public opinion toward immigration policy.

There are some important caveats, however. First, the effects of the double-negative illegal alien frame were significantly different from the other conditions on occasion and led to more restrictionist preferences, especially among independents and Republicans. We also find some reactions *against* the illegal immigrant frame among immigrants in the first and second generations, particularly in our 2007 and 2012 studies, when immigration was very salient in the news and many elites were promoting restrictionist stances. Finally, even if these frames were not generally consequential for public opinion on immigration policy, we find strong differences in how elected officials referred to the population without legal status, with Republicans largely preferring the terms "illegal immigrant" or "illegal alien" and Democrats referring to "undocumented immigrants." Still, our findings largely suggest that immigration advocates, whether on the permissive or restrictive side, would have far greater luck in moving public opinion by focusing on issue framing—particularly frames that are more negative, that are more novel, or that come from an unexpected source—than on the terms used to describe immigrants without legal status.

At the same time, it may be too early to detect a sizable effect on the use of "illegal immigrant" versus "undocumented immigrant" in moving public support for legalization policies. The Drop the I-Word Campaign and the immigrant rights movement more generally are still fairly recent; if the African American civil rights movement is any indication, it will take a generation for certain terms to be deemed socially unacceptable (although, as the literature on symbolic racism and racial resentment suggests, immigration restrictionists may simply find a new vocabulary in which to express antipathy toward immigrants). Indeed, the rise and popularity of presidential candidates like Donald Trump and other immigration restrictionists might keep "illegal immigrant" a socially acceptable term among Republican Party identifiers for the foreseeable future and, importantly, to also keep the term viable in news coverage of presidential elections.

Finally, it is important to recognize that "dropping the I-word" might have other salutary effects, including effects on the self-esteem of undocumented immigrants and on how they are treated by their fellow Americans. In addition, campaigns against the use of "illegal immigrant," when embedded in a larger social movement strategy on immigrant rights, might help instill a sense of empowerment among undocumented immigrants. Our survey experiments indicate, for example, that when first- and second-generation immigrants are exposed to the illegal immigrant frame, they react against the label and become more support-ive of pro-immigrant policies. Real-world examples also lend credence to the potentially mobilizing effects of these strategies: the activist Jose An-tonio Vargas, for instance, has capitalized on support for the Drop the I-Word Campaign to generate enthusiasm for an even larger movement framing strategy—seeing undocumented immigrants as fundamentally American.[33]

7

Conclusions

OR THE last decade, undocumented or illegal immigration has been
one of the most contested policy issues in the United States. In this
book, we have analyzed how the issue has been covered in a range
of news media outlets since 2007, paying particular attention to the ways
in which immigrants are framed—as "illegal," "undocumented," and
"unauthorized"—as well as the ways in which immigration policies are
framed, such as with references to opportunities for citizenship or amnesty, to criminals or young children. Ours is the first study to examine
these news frames systematically across conservative, liberal, and mainstream outlets and on key policy issues such as immigrant legalization,
the DREAM Act, Deferred Action for Childhood Arrivals, and mass deportation. Importantly, we also rely on a series of survey experiments
conducted between 2007 and 2014 to test whether these various frames
affect public opinion on a host of policies related to unauthorized migration.

What themes emerge from examining these various policy arenas, and
what are the implications for issue framing and immigration policy? We
find a few key strands that weave across the chapters, helping make
sense of the larger whole. First, frames vary in their importance according to their type, with issue frames far more consequential than episodic
frames or equivalency frames. In addition, negative frames generally
have stronger effects than positive frames, and these effects sometimes
vary by partisanship and family migration history. Finally, immigrant
advocates have limited, yet significant, opportunities to move public
opinion on immigration policy. We elaborate here on each set of findings
and discuss their implications for future research.

The Surprising Weakness of Episodic and Equivalency Frames

Immigration advocates have devoted considerable attention to the ways
in which the news media and political leaders describe immigrants with-

out legal status. Restrictionist groups tend to favor "illegal immigrant," in the belief that this term will get voters to focus on criminality and other forms of illegality, while pro-immigrant groups reject the term for precisely the same reasons. We characterize "illegal," "undocumented," and "unauthorized" (a term often used by social scientists) as equivalency frames, since they are referring to the same group of people and are logically equivalent.

As we saw in chapter 6, however, these efforts to police the use of equivalency frames have produced mixed results: members of Congress divide along party lines when it comes to using "illegal" versus "undocumented," reinforcing the larger partisan divide on immigration policy and hampering any large-scale shifts in terminology. There has been more movement on the news front: mainstream sources reduced their use of "illegal immigrant" after 2012. At the same time, sources like the *New York Times* have continued to employ the term, and there has been a more general uptick in the use of "illegal immigrant" since Donald Trump entered the 2016 presidential race. Finally, our survey experiments show that these equivalency frames have few significant effects on public opinion on immigration policies such as support for legalization or deportation.[1] As we shall see in our discussion of negative and positive frames, invoking illegality through more robust frames such as immigrant criminality and the rule of law is more effective in shaping public opinion than simply referring to immigrants as "illegal."

The relatively weak effects of equivalency frames is surprising because past literature suggests that Americans react very differently to equivalent outcomes depending on how the information is presented to them. One potential reason for this discrepancy might be that past studies have tended to present situations that involve some kind of calculation (with equivalent outcomes such as employment rates versus unemployment rates, or the certainty of losing a certain number of lives versus the small chance of saving everyone), while our equivalency frames do not depend on any similar calculation. In addition, past studies have framed choices in a very positive or very negative way, such as 90 percent employment or 10 percent unemployment, while our equivalency frames are subtler. While "illegal alien" is clearly a quite negative term, "undocumented" and "unauthorized" are not terms that are likely to evoke strong positive reactions or feelings. Finally, as we discussed in chapter 6, social norms around the inappropriateness of saying "illegal immigrant" are shifting only gradually and indeed may have found some resistance among conservative elites and Republican voters. Regardless of the reason, the weakness of these equivalency frames are notable and merit further examination in future years as the American electorate grows more racially diverse and its share of first- and second-generation immigrants increases.

Another aspect of news framing that usually concerns policy advocates is whether an issue is presented vividly and episodically, with human interest stories that illustrate an issue, or more impersonally and thematically, laden with policy details and statistics. We found significant differences in the use of episodic human-interest frames across news sources, with conservative outlets much less likely than mainstream outlets to use these frames when covering pro-integration policies such as the DREAM Act or comprehensive immigration reform. These differences in the use of episodic frames also correspond with empathetic news coverage, with Fox News and the *Washington Times* ranking lowest on both measures. When it comes to deportation coverage, however, conservative sources are more likely than mainstream sources to rely on human interest coverage, running stories that often focus on criminals and other undesirable actors who deserve to be deported. Thus, we found that the use of episodic frames varies by news source, with conservative sources less likely than mainstream outlets to provide human interest coverage when it comes to pro-integration policies but more likely to do so when it comes to restrictionist policies.

Despite these clear differences in the use of episodic and thematic frames by news source, our survey experiments did not reveal many clear differences in their effects on public opinion. In two of the three policies we examined (the DREAM Act and deportations), both frames seemed to resonate with high-empathy individuals. These findings run counter to our expectation, drawn from the literature, that thematic frames would be more effective in moving opinion than episodic frames.[2] We also found one case in which those in the first and second generations were moved by the episodic empathetic frame to become less supportive of deportations. One reason why we may have found few differences between the two frames is that the articles had a positive tone and we manipulated only one-quarter of the article to be episodic or thematic. People may have therefore been drawn much more to the tone of the articles than to the paragraph that varied. Thus, it is possible that more extensive tests of episodic and thematic framing, particularly with respect to negative as well as positive stories on immigration policy, will reveal stronger effects on public opinion.

In contrast to the relative weakness of equivalency frames and thematic frames, we found that issue frames are highly consequential in shaping public opinion. Past studies have shown various ways in which the passage of legislation may be affected by shifts in opinion, such as when the public moves from opposing a given policy to supporting it, and when net support for (or opposition to) a given policy gets stronger or weaker.[3] Our survey experiments show issue frames having several of these types of effects. For example, on shifting opinion from support to opposition, we found that survey respondents support legalization when presented with the "opportunity to become citizens" frame, but oppose legalization when presented with the amnesty frame. At other times, issue frames can shift public opinion away from a neutral position toward a clearer stance. For example, survey respondents were neutral on deportations in our control condition but became increasingly opposed to deportations when asked to think about immigrants living in the United States for five, ten, and twenty years. Similar effects could be found for the "years in residence" frame as applied to immigrant legalization; this frame shifted opinion from neutral to positive. We also found instances where issue frames moved opinion in an even stronger direction when compared to the control condition. For example, respondents in the control condition were supportive of the DREAM Act, and adding a child frame pushed opinion in an even more supportive direction. Finally, issue frames might also move opinion toward a more neutral or ambivalent stance. We found this to be the case with the amnesty frame, which cooled support for the DREAM Act and DACA.

Our findings on the importance of issue frames also help answer the question with which we began this book: how can the American public hold seemingly contradictory opinions on immigration policy, such as favoring both deportation policies and deportation relief, at the same time and in the same survey? Our work shows that variation in media coverage across policy areas might play an important role. For example, the child frame, which has a positive effect on public support for the DREAM Act across many of our experimental studies, is covered far more often than any frames that decrease support on the issue (such as the amnesty frame). However, there is very little coverage in the media of any frames that would lead to lower support for deportations, even though we find in our experiments that an economic cost frame can decrease support. Some of these trends might help explain why some surveys show that the public is supportive of the DREAM Act but also supportive of many deportation policies.

Finally, why do we see a divergence between the importance of issue frames and the relative unimportance of equivalency frames like "undocumented," "illegal," or "unauthorized"? One reason for it may center on the fact that immigration policy is of relatively low salience to the American public; as Gallup monthly polls have shown, immigration rarely ranks high among the most important problems facing the United States.[4] Consequently, the public has relatively low levels of information about particular policies and the ways in which immigration policies are framed can have a significant effect on opinion. By contrast, invoking different terms may make little difference to individuals who are more likely to have a concrete image of an illegal or undocumented immigrant. Indeed, other experimental research on racial and ethnic cues suggests that the default image of an "illegal immigrant" in the minds of U.S. voters is a Mexican immigrant and that cueing Latino instead of European immigrant origins accentuates the restrictive opinions of American voters.[5] While ethnic cue manipulations are not a part of this study, future research with sufficiently large sample sizes should examine whether ethnic cues interact in important ways with the equivalency and issue frames in our analysis.

Which Issue Frames Are Most Effective?

Knowing that issue frames are consequential prompts us to address whether some frames are more consequential than others. Looking across the various chapters, we see some general patterns on the effectiveness of frames that fall in line with our expectations from chapter 2. First, there are large differences in opinions when individuals are exposed to negative versus positive frames on the same issue dimension. We found strong evidence of this in our chapter on legalization. When participants are exposed to the amnesty frame they oppose legalization, while when exposed to the opportunity frame they either have neutral opinions or are mildly supportive of legalization. These findings obtained in *all five* of our studies. We also found a big shift in opinion when using a law-abiding frame (neutral on immigrant legalization) compared to a law-breaking frame (clearly opposed).

We also found strong effects for negative frames in general. For example, we found that frames that focus on the economic costs of comprehensive immigration reform reduce support for legalization. Introducing an amnesty frame to discussions of the DREAM Act or DACA leads to a substantial decline in support. A rule of law frame, in which participants are led to focus on immigrants' lack of authorization to enter the country, is one of the few to consistently increase support for deportation policies. It is important to note, however, that a negative frame need not always lead to more restrictive opinion. For example, support for deportations declines significantly when respondents are exposed to information on the economic cost of deportations.

These strong effects for negative frames are consistent with a long line of scholarship that has shown that negative information is more persuasive than positive information because it is more likely to draw one's attention; as such, it then has a greater impact on the formation of opinions. There are many different arguments for the mechanisms that lead to this pattern. Against a backdrop of mostly positive information, negative information may better capture attention by standing out as extreme or as more novel.[6] Others hold that negative information is more informative since it points out the potential costs of different courses of action and people are more motivated to avoid costs.[7] Finally, drawing from work in neurobiology, George Marcus, Russell Neuman, and Michael MacKuen argue that the human brain processes positive and negative information differently.[8] Negative information produces a stronger effect on opinion because it is more likely to cause individuals to stop, pay attention, and process information.

This does not mean that positive frames are never effective. As noted earlier, they can serve as an important counterpoint to negative frames. We also know that positive frames can be more effective if they are novel or come from an unexpected source. As we noted in our review of the framing literature in chapter 2, individuals are more likely to be moved by frames to which they have not yet been exposed or frames that come from an unexpected source.[9]

In our study, we found a few instances where a novelty effect was probably at play. First, with the "length of stay" manipulation we consistently found that individuals become more supportive of legalization and less supportive of deportations the longer the undocumented have lived in the United States. We also found that highlighting the economic costs of deporting millions of immigrants decreases support for deportation policies. These frames were largely absent in our analysis of media coverage, making it quite likely that they were relatively novel to survey respondents. Meanwhile, more commonly used frames, such as deportations breaking families apart, had no significant effect in moving public opinion.

We also found a few cases in which a positive frame advanced by an unexpected source moved opinion in either a more progressive or a less restrictionist direction. For example, an argument for legalization delivered from the Republican Party and Fox News made the public less resistant to legalization. As another example, an anti-deportation argument advanced by commentators at Fox News moved public opinion against deportations.

Sometimes positive frames may not be novel but nevertheless are effective if they refer to vulnerable groups such as children. As we pointed out in chapter 4, past studies have shown the child frame to be important for a range of policy issues.[10] Here we found that invoking the child frame increased support for the DREAM Act. In our early studies, the child frame actually had the strongest effects among those more inclined to be less supportive of the policy: independents and Republicans. Our studies do not enable us to identify the particular reasons why the child frame is so effective. It could be that survey respondents viewed undocumented children as lacking agency and thus were reluctant to blame them for their situation (and blamed their parents instead). It is also possible that referencing children leads to greater empathy or perhaps even triggers an instinctual response to protect them.

Whatever the reason, it is unlikely that the effectiveness of the child frame is related to more general concerns about families; indeed, we found that survey respondents did not waver in their support for deportations when told that it would break up families. Notably, the effects of the child frame also diminished over time as the frame probably became less novel and the DREAM Act itself became highly politicized in Congress. Still, it is important to recognize that while negative frames tend to be more effective than positive frames in moving public opinion, positive frames can still be effective when they are novel, come from an unexpected source, or connect to vulnerable populations such as children.

The Effects of Frames Can Vary Across Groups

Although we find very strong issue framing effects, that is not to say that individuals always blindly follow frames. As we discussed in chapter 2, individuals may resist frames that run counter to their predispositions and values and follow those that are consistent with them, though they may need contextual information to challenge frames that run counter to their predispositions and values.[11] This type of contextual information may be provided by the presence of source cues attached to a frame or by the broader political environment in which the study is taking place.[12] For example, if frames are already in the public space and are connected with particular political actors, individuals may have the background knowledge about who supports particular frames to follow or resist them.

In this book, we have focused on two types of dispositions that may affect whether people are influenced by frames. First, we have examined individuals for whom the issue is high in relevance: first- and second-generation immigrants. This group is generally supportive of attempts at more progressive immigration reforms and may therefore be more receptive to frames that support such policies and resistant to frames that argue against them. Our look at moderating effects among this group (as well as Latinos) is more novel in the study of framing effects, which has primarily looked at how values and political dispositions affect reaction to frames. However, we also consider whether people respond differently to frames depending on their partisanship.

Among those for whom immigration is high in relevance, we did find some evidence of resistance compared to those for whom the issue is likely to be lower in relevance. For example, in 2007 individuals who were recent immigrants or the children of immigrants showed more resistance to the negative amnesty frame. Moreover, they were less affected by a frame that claimed that the undocumented were lawbreakers. In our 2010 study, those in the first generation also reacted against the argument that illegal immigrants take jobs away from Americans, and they became less supportive of deportations.

We also found clear evidence, in some years, of first- and second-generation immigrants reacting against "illegal immigrant," and these were some of the only cases in which we found any effects for these equivalency frames. For example, in 2007 those in the first and second generations became even more supportive of legalization and the DREAM Act when exposed to the illegal immigrant frame compared to the undocumented or unauthorized frame. The same effect obtained in 2011 for legalization.

It is important to note that although we saw some evidence of resistance to and rejection of negative frames among those in the first and second generations, we found this evidence only in a handful of cases. It does seem that the more consistent pattern of resistance on this dimension came in 2007, on the heels of the immigration marches, and in 2010, when immigration was also salient. These highly salient immigration contexts may have given participants the contextual information necessary to resist the negative frames in these two years.[13]

More research needs to be done to better understand the circumstances under which those from newer immigrant families follow frames that lead to more progressive policies or resist, and even reject, those that would lead to more restrictive policies. That we find rejection of some frames, even in the absence of cueing information, does suggest that individuals for whom an issue is very high in relevance may be more apt to critically react to frames in the environment, and this may especially be the case when the issue is salient and polarized (as it was in 2007 and 2010).

If we turn to partisanship, we also found some evidence of acceptance and resistance, in both the absence and presence of clear contextual cues. So, for example, when asked, if we could seal our borders and enforce existing immigration laws, whether the undocumented should be given amnesty or an opportunity to eventually become citizens, those on the right became even less supportive of the policy with the amnesty frame than those on the left did in some years (2007 and 2010). That is, they moved in the direction of the frame that was more consistent with their disposition. In two of the years, however, we found no differences by partisanship. In the absence of clear contextual cues in the question, then, whether we see differential reactions to frames by partisanship may depend on the broader political environment. In 2007 and 2010, immigration was highly salient and respondents may have had some cueing information from that environment to connect the frame to their disposition. The more distinct coverage of frames across media is, the easier it may be for people to connect different frames to their disposition in such an environment.

We saw this play out in some respects with the child frame and the DREAM Act. This frame was never attached to a partisan source in our studies, so the experiment did not provide direct contextual cues to respondents. In our early studies, when the issue was newer on the public agenda, had bipartisan support, and had not been extensively covered, the child frame actually led to even more support for the DREAM Act among independents and Republicans than among Democrats (in 2007 and 2010), probably because the former groups had further to move on the issue. However, over time, as the frame became less novel, its effect diminished, and in 2012, when immigration was highly salient and the DREAM Act had become more politicized, we saw Republicans begin to react against the frame. In this year, we also saw Democrats resist an amnesty frame on the issue. As another example, we found very little evidence of partisan moderation when we looked at support for deportations depending on how long undocumented immigrants have been in the United States. This frame has gotten so little coverage in the media that partisans would not have had any contextual cues from the broader environment to help them connect the frames to their partisan predisposition.

If partisans are directly provided with contextual information by way of source cues attached to frames, we see more evidence of acceptance and resistance. For example, when the positive framing of the legalization question is paired with a source cue, we find that Republicans become more supportive of legalization when it is delivered by the Republican Party or Fox News, but resist the message coming from the Democratic Party. Those in the Democratic camp, however, become more supportive of legalization when the positive message is attached to the Democratic Party. A similar pattern emerges when we manipulate the economic costs and benefits of legalization. Republicans react against a claim of the economic benefits of legalization made by the liberal Center for American Progress, while Democrats move in the direction of the frame. We find the reverse pattern when Democrats and Republicans are exposed to an argument about the economic costs of legalization by the conservative Heritage Foundation. In this case, Republicans follow the cue, while Democrats resist it.

In short, partisans are likely to react differently to frames, but only when the broader information environment provides cues that enable them to link the frames to their values and predispositions. In contexts where immigration is highly salient and media coverage varies substantially across liberal, mainstream, and conservative outlets, we may be more likely to find that partisans react differently to issue frames. However, in contexts where media coverage is more similar, as it is on deportations, it is less surprising that we find less evidence of partisans reacting differently to frames.

What Can Immigration Advocates Do?

Our research points to a few ways in which issue frames can be consequential for shaping public opinion on immigration policy. They can be effective if they are relatively novel, if they are not already subject to intense partisan divisions, or if they involve vulnerable populations, such as children, who cannot be blamed for their condition. Of course, the very factor that makes an issue frame novel (lack of prior news coverage for a particular policy dimension) might also limit the ability of issue advocates to exploit that opportunity, as news outlets are unlikely to highlight a policy dimension that is not being hotly debated in Congress, that is not a crisis, or is otherwise poorly understood by the lay public. For example, research on the flow of unaccompanied alien children (UAC) from Central America across the U.S.-Mexico border reveals that news outlets waited almost two years to give the story significant attention and that they did so only after the phenomenon morphed from large-scale border crossings to overcrowded detention centers that drew condemnation from human rights advocates.[14]

Nevertheless, immigration advocates still have some opportunities to introduce new frames to policy debates. Writing opinion columns, appearing on sympathetic television news programs (such as MSNBC or Fox News programs), filing lawsuits, and engaging in protest activity—these are all ways for interest groups to shape news coverage in ways that are politically advantageous. Thus, for example, pro-immigrant advocates can counter the lack of news coverage of the economic contributions of undocumented immigrants by producing policy reports, opinion pieces, and larger-scale information campaigns highlighting this policy dimension. They can employ similar strategies to frame the legalization debate as one largely involving long-term residents of the United States who have no other place to call their home. Our research indicates that both of these policy dimensions could significantly increase public support for legalization and decrease support for mass deportations.

Importantly, our research also suggests that immigration advocates would be better served by focusing on policy frames rather than getting fixated on equivalency frames such as the use of the terms "illegal" or "undocumented." Indeed, past research on boomerang effects suggests that publicly trying to counter a frame may inadvertently reinforce its perceived validity and importance.[15] Thus, pro-immigrant advocates might be more effective in achieving their policy aims if they were to introduce new policy dimensions (for example, immigrants as long-term community members and economic contributors) rather than continue to resist the "illegal" label, an effort that might even elevate the importance of "rule of law" considerations in the minds of voters.[16] Of course, restrictionists can also get into the framing game. Indeed, the results from our survey experiments show that their well-researched efforts on the amnesty frame have been very successful in blunting support for a variety of pro-integration policies, from comprehensive immigration reform to the DREAM Act and DACA.

Finally, larger-scale political developments can also play a significant role in expanding or contracting opportunities for pro-immigration advocates to sway public opinion. For example, in early 2013 Republican leaders and many Fox News hosts seemed to be reading from a new playbook, favoring terms like "undocumented immigrants" over "illegal immigrants" and "amnesty," in an attempt to win support among Latino voters.[17] On the congressional front, Senator Marco Rubio and House Majority Leader Eric Cantor led the charge on reframing immigration and pushing for comprehensive reform, while Fox News president Roger Ailes and anchors Bill O'Reilly and Sean Hannity also softened their rhetoric on immigration during this period.[18]

As we have noted several times in this book, however, the electoral logic of Republican primaries has also tended to reward restrictive rhetoric on immigration, with respect to both immigration policy and the terms used to describe immigrants. Thus, not only did the amnesty frame make a strong comeback in 2015, but Republican candidates like Donald Trump made previously fringe policy ideas—like revoking birthright citizenship and engaging in mass deportations—much more mainstream, while at the same time introducing more explicitly racial frames about immigrants themselves, such as branding Mexican immigrants as drug dealers and rapists. Trump was wildly successful in marshaling anti-immigrant rhetoric to gain early support among Republican primary voters, but he was not alone in these restrictive framing attempts: former Florida governor Jeb Bush brought terms like "anchor baby" into presidential news coverage, while businesswoman Carly Fiorina decried birth tourism among Chinese visitors and New Jersey governor Chris Christie called for FedEx-like tracking of immigrants in the United States.[19]

These comments and proposals are just the latest installment in America's continuing fight over immigration, including the frames used to describe immigrants as well as immigration policy. Given the dynamic nature of immigration framing, it will be important to continue studying immigration opinion in the context of changing media frames and, just as importantly, their potential consequences for public opinion and electoral politics.

Appendices

Appendix to Chapter 1

History of Immigration Reform Prior to 2006

In 1965 the United States passed what is widely seen as the most sweeping revision to its immigration laws. Previously, federal immigration law had been highly restrictive, with national-origin bans that started with the Chinese Exclusion Act of 1882 and expanded to include other Asian countries with the Gentlemen's Agreement of 1907 and the creation of the Asiatic Barred Zone in 1917. By 1924 the United States had effectively shut down all immigration from Asia and severely curtailed immigration from eastern and southern Europe. Throughout this period, Asian immigrants were excluded from eligibility for naturalization. Starting during World War II, however, the United States began to loosen some of these national-origin restrictions, allowing a limited number of migrants from Asia and granting them the right to naturalize. Still, the volume of immigration under these national quotas remained very low until 1965, when Congress abolished the national-origin quota system and replaced it with a system based primarily on family unification and job skills.

Interestingly, however, just as the United States was abolishing national-origin quotas, it also introduced for the first time limitations on the number of people who could lawfully migrate each year from the Western Hemisphere. This limitation proved particularly severe for immigrants from Mexico and Central America, as agricultural employers had grown dependent on migrant workers under the Bracero Program.[1] The continued dependence of growers on immigrant labor is understandable, given the sheer scale of the Bracero Program—in just twenty-two years the program had processed over 4 million workers—and the fact that a postwar economic boom and a rising middle class in the United States had left significant labor shortages in agriculture. Thus, even though the Bracero Program was no longer in place, the networks of employer recruitment and Mexican migration still remained strong, leading to a rapid increase in the undocumented population in the United States.

The issue of undocumented immigration soon became a politically salient issue in states like California and Texas. California passed a law in 1971 that penalized employers for knowingly hiring undocumented immigrants, and several other states soon followed suit, including Florida, Virginia, and most states in New England. Texas went even further in its attempt to discourage undocumented immigrants from settling in the state. In 1975 the state passed revisions to its education code that allowed local school districts to charge tuition to the parents of undocumented immigrant children, thereby practically denying them the ability to access public education. The U.S. Supreme Court struck down this law in its 1982 *Plyler v. Doe* decision, arguing that states could not deny free public education based on immigration status. At the same time, the Court upheld the constitutionality of state employer sanctions laws in its 1976 *DeCanas v. Bica* decision.[2]

Despite the existence of these state sanctions, employers found ways to bypass them and the number of undocumented immigrants in the United States continued to increase, reaching about 3 million by 1980 and nearly 4 million by 1986.[3] Thus, by the early 1980s there was a growing, settled population of undocumented immigrants in the United States, and Congress began debating the merits of a program to legalize these residents. After a few years of negotiation, and with the support of a Republican president and bipartisan votes in Congress, the United States passed the Immigration Reform and Control Act (IRCA) in 1986. IRCA had two key provisions that were unprecedented in federal immigration law: it provided a system of legalization to those undocumented immigrants who had entered the United States before 1982, and it instituted a set of federal sanctions for employers who knowingly hired undocumented immigrants. In the previous great waves of migration, the United States had provided legalization only on a limited basis and as a matter of executive discretion. (In any event, the vast majority of those who were illegally present in the United States prior to 1965 would have been from Asia, not Mexico or other parts of Latin America.) The use of federal employer sanctions in the 1986 immigration reform was also unprecedented. As noted before, a few states had passed employer sanctions laws in the 1970s, but there was no federal law imposing employer penalties at the time. The 1986 IRCA effectively wiped out those state laws by instituting a federal scheme of employer sanctions.

As was soon apparent, however, those employer sanctions were relatively weak: the penalties were fairly small, and it was very difficult to prove that an employer was knowingly hiring undocumented immigrants. Perhaps just as importantly, the United States had by the 1980s developed a fairly robust network of recruitment between sending regions in Mexico and particular receiving regions in the United States, and these regional connections grew stronger as they intersected with extended family networks.[4] The U.S.-Mexico border was also only lightly enforced, and ongoing political dislocations in Mexico and other Central

American countries ensured a continued flow of undocumented immigrants to the United States.[5] Thus, while the number of undocumented immigrants had dropped from 4 million in 1986 to about 2.5 million in 1990, thanks to the legalization under IRCA, the number of unauthorized soon began to rise once again—to about 5 million in 1996 and then 8 million by 2000.[6] Importantly, this increase in the unauthorized occurred despite the passage of federal legislation in 1996 that cut back on welfare eligibility for immigrants, made undocumented immigrants ineligible for federal welfare programs, and greatly increased Border Patrol staffing and enforcement activity, particularly in California and Texas.

By 2000, then, it was clear that an enforcement-heavy strategy was not cutting down on the number of unauthorized immigrants in the United States; there were too many entrenched factors, ranging from the needs of growers to labor shortages in agriculture and construction and the well-established networks of migration between sending regions in Mexico and receiving regions in the United States. The elections of George W. Bush and Mexican president Vicente Fox in 2000 provided hope for a new solution to the problem of undocumented immigration in the United States, this time centered on a program of mass legalization. Not only did President Bush have prior business ties with Mexico and a close friendship with Fox, but he had also made outreach to Latinos a cornerstone of his electoral strategy as governor of Texas. Given this background, and with strong backing from U.S. senators such as Sam Brownback (R-KS) and Edward Kennedy (D-MA), it seemed that immigration reform might once again pass the U.S. Congress.

Immigration reform was high on the Bush administration's legislative agenda in the summer of 2001. Having passed a contentious and ambitious ten-year tax reduction plan, the administration was gearing up to work on a way to regularize the flow of migrants from Mexico and provide a path to legalization for those already residing in the United States. The administration was especially eager to show progress on this issue in advance of the state visit of President Vicente Fox in early September.[7] However, the timing of the reform effort was not fortuitous: within two weeks of the Fox visit, the United States was attacked on September 11, 2001. Even though the attackers were predominantly immigrants from the Middle East who were on temporary visas in the United States, immigration conservatives in Congress were able to seize the moment to argue for greater border security and delay any attempt at immigrant legalization until at least 2006.[8]

Appendix to Chapter 3

In addition to the policy dimensions noted in the text, we also wanted to explore whether beefing up the enforcement component of comprehensive immigration reform would lead to higher levels of support. (We deal more comprehensively with enforcement policy attitudes in chapter 5.) That is, does legislation that incorporates a security component or employer fines lead to more support for CIR?

In the SSI study, we gave one group of respondents this baseline question:

> As you may know, the U.S. Senate passed a bill, S744, that would give [*randomize:* illegal immigrants/undocumented immigrants/illegal aliens] the opportunity to eventually become U.S. citizens. To what extent do you agree or disagree with this Senate immigration bill?

We gave an additional statement to another group of respondents (randomly assigned):

> The bill also [*randomize:* adds 20,000 Border Patrol agents to our southern border with Mexico/builds a 700-mile fence along the U.S.-Mexico border/fines employers up to $25,000 for any future violation of immigration and work laws]. To what extent do you agree or disagree with this Senate immigration bill?

We designed this particular question in light of the immigration debate that was occurring in the Senate, namely, the amendment proposed by Senator Bob Corker (R-TN) to try to generate more Republican support for immigration reform. The logic behind these amendments was that Republican senators might become more supportive of the bill if border security and employer fines were strengthened. However, respondents who preferred more progressive policies might actually become less supportive of legalization given this additional information. Support for legalization is coded in the same manner as in the prior analyses, from -2 to 2. In figure A3.1, we show mean support for legalization across the experimental conditions.

Mean support is above the neutral point in the control group, at 0.314, thus respondents are between neutral and somewhat supportive of the bill. The addition of a security component, in the form of more agents or a fence, increases mean support to 0.55 and 0.52, respectively, and these effects are statistically different from the control group ($p < 0.05$ in both cases). The addition of fines for employers also increases support, to 0.511, and this effect is also significantly different from the control group ($p = 0.06$). It therefore appears that information about these amendments does slightly increase public support above the generic question in the control condition. The lukewarm support for CIR in the control group may be related to the question wording: respondents read that the Senate had already passed the bill. These results hold up if we run a regression

Figure A3.1   Mean Support for Senate Bill 744 by Experimental Condition, 2014

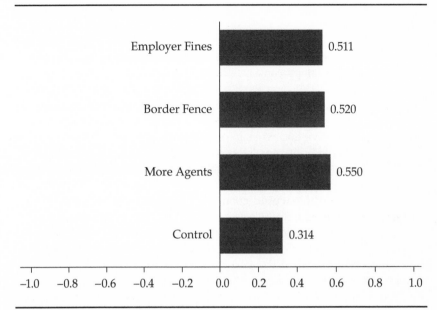

Source: Authors' analysis of 2014 SSI survey data.

controlling for the variables that are unevenly distributed (see table A3.9).[9]

Of course, the main goal of the amendments was to increase support among Republicans, so we next look at whether there was any moderating effect by partisanship (in addition to the other potential moderators that we are considering for each dependent variable). We find that none of the treatments are effective among Democrats, which makes sense given that these particular amendments are meant to appeal to Republicans. However, all three of the treatment conditions are significant among independents as well as Republicans, with the effects being more pronounced for the latter. For example, adding mention of a border fence increases support by about one-quarter of a unit among independents and by half a unit among Republicans (see table A3.9 for OLS results). We find similar moderating effects by Fox News viewership for the fence and fines manipulations: only Fox News viewers become more supportive of CIR given these additional manipulations, though mention of adding more agents increases support for CIR among both Fox News viewers and non–Fox News viewers (see table A3.9 for OLS results).

In the same SSI survey, we also introduced a question about whether individuals would support a policy of allowing the undocumented to stay in the country, but without extending citizenship rights to them. More specifically, half of the sample received the following question:

> In the congressional debate on immigration reform, some are arguing that we can legalize illegal or undocumented immigrants without necessarily allowing them to later become U.S. citizens.

The response options were: "Allow people to live and work in our country, and *don't* give them an opportunity to become U.S. citizens"; and "Allow people to live and work in our country, and give them an opportunity to become U.S. citizens." Respondents were not provided with the option of deporting those without legal status. Another half of the sample answered the same type of question with one additional counterframe: "Others argue that this would create a permanent underclass of people who are treated unequally."

We coded the dependent variable such that a 1 indicated support for providing citizenship and was 0 otherwise. We find essentially no difference in support between the two questions. Seventy-seven percent of respondents in the condition without the counterframe support providing citizenship, while 76 percent of respondents in the counterframe condition do. These effects are also not moderated by education, family immigration history, Fox News viewership, or partisanship, though Fox News viewers and Republicans are less likely to support providing citizenship in general. The only case in which we find some support for a moderating relationship is among Latinos, who become slightly more supportive of providing citizenship when exposed to the counterframe condition (see table A3.10 for full results).[10]

Table A3.1 Support for Legalization, Given Amnesty (Versus Opportunity) Wording, and Moderating Effects by Family Immigration History and Ideology, 2007

	Model 1 (OLS)	Model 2 (OLS)	Model 3 (OLS)	Model 4 (Ordered Probit)	Model 5 (Ordered Probit)	Model 6 (OLS)	Model 7 (OLS)
Undocumented	-0.013	-0.018	-0.650**	-0.099	-0.089	-0.603**	-0.097
	(0.067)	(0.068)	(0.304)	(0.149)	(0.149)	(0.301)	(0.163)
Unauthorized	-0.008	-0.014	-0.489*	-0.481**	-0.477**	-0.456[+]	-0.537**
	(0.066)	(0.068)	(0.294)	(0.146)	(0.147)	(0.291)	(0.161)
Amnesty	-0.678**	-0.656**	-0.142	-0.350**	-0.347**	-0.121	-0.494**
	(0.055)	(0.055)	(0.246)	(0.120)	(0.121)	(0.243)	(0.132)
Female	0.111**	—	—	—	-0.032	0.122**	-0.032
	(0.056)				(0.049)	(0.056)	(0.053)
Protestant	-0.137*	—	—	—	-0.106*	-0.117[+]	-0.093[+]
	(0.074)				(0.064)	(0.075)	(0.069)
Other Christian	-0.039	—	—	—	-0.070	-0.011	0.081
	(0.108)				(0.094)	(0.109)	(0.102)
Other religion	0.436**	—	—	—	0.012	0.441**	0.031
	(0.098)				(0.086)	(0.098)	(0.094)
No religion	0.322**	—	—	—	-0.085	0.329**	-0.062
	(0.082)				(0.073)	(0.083)	(0.094)
Family history	—	—	-0.118*	—	—	-0.076	—
			(0.070)			(0.070)	

(continued)

Table A3.1 *(continued)*

	Model 1 (OLS)	Model 2 (OLS)	Model 3 (OLS)	Model 4 (Ordered Probit)	Model 5 (Ordered Probit)	Model 6 (OLS)	Model 7 (OLS)
Family history * undocumented	—	—	0.184**	—	—	0.172**	—
			(0.087)			(0.086)	
Family history * unauthorized	—	—	0.138*	—	—	0.130+	—
			(0.084)			(0.083)	
Family history * amnesty	—	—	−0.151**	—	—	−0.163**	—
			(0.070)			(0.069)	
Ideology	—	—	—	−0.596**	−0.596**	—	−0.695**
				(0.057)	(0.058)		(0.062)
Ideology * undocumented	—	—	—	0.038	0.035	—	0.038
				(0.069)	(0.069)		(0.074)
Ideology * unauthorized	—	—	—	0.223**	0.223**	—	0.246**
				(0.068)	(0.068)		(0.074)
Ideology * amnesty	—	—	—	−0.127**	−0.131**	—	−0.088+
				(0.056)	(0.056)		(0.060)
Constant	−0.138*	−0.033	0.370+	—	—	0.105	1.443**
	(0.078)	(0.055)	(0.247)			(0.248)	(0.150)
N	2,180	2,180	2,168	2,114	2,114	2,168	2,114
R-squared/pseudo-R-squared	0.089	0.061	0.068	0.082	0.083	0.095	0.235

Source: Authors' analysis of 2007 YouGov survey data.

**p < 0.05; *p < 0.10; +p < 0.20

Table A3.2 OLS on Support for Legalization, Given Amnesty (Versus Opportunity) Wording, and Moderating Effects by Education and Partisanship, 2010

	Model 1	Model 2	Model 3	Model 4	Model 5	Model 6
Undocumented	-0.079	-0.068	-0.041	0.045	0.041	-0.055
	(0.091)	(0.092)	(0.226)	(0.125)	(0.124)	(0.225)
Unauthorized	-0.051	-0.047	0.031	0.132	0.126	0.021
	(0.092)	(0.093)	(0.232)	(0.126)	(0.125)	(0.231)
Amnesty	-0.658**	-0.614**	-0.312*	-0.776**	-0.799**	-0.345*
	(0.075)	(0.075)	(0.188)	(0.103)	(0.103)	(0.188)
Education	0.075	—	—	—	—	0.045*
	(0.026)					(0.025)
Homeowner	-0.391**	—	—	—	-0.380**	-0.296**
	(0.084)				(0.084)	(0.079)
High education	—	—	—	0.171	0.218[+]	—
				(0.153)	(0.153)	
Education * undocumented	—	—	—	-0.259[+]	-0.261[+]	—
				(0.183)	(0.181)	

(continued)

Table A3.2 *(continued)*

	Model 1	Model 2	Model 3	Model 4	Model 5	Model 6
Education * unauthorized	—	—	—	-0.390**	-0.381**	—
				(0.185)	(0.184)	
Education * amnesty	—	—	—	0.323**	0.316**	—
				(0.151)	(0.150)	
Party ID (three-point)	—	—	-0.532**	—	—	-0.517**
			(0.089)			(0.089)
Party ID * undocumented	—	—	-0.005	—	—	-0.001
			(0.106)			(0.106)
Party ID * unauthorized	—	—	-0.022	—	—	-0.018
			(0.109)			(0.108)
Party ID * amnesty	—	—	-0.159*	—	—	-0.157*
			(0.088)			(0.088)
Constant	0.176+	0.144*	1.190**	-0.071	0.337**	1.226**
	(0.128)	(0.076)	(0.189)	(0.100)	(0.116)	(0.212)
N	1,355	1,355	1,355	1,355	1,355	1,355
R-squared	0.066	0.047	0.173	0.056	0.070	0.182

Source: Authors' analysis of 2010 YouGov survey data.
**$p < 0.05$; *$p < 0.10$; +$p < 0.20$

Table A3.3   OLS on Support for Legalization, Given Amnesty (Versus Opportunity) Wording, 2011

	Model 1	Model 2
Undocumented	−0.157	−0.157
	(0.189)	(0.190)
Illegal alien	−0.216	−0.220
	(0.193)	(0.193)
Amnesty	−1.012**	−1.029**
	(0.157)	(0.158)
Male	—	−0.317**
		(0.157)
Education	—	0.023
		(0.053)
Constant	0.914**	1.017**
	(0.150)	(0.215)
N	799	799
R-squared	0.061	0.067

Source: Authors' analysis of 2011 YouGov survey data.
**p < 0.05; *p < 0.10; +*p* < 0.20

Table A3.4 OLS on Support for Legalization, Given Amnesty (Versus Opportunity) Wording and Source Cues, and Moderating Effects by Partisanship and Being Latino, 2012

	Model 1	Model 2	Model 3	Model 4	Model 5	Model 6
Democrat source	0.125	0.122	0.516**	0.099	0.103	0.526**
	(0.107)	(0.107)	(0.257)	(0.116)	(0.116)	(0.257)
Republican source	0.225**	0.221**	-0.029	0.240**	0.241**	-0.024
	(0.100)	(0.101)	(0.252)	(0.110)	(0.110)	(0.253)
Fox News source	0.194*	0.194**	-0.114	-0.198*	0.199*	-0.114
	(0.099)	(0.099)	(0.253)	(0.108)	(0.108)	(0.253)
Amnesty	-0.539**	-0.530**	-0.582**	-0.535**	-0.544**	-0.594**
	(0.731)	(0.073)	(0.183)	(0.079)	(0.079)	(0.183)
Female	0.115+	—	—	—	0.125*	0.080
	(0.774)				(0.073)	(0.073)
Latino	—	—	—	0.581**	0.586**	—
				(0.192)	(0.192)	
Latino * Democratic source	—	—	—	0.437*	0.435*	—
				(0.247)	(0.248)	
Latino * Republican source	—	—	—	-0.077	-0.065	—
				(0.247)	(0.248)	

	(1)	(2)	(3)	(4)	(5)
Latino * Fox News	—	—	0.021	0.015	—
			(0.260)	(0.258)	
Latino * Amnesty	—	—	-0.023	-0.026	—
			(0.183)	(0.182)	
Party ID	—	-0.445**	—	—	-0.442**
		(0.091)			(0.091)
Party ID * Democratic source	—	-0.232*	—	—	-0.236*
		(0.124)			(0.124)
Party ID * Republican source	—	0.116	—	—	0.115
		(0.122)			(0.122)
Party ID * Fox News	—	0.141	—	—	0.141
		(0.122)			(0.122)
Party ID * amnesty	—	0.011	—	—	0.015
		(0.088)			(0.088)
Constant	-0.039	0.840**	-0.119+	-0.181*	0.796**
	(0.080)	(0.187)	(0.088)	(0.094)	(0.193)
N	1,299	1,241	1,299	1,299	1,241
R-squared	0.047	0.132	0.078	0.080	0.132

Source: Authors' analysis of 2012 YouGov survey data.
**$p < 0.05$; *$p < 0.10$; +$p < 0.20$

Table A3.5   OLS on Support for Legalization, Given Amnesty (Versus Opportunity) Wording and Style of Frames, and Moderating Effects by Education, 2014

	Model 1	Model 2	Model 3	Model 4
Episodic, no empathy	−0.098	−0.143+	−0.119	−0.140
	(0.105)	(0.106)	(0.165)	(0.171)
Episodic, empathy	−0.035	−0.088	−0.016	−0.009
	(0.106)	(0.107)	(0.165)	(0.170)
Thematic, no empathy	−0.073	−0.115	0.001	0.044
	(0.106)	(0.108)	(0.160)	(0.169)
Thematic, empathy	−0.106	−0.210**	−0.029	−0.118
	(0.107)	(0.108)	(0.164)	(0.170)
Amnesty	−0.519**	−0.475**	−0.368**	−0.340**
	(0.068)	(0.069)	(0.107)	(0.111)
Family immigration history	—	−0.049+	—	−0.043
		(0.037)		(0.037)
Party identification	—	−0.368**	—	−0.367**
		(0.043)		(0.043)
High education	—	—	0.327**	0.362**
			(0.163)	(0.166)
EDU * episodic no empathy	—	—	0.020	−0.020
			(0.214)	(0.218)
EDU * episodic empathy	—	—	−0.046	−0.144
			(0.215)	(0.218)
EDU * thematic no empathy	—	—	−0.154	−0.289+
			(0.213)	(0.219)
EDU * thematic empathy	—	—	−0.163	−0.180
			(0.217)	(0.220)
EDU * amnesty	—	—	−0.268**	−0.234*
			(0.139)	(0.142)
Constant	0.379**	1.266**	0.199+	1.036**
	(0.081)	(0.165)	(0.121)	(0.192)
N	1,121	1,038	1,121	1,038
R-squared	0.050	0.116	0.057	0.123

Source: Authors' analysis of 2014 SSI survey data.
**$p < 0.05$; *$p < 0.10$; +$p < 0.20$

Table A3.6   OLS on Support for Legalization, Given Source Cue and Years Frame, and Moderating Effects Among Latinos, 2013

	Model 1	Model 2	Model 3	Model 4
Illegal	−0.217**	−0.178*	−0.183*	−0.218**
	(0.089)	(0.095)	(0.098)	(0.092)
Undocumented	−0.087	−0.058	−0.022	−0.054
	(0.093)	(0.099)	(0.102)	(0.096)
Democrat source	0.056	0.023	0.007	0.026
	(0.100)	(0.107)	(0.109)	(0.102)
Republican source	0.158[+]	0.160[+]	0.134	0.144[+]
	(0.102)	(0.109)	(0.113)	(0.106)
Fox News source	−0.004	0.016	0.001	−0.014
	(0.104)	(0.111)	(0.115)	(0.107)
Years	0.152**	0.133**	0.136**	0.160**
	(0.033)	(0.035)	(0.036)	(0.034)
Interest	0.091**	—	—	0.090**
	(0.032			(0.032)
Fox News	−1.066**	—	—	−1.077**
	(0.108)			(0.109)
Age	0.020**	—	0.136	0.020**
	(0.003)		(0.036)	(0.003)
Latino	—	—	0.018	−0.063
			(0.668)	(0.623)
Illegal * Latino	—	—	0.232	0.220
			(0.419)	(0.391)
Undocumented * Latino	—	—	−0.583[+]	−0.549[+]
			(0.416)	(0.388)
Democratic source * Latino	—	—	0.592	0.894*
			(0.566)	(0.528)
Republican source * Latino	—	—	0.493	0.464
			(0.542)	(0.506)
Fox News source * Latino	—	—	0.507	0.568
			(0.539)	(0.503)
Years * Latino	—	—	−0.036	−0.091
			(0.149)	(0.139)
Constant	−40.559**	0.269**	0.247*	−39.862**
	(6.526)	(0.133)	(0.137)	(6.560)
N	1,021	1,021	1,021	1,021
R-squared	0.150	0.019	0.027	0.156

Source: Authors' analysis of 2013 Mechanical Turk survey data.
**$p < 0.05$; *$p < 0.10$; +$p < 0.20$

Table A3.7   OLS on Attitudes Toward Legalization, Given Legal Cue, and Moderating Effects by Family Immigration History, 2010

	Model 1	Model 2
Undocumented	−0.041	0.566+
	(0.092)	(0.388)
Unauthorized	−0.137+	0.297
	(0.093)	(0.385)
Lawbreaking frame	−0.914**	−0.359
	(0.076)	(0.320)
Family immigration history	—	0.085
		(0.090)
Family * undocumented	—	−0.175+
		(0.111)
Family * unauthorized	—	−0.123
		(0.110)
Family * lawbreaking	—	−0.161*
		(0.091)
Constant	0.049	−0.252
	(0.076)	(0.314)
N	1,358	1,351
R-squared	0.098	0.105

Source: Authors' analysis of 2010 YouGov survey data.
**$p < 0.05$; *$p < 0.10$; +$p < 0.20$

Table A3.8 OLS on Attitudes Toward Legalization, Given Economic Arguments, and Moderating Effects by Education, Being Latino, and Partisanship, 2013

	Model 1	Model 2	Model 3	Model 4	Model 5	Model 6	Model 7	Model 8
Illegal	0.048	0.058	0.292	0.048	0.038	0.245	0.036	0.067
	(0.092)	(0.094)	(0.256)	(0.097)	(0.238)	(0.251)	(0.095)	(0.236)
Undocumented	-0.093	-0.057	0.022	-0.054	0.166	-0.024	-0.088	0.147
	(0.091)	(0.093)	(0.256)	(0.096)	(0.237)	(0.250)	(0.094)	(0.235)
Cato Institute	0.036	0.041	0.045	0.075	0.520*	0.091	0.078	0.440+
	(0.117)	(0.119)	(0.329)	(0.122)	(0.304)	(0.323)	(0.120)	(0.303)
Heritage Foundation	-0.196*	-0.204*	-0.891**	-0.181+	0.214	-0.827**	-0.168+	0.122
	(0.114)	(0.117)	(0.311)	(0.120)	(0.302)	(0.305)	(0.118)	(0.300)
Center for American Progress	0.067	0.079	-0.040	0.135	0.711**	0.220	0.116	0.666**
	(0.117)	(0.120)	(0.332)	(0.124)	(0.306)	(0.325)	(0.122)	(0.304)
Congressional Budget Office	0.016	0.004	-0.255	0.043	0.328	-0.216	0.058	0.275
	(0.118)	(0.120)	(0.328)	(0.123)	(0.309)	(0.321)	(0.120)	(0.307)
Interest	0.012	—	—	—	—	0.017	0.014	0.004
	(0.034)					(0.034)	(0.034)	(0.035)
Fox News	-0.696**	—	—	—	—	-0.691**	-0.717**	-0.397**
	(0.101)					(0.101)	(0.101)	(0.108)
Education	0.036+	—	0.009	—	—	0.008	0.039+	0.053**
	(0.026)		(0.067)			(0.065)	(0.026)	(0.026)
Income	-0.012	—	—	—	—	-0.012	-0.009	-0.015
	(0.030)					(0.030)	(0.030)	(0.030)
Illegal * education	—	—	-0.061	—	—	-0.053	—	—
			(0.063)			(0.061)		
Undocumented * education	—	—	-0.021	—	—	-0.018	—	—
			(0.062)			(0.061)		

(continued)

Table A3.8 (continued)

	Model 1	Model 2	Model 3	Model 4	Model 5	Model 6	Model 7	Model 8
Cato Institute * education	—	—	-0.002	—	—	-0.013	—	—
			(0.081)			(0.079)		
Heritage Foundation * education	—	—	0.179**	—	—	0.165**	—	—
			(0.077)			(0.075)		
Center for American Progress * education	—	—	0.031	—	—	0.013	—	—
			(0.082)			(0.080)		
Congressional Budget Office * education	—	—	0.069	—	—	0.062	—	—
			(0.082)			(0.080)		
Latino	—	—	—	0.787**	—	—	0.930**	—
				(0.400)			(0.391)	
Illegal * Latino	—	—	—	0.245	—	—	0.256	—
				(0.426)			(0.417)	
Undocumented * Latino	—	—	—	0.061	—	—	-0.006	—
				(0.417)			(0.408)	
Cato Institute * Latino	—	—	—	-0.402	—	—	-0.565	—
				(0.539)			(0.526)	
Heritage Foundation* Latino	—	—	—	-0.475	—	—	-0.554	—
				(0.499)			(0.487)	
Center for American Progress * Latino	—	—	—	-0.933**	—	—	-0.920**	—
				(0.463)			(0.452)	

Congressional Budget Office * Latino	—	—	—	-0.435	—	—	-0.440	—
				(0.607)			(0.592)	
Party ID	—	—	—	—	-0.211+	—	—	-0.179+
					(0.137)			(0.137)
Illegal * Party ID	—	—	—	—	-0.020	—	—	-0.032
					(0.127)			(0.127)
Undocumented * Party ID	—	—	—	—	-0.132	—	—	-0.128
					(0.126)			(0.125)
Cato Institute * Party ID	—	—	—	—	-0.282*	—	—	-0.239+
					(0.161)			(0.160)
Heritage Foundation * Party ID	—	—	—	—	-0.277*	—	—	-0.220+
					(0.163)			(0.163)
Center for American Progress * Party ID	—	—	—	—	-0.391**	—	—	-0.368**
					(0.164)			(0.163)
Congressional Budget Office * Party ID	—	—	—	—	-0.168	—	—	-0.135
					(0.161)			(0.161)
Constant	0.554**	0.557**	0.522**	0.506**	0.961**	0.641**	0.466**	0.807**
	(0.180)	(0.099)	(0.268)	(0.102)	(0.261)	(0.293)	(0.181)	(0.298)
N	1,000	1,000	1,000	1,000	924	1,000	1,000	924
R-squared	0.057	0.008	0.020	0.019	0.107	0.064	0.070	0.125

Source: Authors' analysis of 2013 Mechanical Turk survey data.
**$p < 0.05$; *$p < 0.10$; +$p < 0.20$

Table A3.9   OLS on Attitudes Toward Senate Bill 744, Given Additional Enforcement Components, and Moderating Effects, 2014

	Model 1	Model 2	Model 3	Model 4	Model 5	Model 6
Agents	0.236**	0.235**	-0.079	-0.078	0.193*	0.191*
	(0.010)	(0.010)	(0.253)	(0.253)	(0.113)	(0.113)
Border fence	0.205**	0.203**	-0.252	-0.254	0.046	0.043
	(0.104)	(0.104)	(0.265)	(0.265)	(0.117)	(0.117)
Employer fines	0.197*	0.194*	-0.058	-0.056	0.040	0.036
	(0.102)	(0.103)	(0.264)	(0.264)	(0.115)	(0.115)
Have children	—	0.026	—	-0.020	—	0.031
		(0.075)		(0.077)		(0.074)
Party ID	—	—	-0.479**	-0.480**	—	—
			(0.091)	(0.091)		
Party ID * agents	—	—	0.189+	0.190+	—	—
			(0.124)	(0.124)		
Party ID * border fence	—	—	0.266**	0.165**	—	—
			(0.131)	(0.124)		
Party ID * employer fines	—	—	0.165+	0.165+	—	—
			(0.128)	(0.128)		
Fox News	—	—	—	—	-0.843**	-0.843**
					(0.162)	(0.162)
Fox News * agents	—	—	—	—	0.102	0.102
					(0.225)	(0.225)

	(1) Coefficient (SE)	(2) Coefficient (SE)	(3) Coefficient (SE)	(4) Coefficient (SE)	(5) Coefficient (SE)	(6) Coefficient (SE)
Fox News * border fence	—	—	—	—	0.591** (0.234)	0.590** (0.234)
Fox News * employer fines	—	—	—	—	0.556** (0.235)	0.559** (0.235)
Constant	0.314** (0.073)	0.307** (0.076)	1.183** (0.185)	1.190** (0.188)	0.534** (0.083)	0.525** (0.085)
N	1,083	1,083	1,003	1,003	1,083	1,083
R-squared	0.006	0.006	0.062	0.062	0.054	0.054

	Coefficient	Standard Error		Coefficient	Standard Error
Effect of the agent condition on …			**Effect of the employer fines condition on …**		
Democrats	0.111	0.148	Democrats	0.107	0.155
Independents	0.300**	0.103	Independents	0.272**	0.105
Republicans	0.490**	0.174	Republicans	0.438**	0.175
Effect of the border fence condition on …			**Effect of all conditions on Fox News viewers**		
Democrats	0.013	0.153	Agents	0.295+	0.195
Independents	0.279**	0.107	Border fence	0.637**	0.203
Republicans	0.545**	0.184	Employer fines	0.597**	0.205

Source: Authors' analysis of 2014 SSI survey data.
**$p < 0.05$; *$p < 0.10$; +$p < 0.20$

Table A3.10   Probit on Support for a Path to Citizenship Relative to Noncitizenship by Frame and Moderating Effect Among Latinos, 2014

	Model 1
Con argument	–0.071
	(0.085)
Latino	–0.113
	(0.268)
Latino * con argument	0.646*
	(0.389)
Constant	0.759**
	(0.062)
N	1,121
Pseudo-R-squared	0.004

Source: Authors' analysis of 2014 SSI survey data.
**$p < 0.05$; *$p < 0.10$; +$p < 0.20$

Appendix to Chapter 4

Table A4.1   OLS on Support for the DREAM Act, 2007

	Model 1 Coefficient (Standard Error)	Model 2 Coefficient (Standard Error)	Model 3 Coefficient (Standard Error)	Model 4 Coefficient (Standard Error)
Undocumented	0.025	0.032	0.079	0.076
	(0.071)	(0.071)	(0.173)	(0.174)
Unauthorized	0.041	0.038	−0.122	−0.118
	(0.070)	(0.071)	(0.172)	(0.172)
Child frame	0.343***	0.340***	0.035	0.033
	(0.058)	(0.058)	(0.141)	(0.142)
Female	—	0.153***	—	0.030
		(0.059)		(0.057)
Church attendance	—	−0.089***	—	−0.002
		(0.023)		(0.022)
Party ID (three-point)	—	—	−0.658***	−0.654***
			(0.068)	(0.069)
Party ID x undocumented	—	—	−0.025	−0.023
			(0.083)	(0.083)
Party ID x unauthorized	—	—	0.096	0.092
			(0.082)	(0.082)
Party ID x child frame	—	—	0.159**	0.161**
			(0.067)	(0.068)
Constant	0.047	0.186**	1.308***	1.296***
	(0.058)	(0.078)	(0.142)	(0.148)
N	2,182	2,157	2,145	2,122
R-squared	0.016	0.026	0.130	0.130

Source: Authors' analysis of 2007 CCES survey data.
***$p < 0.01$; ** $p \leq 0.05$; *$p \leq 0.10$

Table A4.2   OLS on Support for the DREAM Act, 2010

	Model 1 Coefficient (Standard Error)	Model 2 Coefficient (Standard Error)	Model 3 Coefficient (Standard Error)	Model 4 Coefficient (Standard Error)
Undocumented	0.097	0.090	0.342	0.387*
	(0.096)	(0.089)	(0.235)	(0.233)
Unauthorized	0.085	0.097	0.328	0.389*
	(0.097)	(0.090)	(0.242)	(0.239)
Child frame	0.258***	0.322***	–0.131	–0.075
	(0.079)	(0.073)	(0.196)	(0.194)
Ideology (five-point)	—	–0.578***	—	–0.465***
		(0.032)		(0.041)
Party ID (three-point)	—	—	–0.708***	–0.256***
			(0.090)	(0.096)
Party ID x undocumented	—	—	–0.110	–0.144
			(0.110)	(0.108)
Party ID x unauthorized	—	—	–0.102	–0.138
			(0.113)	(0.111)
Party ID x child frame	—	—	0.218**	0.200**
			(0.092)	(0.090)
Constant	0.081	1.975***	1.440***	2.095***
	(0.077)	(0.127)	(0.188)	(0.195)
N	1,352	1,271	1,352	1,271
R-squared	0.009	0.212	0.148	0.227

Source: Authors' analysis of 2010 YouGov survey data.
***$p < 0.01$; **$p \leq 0.05$; *$p \leq 0.10$

Table A4.3 Support for the DREAM Act, 2012

	Model 1 (OLS) Coefficient (Standard Error)	Model 2 (OLS) Coefficient (Standard Error)	Model 3 (Ordered Probit) Coefficient (Standard Error)	Model 4 (OLS) Coefficient (Standard Error)	Model 5 (OLS) Coefficient (Standard Error)
Illegal	0.167 (0.144)	0.147 (0.146)	-0.087 (0.284)	-0.167 (0.329)	-0.214 (0.331)
Undocumented	-0.019 (0.151)	-0.038 (0.152)	-0.073 (0.229)	-0.107 (0.352)	-0.060 (0.354)
Age	-0.012*** (0.004)	—	-0.008*** (0.003)	-0.010*** (0.004)	—
Child frame	0.035 (0.121)	0.018 (0.122)	0.505** (0.241)	0.432+ (0.278)	0.381 (0.279)
Party ID	—	—	-0.356*** (0.119)	-0.516*** (0.149)	-0.542 (0.152)
Party ID x illegal	—	—	0.112 (0.136)	0.164 (0.169)	0.179 (0.171)
Party ID x undocumented	—	—	0.019+ (0.143)	0.016* (0.178)	-0.020 (0.180)
Party ID x child frame	—	—	-0.226** (0.116)	-0.185+ (0.142)	-0.165 (0.144)

(continued)

Table A4.3 *(continued)*

	Model 1 (OLS) Coefficient (Standard Error)	Model 2 (OLS) Coefficient (Standard Error)	Model 3 (Ordered Probit) Coefficient (Standard Error)	Model 4 (OLS) Coefficient (Standard Error)	Model 5 (OLS) Coefficient (Standard Error)
Constant	0.869***	0.351***	—	1.775***	1.375
	(0.205)	(0.125		(0.329)	(0.296)
Cut 1	—	—	-2.034	—	—
			(0.281)		
Cut 2	—	—	-1.611	—	—
			(0.278)		
Cut 3	—	—	-1.115	—	—
			(0.278)		
Cut 4	—	—	-0.428	—	—
			(0.279)		
N	624	624	599	599	599
R-squared	0.020	0.003	—	0.121	0.109

Change in support for the DREAM Act moving from the control to the child frame, by partisanship, model 4

	Coefficient	Standard Error
Democrats	0.280**	0.143
Independents	0.054	0.097
Republicans	-0.172	0.159

Source: Authors' analysis of 2012 YouGov survey data.
***$p < 0.01$; **$p \leq 0.05$; *$p \leq 0.10$; +$p \leq 0.20$

Table A4.4 Support for the DREAM Act Adding in Amnesty Conditions, 2012

	Model 1 (OLS) Coefficient (Standard Error)	Model 2 (OLS) Coefficient (Standard Error)	Model 3 (Ordered Probit) Coefficient (Standard Error)	Model 4 (OLS) Coefficient (Standard Error)	Model 5 (Ordered Probit) Coefficient (Standard Error)	Model 6 (OLS) Coefficient (Standard Error)
Illegal	-0.084	-0.095	-0.077	-0.086	-0.081	-0.098
	(0.236)	(0.237)	(0.200)	(0.236)	(0.200)	(0.238)
Undocumented	0.293	0.304	0.242	0.288	0.254	0.298
	(0.249)	(0.251)	(0.216)	(0.249)	(0.216)	(0.251)
Age	-0.009***	—	-0.007***	-0.009***	—	—
	(0.003)		(0.002)	(0.003)		
Party ID	-0.467***	-0.482***	0.157***	-0.509***	-0.371***	-0.531***
	(0.114)	(0.115)	(0.097)	(0.128)	(0.103)	(0.129)
Party ID x illegal	0.194*	0.194*	-0.047	0.196*	0.154+	0.196*
	(0.118)	(0.119)	(0.104)	(0.118)	(0.010)	(0.119)
Party ID x undocu- mented	-0.065	-0.077	-0.047	-0.060	-0.059	-0.072
	(0.124)	(0.125)	(0.104)	(0.124)	(0.104)	(0.125)
Child frame	0.526***	0.517***	—	—	—	—
	(0.193)	(0.194)				
Amnesty frame	0.244+	0.245	—	—	—	—
	(0.192)	(0.193)				
Party ID x child frame	-0.247***	-0.243***	—	—	—	—
	(0.096)	(0.097)				
Party ID x amnesty frame	-0.225**	-0.230**	—	—	—	—
	(0.096)	(0.097)				

(continued)

Table A4.4 *(continued)*

	Model 1 (OLS) Coefficient (Standard Error)	Model 2 (OLS) Coefficient (Standard Error)	Model 3 (Ordered Probit) Coefficient (Standard Error)	Model 4 (OLS) Coefficient (Standard Error)	Model 5 (Ordered Probit) Coefficient (Standard Error)	Model 6 (OLS) Coefficient (Standard Error)
Child, no amnesty	—	—	0.495*** (0.241)	0.418+ (0.279)	0.461* (0.240)	0.378+ (0.279)
Party ID x child, no amnesty	—	—	-0.216* (0.116)	-0.172 (0.142)	-0.202* (0.116)	-0.155 (0.143)
Amnesty, no child	—	—	—	0.137 (0.272)	0.179 (0.222)	0.107 (0.274)
Party ID x amnesty, no child	—	—	-0.162+ (0.109)	-0.151 (0.138)	-0.156+ (0.109)	-0.143 (0.139)
Child and amnesty	—	—	—	0.763*** (0.263)	0.680*** (0.225)	0.754*** (0.263)
Party ID x child and amnesty	—	—	-0.416*** (0.110)	-0.465*** (0.133)	-0.415*** (0.110)	-0.466*** (0.134)
Constant	1.495*** (0.253)	1.136*** (0.228)	—	1.551*** (0.275)	—	1.211*** (0.252)
Cut 1	—	—	-1.857 (0.231)	—	-1.578 (0.211)	—
Cut 2	—	—	-1.440 (0.230)	—	-1.163 (0.210)	—
Cut 3	—	—	-0.950 (0.229)	—	-0.676 (0.209)	—
Cut 4	—	—	-0.248 (0.229)	—	0.022 (0.209)	—
N	1,240	1,240	1,240	1,240	1,240	1,240
R-squared	0.169	0.161	—	0.170	—	0.162

Source: Authors' analysis of 2012 YouGov survey data.

***$p < 0.01$; **$p \leq 0.05$; *$p \leq 0.10$; +$p \leq 0.20$

Table A4.5   Change in Support for the DREAM Act Moving from the Control Group to the Given Frame, by Partisan Group, from Model 6, 2012

	Coefficient	Standard Error
Child frame only		
Democrats	0.223*	0.162
Independents	0.068	0.124
Republicans	–0.087	0.213
Amnesty frame only		
Democrats	–0.035	0.159
Independents	–0.178	0.121
Republicans	–0.320*	0.206
Both child and amnesty frames		
Democrats	0.288*	0.154
Independents	–0.178	0.119
Republicans	–0.645***	0.201

Source: Authors' analysis of 2012 YouGov survey data.
***$p < 0.01$; **$p \leq 0.05$; *$p \leq 0.10$

Table A4.6 OLS on Support for the DREAM Act, 2014

	Model 1 Coefficient (Standard Error)	Model 2 Coefficient (Standard Error)	Model 3 Coefficient (Standard Error)	Model 4 Coefficient (Standard Error)	Model 5 Coefficient (Standard Error)	Model 6 Coefficient (Standard Error)
Episodic, no empathy	-0.102 (0.113)	-0.163+ (0.113)	-0.181 (0.290)	-0.175 (0.291)	-0.108 (0.111)	-0.166+ (0.112)
Episodic, empathy	-0.017 (0.114)	-0.103 (0.114)	-0.074 (0.297)	-0.062 (0.298)	-0.010 (0.112)	-0.090 (0.112)
Thematic, no empathy	-0.075 (0.114)	-0.119 (0.115)	-0.124 (0.292)	-0.120 (0.292)	-0.065 (0.112)	-0.101 (0.113)
Thematic, empathy	0.081 (0.116)	-0.048 (0.116)	0.070 (0.300)	0.075 (0.300)	0.099 (0.114)	-0.026 (0.114)
Child frame	0.166** (0.073)	0.118+ (0.074)	-0.036 (0.186)	-0.036 (0.186)	0.214** (0.104)	0.253** (0.105)
Age	—	0.002 (0.002)	—	0.002 (0.002)	—	0.001 (0.002)
Family immigration history	—	-0.015 (0.040)	—	-0.015 (0.040)	—	-0.021 (0.039)
Party ID (three-point)	—	-0.435*** (0.046)	-0.471*** (0.109)	-0.464*** (0.110)	—	-0.413*** (0.046)
Party ID x episodic, no empathy	—	—	0.009 (0.141)	0.006 (0.141)	—	—

	(1)	(2)	(3)	(4)	(5)	(6)
Party ID x episodic, empathy	—	—	-0.016 (0.143)	-0.021 (0.143)	—	—
Party ID x thematic, no empathy	—	—	0.001 (0.140)	0.001 (0.140)	—	—
Party ID x thematic, empathy	—	—	-0.066 (0.148)	-0.067 (0.149)	—	—
Party ID x child frame	—	—	0.083 (0.091)	0.081 (0.091)	—	—
High empathy	—	—	—	—	0.134 (0.127)	0.162 (0.128)
Trait empathy x episodic, no empathy	—	—	—	—	0.127+ (0.085)	0.120+ (0.087)
Trait empathy x episodic, empathy	—	—	—	—	0.186** (0.091)	0.143+ (0.090)
Trait empathy x thematic, no empathy	—	—	—	—	0.345*** (0.094)	0.277*** (0.097)
Trait empathy x thematic, empathy	—	—	—	—	0.301*** (0.093)	0.306*** (0.092)
Trait empathy x child frame	—	—	—	—	-0.119 (0.144)	-0.256* (0.146)
Constant	0.291*** (0.087)	-2.419 (4.829)	1.276*** (0.231)	-2.304 (4.857)	0.229** (0.108)	-0.686 (4.776)
N	1,123	1,039	1,040	1,039	1,123	1,039
R-squared	0.007	0.090	0.090	0.091	0.048	0.120

Source: Authors' analysis of 2014 SSI survey data.
***p < 0.01; **p ≤ 0.05; *p ≤ 0.10; +p ≤ 0.20

Table A4.7 OLS on Support for DACA, 2012

	Model 1 Coefficient (Standard Error)	Model 2 Coefficient (Standard Error)	Model 3 Coefficient (Standard Error)	Model 4 Coefficient (Standard Error)
Illegal	0.192*	0.209**	-0.117	-0.111
	(0.100)	(0.100)	(0.217)	(0.219)
Undocumented	0.108	0.129	0.086	0.078
	(0.104)	(0.102)	(0.228)	(0.227)
Amnesty frame	-0.339***	-0.342***	-0.254+	-0.271+
	(0.083)	(0.083)	(0.182)	(0.183)
Age	—	-0.011***	—	-0.007***
		(0.003)		(0.002)
Party ID	—	—	-0.849***	-0.841***
			(0.094)	(0.094)
Party ID x illegal	—	—	0.157+	0.159+
			(0.111)	(0.111)
Party ID x undocumented	—	—	0.028	0.038
			(0.114)	(0.113)
Party ID x amnesty frame	—	—	-0.018	-0.009
			(0.092)	(0.092)
Constant	0.260***	0.763***	1.851***	2.137***
	(0.083)	(0.144)	(0.178)	(0.202)
N	1,300	1,300	1,241	1,241
R-squared	0.018	0.032	0.216	0.221

Source: Authors' analysis of 2012 YouGov survey data.
***$p < 0.01$; **$p \leq 0.05$; *$p \leq 0.10$; +$p \leq 0.20$

Table A4.8 OLS on Support for DACA, 2014

	Model 1 Coefficient (Standard Error)	Model 2 Coefficient (Standard Error)	Model 3 Coefficient (Standard Error)	Model 4 Coefficient (Standard Error)	Model 5 Coefficient (Standard Error)
Episodic, no empathy	0.130	0.018	0.122	0.017	0.309**
	(0.123)	(0.114)	(0.122)	(0.114)	(0.151)
Episodic, empathy	0.090	-0.016	0.093	-0.011	0.205+
	(0.125)	(0.115)	(0.123)	(0.114)	(0.151)
Thematic, no empathy	0.005	-0.058	0.011	-0.044	0.046
	(0.124)	(0.116)	(0.123)	(0.115)	(0.151)
Thematic, empathy	0.186+	0.000	0.194+	0.012	0.314**
	(0.126)	(0.116)	(0.125)	(0.116)	(0.154)
Context	-0.053	-0.022	-0.004	0.104	0.017
	(0.080)	(0.074)	(0.114)	(0.106)	(0.099)
Family immigration history	—	-0.051+	—	-0.058+	—
		(0.040)		(0.040)	
Party ID (three-point)	—	-0.787***	—	-0.773***	—
		(0.046)		(0.046)	
High empathy	—	—	0.157	0.096	—
			(0.136)	(0.126)	
Trait empathy x episodic, no empathy	—	—	0.132+	0.102	—
			(0.093)	(0.088)	
Trait empathy x episodic, empathy	—	—	0.172*	0.115	—
			(0.100)	(0.091)	
Trait empathy x thematic, no empathy	—	—	0.305***	0.282***	—
			(0.103)	(0.098)	

(continued)

Table A4.8 (continued)

	Model 1 Coefficient (Standard Error)	Model 2 Coefficient (Standard Error)	Model 3 Coefficient (Standard Error)	Model 4 Coefficient (Standard Error)	Model 5 Coefficient (Standard Error)
Trait empathy x thematic, no empathy	—	—	0.305*** (0.103)	0.282*** (0.098)	—
Trait empathy x thematic, empathy	—	—	0.142+ (0.102)	0.151+ (0.093)	—
Trait empathy x context	—	—	-0.106 (0.159)	-0.245* (0.147)	—
Have children	—	—	—	—	0.597*** (0.202)
Have children x episodic, no empathy	—	—	—	—	-0.601** (0.263)
Have children x episodic, empathy	—	—	—	—	-0.393+ (0.267)
Have children x thematic, no empathy	—	—	—	—	-0.209 (0.266)
Have children x thematic, empathy	—	—	—	—	-0.445* (0.269)
Have children x context	—	—	—	—	-0.213 (0.169)
Constant	-.053 (.080)	1.623*** (.175)	-.184+ (.113)	1.567*** (.187)	-0.283*** (0.110)
N	1,122	1,039	1,122	1,039	1,122
R-squared	0.003	0.230	0.029	0.243	0.013

Source: Authors' analysis of 2014 YouGov survey data.
***$p < 0.01$; **$p \leq 0.05$; *$p \leq 0.10$; +$p \leq 0.20$

Appendix to Chapter 5

Table A5.1   OLS on Support for Deportation, 2007

	Model 1 Coefficient (Standard Error)	Model 2 Coefficient (Standard Error)
Legal frame	0.202+	0.139
	(0.125)	(0.189)
Security frame	–0.020	–0.111
	(0.128)	(0.189)
Cost frame	–0.307**	–0.591***
	(0.126)	(0.186)
Family frame	–0.148	–0.234
	(0.127)	(0.192)
High education	–1.430***	–1.749***
	(0.104)	(0.233)
Education x legal	—	0.110
		(0.252)
Education x security	—	0.160
		(0.256)
Education x cost	—	0.525**
		(0.252)
Education x family	—	0.155
		(0.256)
Constant	1.270***	1.451***
	(0.129)	(0.175)
N	2,163	2,163
R-squared	0.084	0.086

Source: Authors' analysis of 2007 CCES survey data.
***$p < 0.01$; **$p \leq 0.05$; *$p \leq 0.10$; +$p \leq 0.20$

Table A5.2   OLS on Support for Deportation, 2007

	Coefficient (Standard Error)	Test of equality of coefficients between conditions	p-Value on Test
Family only	−0.032	Family none v. cost none	0.19
	(0.231)	Family none v. legal none	0.36
Cost only	−0.332+	Family none v. security none	0.77
	(0.228)	Family none v. legal family	0.90
Legal only	0.179	Family none v. legal cost	0.71
	(0.225)	Family none v. security family	0.65
Security only	0.036	Family none v. security cost	0.29
	(0.231)	Cost none v. legal none	0.02
Legal and family	−0.061	Cost none v. security none	0.11
	(0.226)	Cost none v. legal family	0.23
Legal and cost	0.054	Cost none v. legal cost	0.09
	(0.227)	Cost none v. security family	0.40
Security and family	−0.137	Cost none v. security exposure	0.81
	(0.233)	Legal none v. security none	0.53
Security and cost	−0.277	Legal none v. legal family	0.28
	(0.227)	Legal none v. legal cost	0.58
Constant	0.464***	Legal none v. security family	0.17
	(0.162)	Legal none v. security cost	0.04
N	2,167	Security none v. legal family	0.67
R-squared	0.004	Security none v. legal cost	0.94
		Security none v. security family	0.46
		Security none v. security cost	0.17
		Legal family v. legal cost	0.61
		Legal family v. security family	0.74
		Legal family v. security cost	0.34
		Legal cost v. security family	0.41
		Legal cost v. security cost	0.14
		Security family v. security cost	0.55

Source: Authors' analysis of 2007 CCES survey data.
***$p < 0.01$; **$p \leq 0.05$; *$p \leq 0.10$; +$p \leq 0.20$

Table A5.3   OLS on Support for Deportation, 2010

	Model 1 Coefficient (Standard Error)	Model 2 Coefficient (Standard Error)
Undocumented	−0.031	−0.112
	(0.107)	(0.099)
Unauthorized	0.031	−0.024
	(0.109)	(0.101)
Legal frame	0.265**	0.260**
	(0.137)	(0.127)
Culture frame	0.015	0.034
	(0.137)	(0.128)
Security frame	−0.069	−0.010
	(0.142)	(0.131)
Economic frame	−0.171	−0.019
	(0.142)	(0.131)
Interest	—	0.075+
		(0.047)
Party ID (three-point)	—	0.713***
		(0.046)
Female	—	−0.097
		(0.078)
Constant	0.590***	−1.032***
	(0.089)	(0.212)
N	1,363	1,331
R-squared	0.010	0.176

Source: Authors' analysis of 2010 CCES survey data.
***$p < 0.01$; **$p \leq 0.05$; *$p \leq 0.10$; +$p \leq 0.20$

Table A5.4   OLS on Support for Deportation Moderated by Family Immigration History, 2010

	Model 1 Coefficient (Standard Error)	Model 2 Coefficient (Standard Error)
Undocumented	−0.877**	−1.105***
	(0.438)	(0.408)
Unauthorized	−0.463	−0.633+
	(0.452)	(0.427)
Family history	−0.097	−0.106
	(0.111)	(0.102)
Family history* undocumented	0.249**	0.292***
	(0.125)	(0.117)
Family history * unauthorized	0.140	0.175+
	(0.128)	(0.121)
Culture frame	−0.277	−0.066
	(0.578)	(0.535)
Security frame	−0.532	−0.505
	(0.578)	(0.535)
Legal frame	0.018	0.139
	(0.587)	(0.545)
Economic frame	−1.468**	−1.040*
	(0.606)	(0.560)
Family history * culture frame	0.089	0.033
	(0.165)	(0.153)
Family history * economic frame	0.376**	0.297*
	(0.171)	(0.159)
Family history * security frame	0.136	0.145
	(0.166)	(0.154)
Family history * legal frame	0.071	0.035
	(0.166)	(0.154)
Interest	—	0.075+
		(0.047)
Party ID (three-point)	—	0.716***
		(0.046)
Female	—	−0.101+
		(0.078)
Constant	0.919**	−0.682*
	(0.394)	(0.411)
N	1,356	1,324
R-squared	0.025	0.192

Source: Authors' analysis of 2010 CCES survey data.
***$p < 0.01$; **$p \leq 0.05$; *$p \leq 0.10$; +$p \leq 0.20$

Table A5.5   OLS on Whether Immigrants Should Be Given Special Consideration, 2012

	Model 1 Coefficient (Standard Error)	Model 2 Coefficient (Standard Error)
Ten years	−0.015	−0.140
	(0.091)	(0.223)
Twenty years	−0.251***	−0.271
	(0.091)	(0.225)
Republican source	−0.088	0.229
	(0.105)	(0.258)
Democratic source	−0.128	−0.312
	(0.105)	(0.259)
Fox News source	−0.255***	−0.038
	(0.104)	(0.258)
High education	−0.164**	—
	(0.075)	
Party ID	—	0.557***
		(0.109)
Party ID x ten years	—	0.079
		(0.108)
Party ID x twenty years	—	0.020
		(0.110)
Party ID x Republican source	—	−0.168+
		(0.125)
Party ID x Democratic source	—	0.128
		(0.126)
Party ID x Fox News source	—	−0.104
		(0.125)
Constant	0.096	−1.081***
	(0.099)	(0.227)
N	1,299	1,240
R-squared	0.017	0.129

Source: Authors' analysis of 2012 YouGov survey data.
***$p < 0.01$; **$p \leq 0.05$; *$p \leq 0.10$; +$p \leq 0.20$

Table A5.6   OLS on Whether Immigrants Should Be Given Special Consideration, 2014

	Party ID Coefficient (Standard Error)	Family History Coefficient (Standard Error)	Fox News Coefficient (Standard Error)	Trait Empathy Coefficient (Standard Error)
Episodic, no empathy	0.262	-0.532+	0.013	-0.060
	(0.295)	(0.396)	(0.128)	(0.114)
Episodic, empathy	0.144	-0.768*	0.052	-0.016
	(0.302)	(0.436)	(0.127)	(0.115)
Thematic, no empathy	0.285	-0.037	-0.023	-0.083
	(0.296)	(0.467)	(0.128)	(0.114)
Thematic, empathy	0.065	0.128	-0.076	-0.067
	(0.304)	(0.434)	(0.130)	(0.116)
Ten years	-0.492**	0.168	-0.179*	0.094
	(0.235)	(0.357)	(0.102)	(0.131)
Twenty years	-0.716***	0.167	-0.381***	-0.157
	(0.224)	(0.347)	(0.100)	(0.130)
Moderator	0.389***	0.133+	0.850***	0.118
	(0.122)	(0.104)	(0.242)	(0.151)

Moderator x episodic, no empathy	-0.135	0.142	-0.510*	-0.187**
	(0.143)	(0.114)	(0.267)	(0.087)
Moderator x episodic, empathy	-0.051	0.217*	-0.410+	-0.077
	(0.145)	(0.124)	(0.274)	(0.093)
Moderator x thematic, no empathy	-0.175	-0.017	-0.442*	-0.329***
	(0.142)	(0.131)	(0.270)	(0.096)
Moderator x thematic, empathy	0.001	0.020	-0.138	-0.229**
	(0.151)	(0.124)	(0.275)	(0.095)
Moderator x ten years	0.222*	-0.064	0.373*	-0.294+
	(0.116)	(0.101)	(0.213)	(0.183)
Moderator x twenty years	0.197*	-0.140+	0.151	-0.303*
	(0.110)	(0.098)	(0.209)	(0.179)
Constant	-0.910***	-0.585+	-0.279***	-0.196+
	(0.253)	(0.362)	(0.105)	(0.124)
N	1,038	1,121	1,121	1,121
R-squared	0.104	0.029	0.080	0.047

Source: Authors' analysis of 2014 SSI survey data.
Note: The top of each column lists the moderator in the given model.
***p < 0.01; **p ≤ 0.05; *p ≤ 0.10; +*p* ≤ 0.20

Appendix to Chapter 6

Table A6.1   OLS Regression on Support for Legalization by Condition and Family Immigration History, 2007 and 2011

	2007 Coefficient (Standard Error)	2011 Coefficient (Standard Error)
Undocumented	−0.603**	−1.035*
	(0.301)	(0.556)
Unauthorized	−0.456+	—
	(0.291)	
Female	0.122**	—
	(0.056)	
Protestant	−0.117+	—
	(0.075)	
Other Christian	−0.011	—
	(0.109)	
Other religion	0.441**	—
	(0.098)	
No religion	0.329**	—
	(0.083)	
Amnesty frame	−0.121	−0.741+
	(0.243)	(0.482)
Family history	−0.076	−0.454**
	(0.070)	(0.119)
Family history * undocumented	0.172**	0.265+
	(0.086)	(0.166)
Family history * unauthorized	0.130+	—
	(0.083)	
Family history * amnesty	−0.163**	−0.090
	(0.070)	(0.142)
Illegal alien	—	−0.445
		(0.560)
Family history * illegal alien	—	0.073
		(0.165)
Education	—	0.044
		(0.509)
Male	—	−0.340**
		(0.152)
Constant	0.105	2.456**
	(0.248)	(0.431)
N	2,168	796
R2	0.0945	0.1130

Source: Authors' analysis of 2007 CCES and 2011 YouGov survey data.
Note: 2011 is weighted.
**$p < 0.05$; *$p < 0.10$; +$0 < 0.20$

Table A6.2   OLS on Support for the DREAM Act and DACA, 2011 and 2012

	2011 DREAM Act Coefficient (Standard Error)	2012 DREAM Act Coefficient (Standard Error)	2012 DACA Coefficient (Standard Error)
Illegal immigrant	—	0.262**	0.209**
		(0.102)	(0.100)
Undocumented	0.269+	0.123	0.129
	(0.197)	(0.109)	(0.102)
Age	—	–0.013**	–0.011**
		(0.003)	(0.003)
Child	—	0.035	—
		(0.086)	
Amnesty	—	–0.199**	–0.342**
		(0.085)	(0.083)
Illegal alien	0.009	—	—
	(0.203)		
Came as children	–0.013	—	—
	(0.164)		
Education	0.034	—	—
	(0.057)		
Constant	0.706**	0.827**	0.763**
	(0.229)	(0.155)	(0.144)
N	800	1,299	1,300
R-squared	0.004	0.028	0.032

Source: Authors' analysis of YouGov survey data.
**$p < 0.05$; *$p < 0.10$; +$p < 0.20$

Table A6.3   OLS on the DREAM Act by Given Moderator, 2007, 2011, and 2012

	2007 Family History Coefficient (Standard Error)	2011 Party Identification Coefficient (Standard Error)	2011 Fox Viewership Coefficient (Standard Error)	2011 Latino Coefficient (Standard Error)	2012 Party Identification Coefficient (Standard Error)
Undocumented	-0.570*	0.219	0.541**	0.547*	0.377
	(0.317)	(0.194)	(0.216)	(0.289)	(0.232)
Unauthorized	-0.773**	—	—	—	—
	(0.306)				
Illegal alien	—	0.041	0.275	0.286	0.096
		(0.202)	(0.226)	(0.289)	(0.236)
Child frame	0.418+	0.068	-0.259+	0.277	0.062
	(0.255)	(0.162)	(0.179)	(0.237)	(0.083)
Amnesty frame	—	—	—	—	-0.178
					(0.082)
Given moderator	-0.246**	-0.971**	-1.323**	1.889**	-0.515
	(0.071)	(0.196)	(0.386)	(0.304)	(0.077)
Moderator * undocumented	0.172*	-0.257	-0.605+	-0.522+	-0.258
	(0.090)	(0.218)	(0.451)	(0.372)	(0.116)

Moderator * unauthorized	0.237** (0.087)	0.019 (0.245)	—	—	—
Moderator * alien	—	—	-0.517 (0.462)	-0.386 (0.374)	-0.195 (0.118)
Moderator * child	-0.167 (0.073)	0.231 (0.189)	0.684* (0.362)	-0.367 (0.307)	—
Education	—	0.048 (0.054)	-0.007 (0.055)	0.165** (0.055)	—
Female	0.148** (0.059)	—	—	—	—
Age	—	—	—	—	-0.008 (0.003)
Constant	0.823** (0.250)	0.517** (0.232)	1.200** (0.228)	-0.714** (0.291)	1.856 (0.197)
N	2,169	800	800	800	1,240
R-squared	0.0282	0.1282	0.0961	0.1081	0.1610

Source: Authors' analysis of CCES survey data.
Note: All models except for 2007 are weighted. The top of each column lists the moderator in the given model.
**$p < 0.05$; *$p < 0.10$; +$p < 0.20$

Table A6.4 Change in Support for the DREAM Act Moving from One Condition to Another by Different Levels of the Moderating Variable, 2007, 2011, and 2012

	Illegal Immigrant to Undocumented Coefficient (p-Value)	Illegal Immigrant to Unauthorized Coefficient (p-Value)	Illegal Immigrant to Illegal Alien Coefficient (p-Value)
2007—Family immigration history			
First generation	−0.398	−0.536	—
	(0.083)	(0.222)	
Second generation	−0.226	−0.299	—
	(0.123)	(0.035)	
Third generation	−0.054	−0.061	—
	(0.499)	(0.436)	
Fourth generation and higher	0.118	0.176	—
	(0.178)	(0.044)	
	—	—	—
2011—Party ID			
Democrat	—	—	—
	0.476		
	(0.040)		
Independent	0.219	—	—
	(0.258)		
Republican	−0.038	—	—
	(0.911)		
	—		—

2011—Fox News viewers	—	—
Non-Fox News viewer	0.541	—
	(0.013)	
Fox News viewer	−0.064	—
	(0.872)	
2011—Latinos	—	—
Non-Latinos	0.547	—
	(0.058)	
Latino	0.025	—
	(0.915)	
2012—Party ID	—	—
Democrat	0.119	−0.099
	(0.385)	(0.472)
Independent	−0.140	−0.294
	(0.169)	(0.004)
Republican	−0.398	−0.489
	(0.019)	(0.005)

Source: Authors' analysis of CCES survey data.
Note: These coefficients were estimated from the results reported in table A5.3.

Table A6.5   OLS Regression on Deportations by Given Moderator, 2010 and 2014

	2010 Coefficient (Standard Error)	2014 Coefficient (Standard Error)	2014 Coefficient (Standard Error)
Undocumented	−0.877**	−0.055	−0.118
	(0.438)	(0.134)	(0.137)
Unauthorized	−0.463	—	—
	(0.452)		
Illegal alien	—	−0.123	−0.122
		(0.135)	(0.139)
Family history	−0.097	—	—
	(0.111)		
Family * undocumented	0.249**	—	—
	(0.125)		
Family * unauthorized	0.140	—	—
	(0.128)		
Culture frame	−0.277	—	—
	(0.578)		
Security frame	−0.532	—	—
	(0.578)		
Legal frame	0.018	—	—
	(0.587)		
Economic frame	−1.468**	—	—
	(0.606)		
Family * culture	0.089	—	—
	(0.165)		
Family * economic frame	0.376**	—	—
	(0.171)		
Family * security	0.136	—	—
	(0.166)		
Family * legal	0.071	—	—
	(0.166)		
Latino	—	—	−1.039
			(0.456)
Latino * illegals	—	—	0.200
			(0.576)
Latino * undocumented	—	—	1.233*
			(0.629)
Family immigration history	—	0.024	−0.001
		(0.061)	(0.062)
Age	—	0.003	0.005
		(0.004)	(0.004)
White	—	0.283	0.220
		(0.146)	(0.148)
Constant	0.919**	−6.530	−9.221
	(0.394)	(7.284)	(7.329)
N	1,356	1,119	1,119
R-squared	0.0254	0.0054	0.0145

Source: Authors' analysis of 2010 YouGov and 2014 SSI survey data.
**$p < 0.05$; *$p < 0.10$; +$p < 0.20$

Table A6.6   Change in Support for Deportations Moving from Illegal to Undocumented Condition by Moderating Variable, 2010 and 2011

	Coefficient (p-Value)
2010—Family immigration history	
First generation	−0.628
	(0.049)
Second generation	−0.380
	(0.064)
Third generation	−0.131
	(0.265)
Fourth generation and higher	0.118
	(0.370)
2011—Latino	
Non-Latino	−0.118
	(0.389)
Latino	1.115
	(0.070)

Source: Authors' analysis of CCES and YouGov survey data.
Note: These coefficients were estimated from the results reported in table A6.4.

Notes

Chapter 1: Introduction

1. Gulasekaram and Ramakrishnan 2015.
2. Farley 2010.
3. Archibold 2010; Shahid 2010.
4. Gulasekaram and Ramakrishnan 2015.
5. The White House 2010.
6. Quinnipiac University Poll 2012.
7. Rogers Smith 1993, 1997.
8. Franklin 1760; Ngai 2004; Zolberg 2005.
9. We use the terms "illegal," "undocumented," and "unauthorized" inter-changeably in our work. As we elaborate in chapter 5, these terms can be considered equivalency frames: there are strong variations in usage among partisans, but their implications for public opinion on immigration policy are relatively weak.
10. Ngai 2004; Massey, Durand, and Malone 2002.
11. Passel 2006.
12. We say more about the legislative history of the DREAM Act in chapter 4.
13. We provide more details on these shifting stances on immigrant legalization among Republican legislators and conservative media personalities in chapter 3.
14. Indeed, even uncertain beliefs may be sufficient to affect congressional be-havior, because members try to minimize risk when running for reelection (Arnold 1990; Druckman, Kifer, and Parkin 2009).
15. Waters and Pineau 2015.
16. Scheve and Slaughter 2001; Citrin, Reingold, and Green 1990; Brader, Valen-tino, and Suhay 2008.
17. Scheve and Slaughter 2001; Hainmueller and Hiscox 2010; Hainmueller and Hopkins 2014.
18. On stereotypes about immigrants, see Burns and Gimpel 2000; Hainmueller and Hiscox 2010; Hainmueller and Hopkins 2014. On English as the official language of the United States, see Espenshade and Calhoun 1993; Schild-kraut 2001, 2005.
19. See, for example, Knoll, Redlawsk, and Sanborn 2010; Druckman, Peterson, and Slothuus 2013; Masuoka and Junn 2013.
20. Abrajano and Singh 2008a; Dunaway et al. 2011; Dunaway, Branton, and Abrajano 2010.
21. Tversky and Kahneman 1981; Druckman 2004.
22. Luntz 2005.

23. Lau 1982; Geer 2006.
24. Republican National Committee 2013.

Chapter 2: Media Framing and Effects on Public Opinion

1. Goffman 1974.
2. Small 2002, 2004.
3. Young 2010.
4. Lee and Zhou 2015.
5. Chong and Druckman 2007c, 100, citing Gamson and Modigliani 1987, 1989.
6. Snow et al. 1986, 464.
7. Ibid., 469.
8. McCaffrey and Keys 2000; Snow et al. 1986; Snow and Byrd 2007; Zavestoski et al. 2004.
9. Pierson 2001.
10. Birney, Graetz, and Shapiro 2006; Bartels 2008; Nyhan, Reifler, and Ubel 2013.
11. Iyengar and Kinder 1987.
12. In addition to framing, the media also play an important role in agenda setting and priming (Iyengar and Kinder 1987; McCombs and Shaw 1972; MacKuen 1984).
13. Gross 2008, 171.
14. Vedantam 2010.
15. Dinan 2012.
16. Dennis Chong and James Druckman (2007b) argue that Shanto Iyengar and Donald Kinder's (1987) conceptualization of priming differs from treatments in psychology. In their review of framing theory, they note that Steven Sherman, Diane Mackie, and Denise Driscoll (1990, 405) define priming as "as a procedure that increases the accessibility of some category or construct in memory." Something can be made accessible even with a brief mention or by emphasizing certain sides of an issue. In that sense, Chong and Druckman see little difference between priming, as conceived in psychology, and framing.
17. Druckman 2004.
18. *Your World with Neil Cavuto*, Fox News, March 5, 2013.
19. *Up with Chris Hayes*, MSNBC, February 2, 2013.
20. Cargile, Merolla, and Pantoja 2014.
21. Chong and Druckman 2007b, 114.
22. Chavez 2013; Santa Ana 2002, 2013.
23. Hamilton 1998, 2004.
24. Branton and Dunaway 2009; Abrajano and Singh 2008; Haynes 2014.
25. Merolla, Ramakrishnan, and Haynes 2013; Haynes 2014.
26. On differences between news anchors, see Haynes 2014; on the differences between news organization, see Merolla, Ramakrishnan, and Haynes 2013.
27. Bloemraad, de Graauw, and Hamlin (2015); Patler and Gonzales (2015).
28. Ramakrishnan and Silva 2015.

29. Prior 2007; Coe et al. 2008; Groseclose and Milyo 2005.
30. On the independent effect of news coverage on opinion, see Levendusky 2013 and Mutz 2006. On whether Americans tend to watch news that reflects their political beliefs, see Iyengar and Hahn 2009 and Stroud 2007. On their choice to opt in or out of partisan news coverage, see Arceneaux and John-son 2013 and Prior 2013.
31. Coe et al. 2008; Morris 2007; Feldman et al. 2011.
32. See "Most Liberal and Conservative American News Media," Mondo Times, available at: http://www.mondotimes.com/rating/politicalusa.html (accessed March 30, 2016); Gentzkow and Shapiro 2010.
33. On Fox News, see DellaVigna and Kaplan 2006; Iyengar and Hahn 2009.
34. Shain 2009; Bauder 2009.
35. Weaver and Scacco 2012.
36. Golan 2006.
37. We used interval sampling for our qualitative content analysis when the number of stories in a given year for a given source (for example, Fox News in 2013) exceeded fifty to ensure that stories in months with less news cover-age would have a greater likelihood of being included in the sample than stories drawn from a simple random sample during the entire year. When sampling was necessary, we applied the following sampling strategy: If the number of stories in a given year and source exceeded one hundred, we sampled every third article. For those populations between fifty-one and one hundred, we sampled every other article. The goal was to maintain a practical number of articles as close to fifty as possible; our sample counts ranged from forty to sixty-five per source per year.
38. Druckman and Parkin 2005.
39. See, for example, Geer 2006; Lau 1982; Lau, Sigelman, and Rovner 2007; Mar-cus, Neuman, and MacKuen 2000; Merolla and Zechmeister 2009.
40. We operationalized episodic frames by focusing on individuals' stories and cases of immigrants caught up in the "illegal" immigration context. This frame excludes from consideration stories that discuss a specific bill or presi-dential action with no accompanying example or story about a specific "il-legal" immigrant. We employed this operationalization, which is narrower than that found in works like Gross (2008), primarily to remain consistent with the way we operationalized episodic and thematic frames in our ex-periments. All stories that do not qualify as episodic were coded as thematic to maintain exclusivity. Additionally, those stories containing both episodic and thematic frames were coded using the dominant frame (in terms of ma-jority coverage in the news article).
41. Tajfel 1982; Tajfel and Turner 1979; Turner 1985.
42. See, for example, Billig and Tajfel 1973; Brewer and Silver 1978.
43. Kaiser and Pratt-Hyatt 2009; Kaiser and Wilkins 2010.
44. Schuman, Steeh, and Bobo 1997.
45. See, for example, Jackman 1978; Kinder and Sanders 1996; Kinder and Sears 1981.
46. On symbolic racism, see Kinder and Sears 1981 and Tarman and Sears 2005; on racial resentment, see Kinder and Sanders 1996; on aversive racism, see Gaertner and Dovidio 1986, 2000.

47. Dovidio and Gaertner 2004.
48. Key 1949; Blumer 1958; Blalock 1967.
49. McClain et al. 2006; Hopkins 2010; Newman 2013.
50. Altemeyer 1988; Feldman and Stenner 1997; Stenner 2005. Members of dominant groups can even perceive identity threat from seemingly positive messages, such as an organization's emphasis that it is pro-diversity (Dover, Major, and Kaiser 2016).
51. Merolla and Zechmeister 2009.
52. For an overview, see Hainmueller and Hopkins 2014.
53. Duckitt and Sibley 2010; Craig and Richeson 2013.
54. Rattan et al. 2012.
55. Eberhardt et al. 2006.
56. Goff et al. 2008.
57. Brader, Valentino, and Suhay 2008.
58. Masuoka and Junn 2013.
59. Payne 2001; Payne, Lambert, and Jacoby 2002.
60. Eberhardt et al. 2004.
61. Pérez 2010.
62. Allport 1954.
63. Islam and Hewstone 1993; Johnson and Jacobson 2005; Kalkan, Layman, and Uslaner 2009; McClain et al. 2006; Oliver and Wong 2003; Pettigrew 1997; Sigelman and Welch 1993; Yancey 1999. For a meta-analysis of these effects, see Pettigrew and Tropp 2006.
64. Paolini, Harwood, and Rubin 2010; Stephan et al. 2002.
65. Richeson and Shelton 2007.
66. Gaertner et al. 1993.
67. Todd et al. 2011.
68. Eccleston, Kaiser, and Kraynak (2010).
69. Zaller 1992.
70. Chong and Druckman 2007b; Nelson, Clawson, and Oxley 1997.
71. Druckman 2001; Druckman and Nelson 2003; Iyengar 1991; Nelson and Kinder 1996; Nelson, Oxley, and Clawson 1997; Nelson and Oxley 1999.
72. Nelson, Clawson, and Oxley 1997.
73. Druckman 2001.
74. Cargile, Merolla, and Pantoja 2014.
75. Druckman and Nelson 2003.
76. Nelson and Oxley 1999.
77. Nelson, Oxley, and Clawson 1997.
78. Kam 2005.
79. Chong and Druckman 2007b; Zaller 1992.
80. For a review of these approaches, see Chong and Druckman 2007b.
81. Iyengar 1991.
82. Fiske and Taylor 1991.
83. On the undocumented as an out-group, see Chavez 2013; Berg 2009; Merolla and Zechmeister 2009; Masuoka and Junn 2013.
84. Tversky and Kahneman 1981, 1986.
85. Masuoka and Junn 2013, 159.
86. Ibid.

87. Pérez 2010. As the fastest-growing immigrant community, Latinos are often associated with the term "illegal immigrant," but this is not the case for Asians (Brader, Valentino, and Suhay 2008; Branton and Dunaway 2008; Knoll, Redlawsk, and Sanborn 2010).
88. Knoll, Redlawsk, and Sanborn 2010.
89. Druckman 2004, 672.
90. Ibid.
91. Druckman, Peterson, and Slothuus 2013; Levendusky 2013.
92. Brader, Valentino, and Suhay 2008.
93. Cargile, Merolla, and Pantoja 2014.
94. Druckman, Peterson, and Slothuus 2013.
95. For example, Bartels 2002; Campbell et al. 1960.
96. Zaller 1992.
97. Ibid.
98. Brewer 2001; Chong and Druckman 2007b.
99. Knoll, Redlawsk, and Sanborn 2010.
100. Masuoka and Junn 2013.
101. Even if in-group identity is not activated, their own personal experiences with discrimination can lead minorities to feel greater closeness and common fate with other racial and ethnic groups (Craig and Richeson 2012), and this may be relevant for attitudes toward immigrants, who are from a variety of backgrounds.
102. Citrin, Green, Muste, and Wong 1997; Espenshade and Calhoun 1993.
103. For studies that find those with low knowledge to be susceptible to framing effects, see, for example, Kinder and Sanders 1990; Haider-Markel and Joslyn 2001. For studies coming to the opposite finding, see Nelson, Oxley, and Clawson 1997; Miller and Krosnick 2000.
104. Druckman and Nelson 2003.
105. Zaller 1992.
106. Espenshade and Calhoun 1993; Citrin et al. 1997; Pantoja 2006.
107. Chong and Druckman 2007a; Druckman 2010.
108. Ledgerwood and Boydstun 2014; Cargile, Merolla, and Pantoja 2014.
109. Druckman and Leeper 2012; Chong and Druckman 2007b. Furthermore, exposure to competing frames can lead to null framing effects, especially if they are of equal strength (Chong and Druckman 2007a; Druckman et al. 2010; Sniderman and Theriault 2004). Exposure to heterogenous discussion groups after receiving a frame can also negate the effects of a frame (Druckman and Nelson 2003).
110. Druckman 2001.
111. Bullock 2011; Druckman et al. 2010; Sniderman and Theriault 2004; Druckman and Nelson 2003.
112. Druckman, Peterson, and Slothuus 2013.
113. Lupia and McCubbins 1998.
114. The 2007 study was conducted over the last two weeks of November 2007, and the 2010 pre-election survey was in the field from late September to late October each year.
115. As the sampling document for CCES notes: "There are three types of strata in the sample: Registered and Unregistered Voters, State Size, and Competi-

tive and Uncompetitive Congressional Districts. The choice of strata guarantees that the study achieves adequate samples in all states and sufficient distribution across congressional districts to measure the differences between competitive and uncompetitive races. . . . Polimetrix further stratifies the sample on age, race, and gender."

116. Although the survey organization provided data weighted to the national population, the sample size for the weighted data is only 1,000 for 2007, 2008, and 2010. We therefore present the unweighted data to increase the power of our experimental manipulations. We report the findings for the weighted data in the notes for relevant chapters.

117. YouGov interviewed 878 respondents who were then matched down to a sample of 800 to produce the final data set. The respondents were matched on gender, age, education, party identification, ideology, and political interest. YouGov then weighted the matched set of survey respondents to known marginals for the general population of the United States from the 2007 American Community Survey (ACS). We present the weighted analyses in the text.

118. YouGov interviewed 1,420 respondents, who were then matched down to a sample of 1,300 to produce the final data set. The respondents were matched on gender, age, race, education, party identification, ideology, and political interest. YouGov then weighted the matched set of survey respondents to known marginals for the general population of the United States from the 2007 ACS. We present the weighted analyses in the text.

119. Druckman and Kam 2011; Berinsky, Huber, and Lenz 2012.

Chapter 3: Comprehensive Immigration Reform

1. Ngai 2004.
2. Kerwin 2010.
3. Massey, Durand, and Malone 2002; Smith 2011.
4. Passel, Cohn, and Gonzalez-Barrera 2013.
5. Much of this chapter relates to the terms used to describe immigrants without legal authorization to stay in the United States. We use these terms interchangeably and in chapter 6 offer a detailed analysis of news coverage and framing effects of the terms "illegal," "undocumented," and "unauthorized."
6. Jachimowicz 2004.
7. Shirley and Devine 2010.
8. Morris 2006; Shirley and Devine 2010.
9. Gulasekaram and Ramakrishnan 2015.
10. On the protests, see Voss and Bloemraad 2010.
11. Pew Research Center 2006.
12. Deparle 2011.
13. Rahman 2008.
14. Dwyer 2012.
15. Schneider 2008.

16. Weiner 2012; Everett 2013.
17. Gregory 2013.
18. On Republican support for the Senate bill, see Congress.gov, "S.744—Border Security, Economic Opportunity, and Immigration Modernization Act," available at: https://www.congress.gov/bill/113th-congress/senate-bill/744; on the bill's reception in the House, see Carroll 2013.
19. Kim 2014.
20. Coe et al. 2008; Morris 2007; Feldman et al. 2011.
21. We use two content analyses to supply the findings for this section. The sample years were selected based on two criteria: years coinciding with our survey experiments and years in which "illegal" immigration was most salient, according to Gallup measures of the "most important problem." The quantitative content analysis included stories appearing between January 1, 2007, and December 31, 2013. The qualitative content analysis included stories from 2007, 2010, 2012, and 2013. The search term used in Lexis-Nexis to supply the stories to code for both the quantitative and qualitative analyses was the following: hlead ("pathway to citizenship") or ("path to citizenship") or ("CIR") or ("comprehensive immigration reform") or ("immigration reform") or ("immigration legalization") or ("legalizing immigrants") or ("immigrant legalization") or ("legalize immigrant!") or ("comprehensive immigra!"). The quantitative analysis used all stories resulting from this search (see table 3.1). The qualitative analysis was based on either a systematic random sample or all stories resulting from this search depending on the size of the search result. Full sets of stories were analyzed for FOX 2007 (n = 39), 2010 (n = 45), and 2012 (n = 6); MSNBC 2007 (n = 11), 2010 (n = 13), 2012 (n = 4), and 2013 (n = 66); CNN 2010 (n = 49) and 2012 (n = 4); WT 2010 (n = 33) and 2012 (n = 26); NYT 2007 (n = 57), 2010 (n = 22), and 2012 (n = 31); and NYP 2007 (n = 12), 2010 (n = 5), 2012 (n = 6), and 2013 (n = 49). Every other story was analyzed for FOX 2013 (n = 40) and WT 2013 (n = 45). Every third story was analyzed for CNN 2007 (n = 49) and 2013 (n = 39); WT 2007 (n = 42); WP 2007 (n = 65), 2010 (n = 47), 2012 (n = 40), and 2013 (n = 63). A simple random sample of stories was analyzed for NYT 2013 (n = 50). The overall inter-coder reliability for qualitative coding on legalization stories was 94 percent for mainstream media sources and 92 percent for conservative news sources.
22. Allen and Vandehei 2013.
23. Weprin 2012.
24. Druckman and Parkin 2005. Tone was coded as part of our qualitative content analysis, which often involved sampling from a larger universe of stories. Inter-coder reliability for the tone of legalization stories was 95 percent for mainstream media sources and 96 percent for conservative news sources.
25. Put another way, we coded article tone based on whether the article cast undocumented immigrants in a net positive or negative light, with stories that had a balanced mix of positive and negative sentiments receiving a neutral rating.
26. Deparle 2011.
27. Ibid.
28. Luntz 2005.

29. Gregory 2013. In addition to examining some of the ways in which these frames are deployed by advocates, we also find support for the non-equivalence of these frames in a validation study we conducted in 2015 with Mechanical Turk participants ($n = 600$). We presented participants with the amnesty frame as well as the pathway frame and asked them to first indicate whether the argument was opposed to or in favor of legalization on a seven-point scale, with higher values being more supportive. We also asked them to rate how effective the argument was, also on a seven-point scale, in making its case. As expected, participants perceived the pathway frame as more supportive of legalization (mean = 4.88) and the amnesty frame as more opposed (mean = 2.77). However, that the perceived direction of the pathway frame is closer to the middle option—neither opposed nor supportive—further supports our argument that this frame is vaguer. With respect to the perceived effectiveness of the frame, participants perceived the pathway frame as more effective (mean = 4.41) than the amnesty frame (mean = 3.60), but this result may reflect the younger, more liberal characteristics of Mechanical Turk samples.

30. The search term used in Lexis-Nexis to supply the stories to code for "amnesty, no pathway," was hlead ("pathway to citizenship") or ("path to citizenship") or ("CIR") or ("comprehensive immigration reform") or ("immigration reform") or ("immigration legalization") or ("legalizing immigrants") or ("immigrant legalization") or ("legalize immigrant!") or ("comprehensive immigra!") and body ("amnesty") and not ("path") and not ("pathway"). Search results for "pathway, no amnesty" were added to the results for "both amnesty and pathway" to produce the measure of any mention of "any pathway." The search term used in Lexis-Nexis to supply the stories to code for "pathway, no amnesty," was hlead ("pathway to citizenship") or ("path to citizenship") or ("CIR") or ("comprehensive immigration reform") or ("immigration reform") or ("immigration legalization") or ("legalizing immigrants") or ("immigrant legalization") or ("legalize immigrant!") or ("comprehensive immigra!") and body ("path" or "pathway") and not ("amnesty").

31. This pattern of findings is also apparent, though less stark, if we code for any mention of amnesty (see table 3.3).

32. This pattern of findings is also consistent if we use any mention of a pathway (see table 3.3).

33. The inter-coder reliability for episodic or thematic framing of legalization stories was 95 percent for mainstream media sources and 92 percent for conservative news sources. For more details about our coding strategy on episodic and thematic framing, see chapter 1, note 40.

34. Cristina Jimenez, *Melissa Harris-Perry*, MSBNC, February 2, 2013.

35. Former congressman Allen West (R-FL), *Your World with Neil Cavuto*, Fox News, March 5, 2013.

36. Gross 2008.

37. Congress.gov, "S.744—Border Security, Economic Opportunity, and Immigration Modernization Act," available at: https://www.congress.gov/bill/113th-congress/senate-bill/744 (accessed May 10, 2016).

38. Cohen 2011, 2013b.

39. The search term used in Lexis-Nexis to supply the stories to code for years in the United States was hlead ("pathway to citizenship") or ("path to citizenship") or ("CIR") or ("comprehensive immigration reform") or ("immigration reform") or ("immigration legalization") or ("legalizing immigrants") or ("immigrant legalization") or ("legalize immigrant!") or ("comprehensive immigra!") and body ("pathway to citizenship") or ("path to citizenship") w/25 (plural[years] or "long time" or "decade" or "decades" or "long term resident!" or "recent! arriv!"). To validate this search, we read each story to determine the accuracy of the initial Lexis-Nexis search. Two new variables were constructed from this qualitative analysis: stories mentioning the number of years an undocumented immigrant has lived in the United States *and* stories mentioning the number of years an undocumented immigrant has lived in the United States or discussion of the number of years it would take an undocumented immigrant to earn U.S. citizenship with some version of CIR. Over the years covered (2007–2013), we retrieved 69 stories in the *Washington Post*, 55 stories in the *Washington Times*, 39 segments on MSNBC, 34 segments on Fox News, and 102 segments on CNN. The inter-coder reliability for mentions of years in the United States in legalization stories was 100 percent for mainstream media sources and 96 percent for conservative news sources.

40. Anchor Rick Sanchez, *CNN Newsroom*, CNN, December 17, 2009.

41. Inter-coder reliability for pro or con framing of legalization stories was 93 percent for mainstream media sources and 92 percent for conservative news sources. The search terms used in Lexis-Nexis to supply the stories to code for these frames were as follows:

Economic frame: hlead ("pathway to citizenship") or ("path to citizenship") or ("CIR") or ("comprehensive immigration reform") or ("immigration reform") or ("immigration legalization") or ("legalizing immigrants") or ("immigrant legalization") or ("legalize immigrant!") or ("comprehensive immigra!") and body ("economic benefit!" or "economic cost!" or "economic growth" or "job!" or "employment" or "unemployment" or "economic impact!" or "economic effect!" or "economic" or "economy") w/25 ("immigra!"). Over the years covered, we retrieved 198 stories in the *Washington Post*, 113 stories in the *Washington Times*, 72 segments on MSNBC, 66 segments on Fox News, and 205 segments on CNN.

Familial frame: hlead ("pathway to citizenship") or ("path to citizenship") or ("CIR") or ("comprehensive immigration reform") or ("immigration reform") or ("immigration legalization") or ("legalizing immigrants") or ("immigrant legalization") or ("legalize immigrant!") or ("comprehensive immigra!") and body ("family" or "families" or "family member!" or "relative!" or "parent!" or "father!" or "mother!" or "brother!" or "sister!") w/25 ("immigra!"). Over the years covered, we retrieved 146 stories in the *Washington Post*, 86 stories in the *Washington Times*, 43 segments on MSNBC, 38 segments on Fox News, and 144 segments on CNN.

Rule of law frame: hlead ("pathway to citizenship") or ("path to citizenship") or ("CIR") or ("comprehensive immigration reform") or ("immigration reform") or ("immigration legalization") or ("legalizing immigrants") or ("immigrant legalization") or ("legalize immigrant!") or ("comprehensive immigra!") and body ("break! w/2 law!") or ("reward! w/3 break!") or ("reward! w/3 law!") or ("incent! w/3 break!") or ("illegal is illegal") or ("what part of illegal") or ("rule of law") w/25 ("immigra!"). Over the years covered, we retrieved 24 stories in the *Washington Post*, 34 stories in the *Washington Times*, 11 segments on MSNBC, 15 segments on Fox News, and 37 segments on CNN.

Criminal frame: hlead ("pathway to citizenship") or ("path to citizenship") or ("CIR") or ("comprehensive immigration reform") or ("immigration reform") or ("immigration legalization") or ("legalizing immigrants") or ("immigrant legalization") or ("legalize immigrant!") or ("comprehensive immigra!") and (body ("crime!" or "criminal!" or "felon!" or "safety" or "gang!" or "violence" or "DUI" or "convict" or "convicted" or "arraign!" or "violent") w/25 ("immigra!"). Over the years covered, we retrieved 109 stories in the *Washington Post*, 94 stories in the *Washington Times*, 48 segments on MSNBC, 64 segments on Fox News, and 130 segments on CNN.

To buttress findings from the quantitative content analysis, we also conducted a qualitative content analysis of amnesty and pathway segments from CNN, Fox News, and MSNBC from 2007, 2010, 2012, and 2013 that allowed us to more accurately describe the use of the restrictive rule of law frame and the restrictive and permissive economic frames.

42. We address this assumption about the familial frame's permissiveness later in this chapter.
43. As noted earlier, the years for our qualitative coding (2007, 2010, 2012, 2013) coincide with the years of our survey experiment coverage and were also the years in the 2007–2013 period when immigration was most salient as an issue, as measured by Gallup polls on the "most important problem."
44. Patrick Buchanan, *Hardball,* MSNBC, May 31, 2007.
45. Thomas Roberts, *MSNBC Special,* MSNBC, February 1, 2013.
46. Steve King, *Hannity,* Fox News, June 20, 2013.
47. Doug McKelway and Charles Grassley, *Fox Special Report with Bret Baier,* Fox News, February 13, 2013.
48. Shannon Travis and "Luis," *CNN Newsroom,* CNN, April 10, 2013.
49. Stories coded as including the familial frame were those that simply included language identifying this familial argument, regardless of whether the reporter, anchor, or guest favored or opposed it.
50. For a review of this research, see Waters and Pineau 2015.
51. Frame prevalence ranged by year from 1 to 9 percent for the rule of law, 18 to 37 percent for economic effects, 69 to 95 percent for crime, and 8 to 37 percent for familial.
52. We used the weighted data for these analyses since we could retain the full sample size; that was not the case for the 2007 and 2010 CCES.

53. In the 2011 study, the terms used to describe immigrants were slightly different, and in 2014 we did not vary the terms used to describe immigrants.
54. Lupia and McCubbins 1998.
55. Bartels 2002; Bullock 2011; Druckman, Peterson, and Slothuus 2013; Zaller 1992.
56. They are also consistent if we run an ordered probit analysis.
57. The results are consistent if we run an analysis controlling for the unevenly distributed variables. They are also consistent if we run an ordered probit analysis.
58. We also find a moderating effect with respect to education in this study and in the 2014 SSI study. In 2010 the effect of the amnesty condition (relative to the opportunity frame) was stronger among those low in education (β = −0.776) compared to those high in education (β = −0.453). However, we find the opposite pattern in 2014: the effect of the amnesty condition was stronger among those high in education (β = −0.636) compared to those low in education (β = −0.368). It is unclear why we would get different effects across the two studies on education (see tables A3.2 and A3.5 for full regression results).
59. Authors' analysis of Gallup "most important question" data from the iPoll archives.
60. We did test for whether there were any interaction effects between these two treatments and the source cues and did not find evidence of that.
61. All of these results are consistent if we control for variables that are unevenly distributed across experimental conditions (see table A3.4). They are also consistent if ordered probit is used instead of OLS.
62. In our 2015 study to test the perceived direction and effectiveness of different frames on legalization (for more details, see note 29), individuals perceived this frame as supportive of legalization (mean = 5.47), as expected, and as somewhat effective (mean = 4.94).
63. The results are also consistent if we control for unevenly distributed variables (see table A3.6 for full regression results). They are also consistent if we use ordered probit instead of OLS.
64. However, this is the case only when we control for variables that are unevenly balanced across experimental conditions.
65. In our 2015 study of the perceived direction and effectiveness of different frames, the latter frame was perceived as more supportive of legalization (mean = 5.55), and the former frame as more opposed to legalization (mean = 1.73), as expected. Individuals perceived the pro-legal frame (mean = 4.62) and the con-legal frame (mean = 4.28) as moderately effective.
66. We do not find any evidence of an interaction between this condition and the terms used to describe those without legal status. We do not find any evidence of imbalance on demographic indicators across experimental conditions. Finally, the results are consistent if ordered probit is used.
67. Masuoka and Junn 2013.
68. In our 2015 study of the perceived direction and effectiveness of different frames on legalization, individuals perceived the statement, "Some say that immigrant legalization will add over $1 trillion to the U.S. economy" as sup-

portive of legalization (mean = 5.41) and as somewhat effective (mean = 4.99). When asked to assess the statement that it will cost the United States over $1 trillion, they perceived the statement as opposed to legalization (mean = 2.06) and as moderately effective (mean = 4.73).

69. This condition is also statistically different from all of the positive economic frame conditions.

70. See, for example, Cargile, Merolla, and Pantoja 2014; Geer 2006; Lau 1982. These results hold up if we add controls for the variables that are unevenly distributed across experimental conditions (see table A3.8). They are also consistent if ordered probit is used instead of OLS.

71. Bullock 2011; Druckman, Peterson, and Slothuus 2013; Zaller 1992. In addition to partisans reacting differently to the frames, we find that Latinos became less supportive of legalization in the "Center for American Progress" condition, while those lower in education were particularly affected by the argument from the Heritage Foundation (see table A3.8 for full results). The finding for Latinos was very unexpected; it may be that Latinos in the control group were quite supportive of legalization, while introducing the "liberal" label turned some off. The stronger effect of the economic cost argument among lower-educated respondents may also have been related to this group facing more perceived competition with immigrants.

72. Luntz 2005.

Chapter 4: The DREAM Act and DREAMers

1. S.1291, 107th Cong., 2nd sess., June 20, 2002; H.R. 1918, 107th Cong., 1st sess., May 21, 2001.

2. S.2075, 109th Cong., 1st sess., November 18, 2005; S.1348, 110th Cong., 1st sess., May 10, 2007.

3. Authors' analysis of DREAM Act question in 2007 CCES immigration module.

4. H.R.5281, 111th Cong., 2nd sess., December 8, 2010. On the role of Latinos in the Reid-Angle race, see Barreto (2010).

5. News coverage in 2007 and 2010 on the DREAM Act represents nearly 30 percent of all such news coverage between 2007 and 2013.

6. Wallsten 2012.

7. Rahman 2012.

8. The White House 2010.

9. Coe et al. 2008; Morris 2007; Feldman et al. 2011.

10. Two content analyses were used to supply the findings for this section. The sample years were selected based on two criteria: years coinciding with our survey experiments and years in which "illegal" immigration was most salient. The quantitative content analysis included stories appearing between January 1, 2007, and December 31, 2013. The qualitative content analysis included stories from 2007, 2010, 2012, and 2013. The search term used in Lexis-Nexis to supply the stories to code for both the quantitative and qualitative analyses was the following: body ("DREAM act"). The quantitative analysis analyzed all stories resulting from this search (see table 4.1). The

qualitative analysis used either an interval sample or all stories resulting from this search depending on the size of the search. Stories unrelated to the DREAM Act were thrown out. Full sets of stories were analyzed for WP 2007 (n = 8), 2010 (n = 46), and 2013 (n = 24); WT 2007 (n = 23), 2010 (n = 33), and 2013 (n = 28); NYT 2007 (n = 11), 2010 (n = 44), and 2013 (n = 34); NYP 2010 (n = 4), 2012 (n = 8), and 2013 (n = 4); FOX 2007 (n = 7), 2010 (n = 96), and 2013 (n = 27); MSNBC 2007 (n = 0), 2010 (n = 83), and 2013 (n = 48); and CNN 2007 (n = 53), 2010 (n = 121), and 2013 (n = 35). Every third story was analyzed for WP 2012 (n = 58), WT 2012 (n = 31), FOX 2012 (n = 91), CNN 2012 (n = 94), and MSNBC 2012 (n = 58). A random sampling was analyzed for NYT 2012 (n = 50). The overall inter-coder reliability for qualitative coding on DREAM Act stories was 93 percent for mainstream media sources and 93 percent for conservative news sources.

11. We draw on data from the qualitative content analysis to evaluate tone.

12. We followed a grounded approach to qualitative coding and arrived at the following scheme and observations: use of language or phraseology that cast undocumented immigrants in a positive light. Following along the lines of previous work (Druckman and Parkin 2005), we decided to code tone by counting the number of positively and negatively slanted terms or combination phrases in each immigration story. Those stories with more than a 55/45 percent positive/negative split were coded as positive. Those stories with more than a 55/45 percent negative/positive split were coded as negative. Those stories falling in between were coded as neutral. Inter-coder reliability for the tone of DREAM Act stories was 88 percent for mainstream media sources and 93 percent for conservative news sources.

13. Although definitions of empathy abound, most scholars agree that it has two general dimensions: cognitive and affective. Cognitive empathy can be divided into three types of perspective-taking: self-focused, other-focused, or dual-focused (Oxley 2011). In self-focused perspective-taking, an individual puts herself in the position of the subject in focus and generates emotions that are similar to the subject's but shaped largely by her own psychology. The other-focused individual imagines how the subject in focus is feeling and generates emotions largely congruent with those of the subject. Finally, a dual-focused individual both puts herself in the position of the subject and imagines how the subject is feeling. Affective or emotional empathy has been defined as the visceral, reactive feelings (empathy, sympathy, sadness, soft-heartedness, concern) that individuals can experience after exposure to empathetic stimuli or in response to experiencing cognitive empathy. For the purposes of this book, we choose not to distinguish between the types of empathy that words or phrases in the media can evoke primarily because empathetic language can often induce multiple types of empathy and the type of empathy evoked is often dependent on the psychological particulars of the reader or viewer. Inter-coder reliability for empathy evoked by DREAM Act stories was 84 percent for mainstream media sources and 80 percent for conservative news sources.

14. Lawrence O'Donnell, *The Last Word with Lawrence O'Donnell*, MSNBC, 2010.

15. Anchor Brian Sullivan, *Your World with Neil Cavuto*, Fox News, December 31, 2010.

16. We find that 80 percent of DREAM Act stories in the *New York Post* included empathetic elements, but this figure is derived from a very small number of stories—only sixteen in total.

17. Amnesty was mentioned in 35 percent of Fox News stories, 29 percent of *Washington Times* stories, 24 percent of CNN stories (in 2010), 21 percent of *New York Times* stories, 16 percent of MSNBC stories, and 15 percent of *Washington Post* stories. As noted earlier, overall amnesty mentions are skewed high owing in large part to the restrictionist coverage of CNN anchors Glenn Beck and Lou Dobbs in 2007.

18. Permissive elements included using the following terms in depicting the DREAM Act: "children," "young," "youth," "kids," "undocumented immigrant," "path to citizenship," and "students." In addition, "Dreamers" were discussed as "deserving" and "less morally culpable." Conversely, restrictive elements included the terms "illegals," "aliens," "illegal immigrants," "anchor babies," "chain migration," "stealth amnesty," and "amnesty." Moreover, "students" were talked about as being part of the problem. More extreme codes were applied to stories using 75 percent or more of these restrictive elements in referring to the DREAM Act, while "slightly" was applied to stories including between 50 and 75 percent of them. Those stories containing an even number of permissive and restrictive terms were coded as "even" and given a value of 0. Inter-coder reliability for the use of permissive or restrictive language in DREAM Act stories was 88 percent for mainstream media sources and 88 percent for conservative news sources.

19. Bill Tucker and Kris Kobach (UM-KC), *Lou Dobbs Tonight*, CNN, March 1, 2007.

20. Jorge Mursuli, *Countdown with Keith Olbermann*, MSNBC, October 6, 2010.

21. Neil Cavuto, interview with Arizona Speaker of the House Kirk Adams, *Your World with Neil Cavuto*, Fox News, November 11, 2010.

22. Inter-coder reliability for episodic or thematic framing of DREAM Act stories was 92 percent for mainstream media sources and 96 percent for conservative news sources.

23. *Washington Post* 2010a.

24. The undocumented immigrant Celso, *The Last Word with Lawrence O'Donnell*, MSNBC, 2010.

25. Rich Lowry of the *National Review*, "The Political War over Immigration Continues," *On the Record with Greta Van Susteren*, Fox News, July 30, 2010.

26. Peri 2011; Ottaviano and Peri 2012; Card 2001.

27. Cullen, Fisher, and Applegate 2000.

28. Oliver 2006; Zivkovic et al. 2010; Miceli 2005.

29. Kiran Chetry, *American Morning*, CNN, December 8, 2010.

30. Gorak 2010.

31. We also included a question on our 2011 study, but used a different scale for the dependent variable. We report on these analyses in the text as well.

32. More specifically, respondents read: "Some say illegal or undocumented immigrants . . ."

33. In a study conducted in June 2015, we tested the perceived direction and effectiveness of this frame for the DREAM Act. We found clear evidence that people perceive this frame as being supportive of the DREAM Act. When

asked to indicate whether the frame reflected opposition or support for the policy on a seven-point scale, mean placement was 6.06. This frame was also rated as highly effective (mean = 5.93 on a seven-point scale).

34. For the 2012 survey, we confined our analysis to those who were not exposed to the amnesty frame. We discuss that frame later in the chapter.

35. We used the weighted data for 2012 since it made no difference for the sample size. The results for the unweighted data show the same pattern.

36. Although randomization worked as intended across most demographic and dispositional indicators, there are one or two variables in each survey year that are not evenly distributed in balance tests. The results remain the same if we run a regression analysis with controls for the few variables that are unbalanced across experimental conditions. See tables A4.1–A4.3 and A4.6. The findings are also the same if ordered probit is used instead of OLS.

37. Druckman and Leeper 2012. Another possibility is that as the public learns more about the issue they may become better able to counterargue with a given frame (Chong and Druckman 2007b).

38. For a review, see Chong and Druckman (2007b).

39. We also tested whether reaction to the frames varies by educational attainment, Latinos, whether the respondent has children in the home, and the immigration history of the respondent's family. We find no evidence of a moderating effect of the child frame according to these measures. We also tested for moderating effects by ideology and find that they mirror the moderating effects for partisanship.

40. Knoll, Redlawsk, and Sanborn 2010.

41. The findings are the same if we include the variables that are unevenly distributed across experimental conditions (see tables A4.1–A4.3 and A4.6). We also ran ordered probit analyses, and the results are the same as with OLS. We use OLS for ease of presentation.

42. That is, the interaction term is significant only in these years. For 2012, this is the case only for the ordered probit analyses. The p-values on the interaction term are just outside of statistical significance for the OLS analyses. To better compare the results across the years, we illustrate the effects from the OLS analyses in the figure but include the ordered probit results in table A4.3.

43. We find a similar pattern if we look at the moderating effects by Fox News viewership in 2007 (the only year for which we had a measure of news viewership). Among non–Fox News viewers, exposure to the child frame increased support for the DREAM Act by about a quarter of a unit ($\beta = 0.362$, $p = 0.026$). Among Fox News viewers, the exposure to the child frame increased support by more than half a unit ($\beta = 0.642, p = 0.000$).

44. In the ordered probit analyses, the p-value on the child frame is statistically significant at 0.046 for Republicans.

45. Druckman, Peterson, and Slothuus (2013) look at different frames on the DREAM Act than those we look at here. For pro-frames, they look at the opportunities that the act would give to young people (strong frame) and the public's support for the DREAM Act (weak frame), while for con-frames they look at the argument that the act would encourage more illegal immigration (strong) and that it is not well designed and too political (weak).

46. In a study conducted in June 2015 in which we tested the perceived direction

and effectiveness of frames on the DREAM Act, we found that participants perceived this frame as clearly opposed to the DREAM Act (mean = 2.89 on a seven-point scale). They also perceived it as less effective (mean = 3.46) than the child frame.

47. Luntz 2005.

48. For the DREAM Act, the control group includes those who were and were not exposed to the child frame. Later in the chapter, we distinguish the effects for the child and amnesty frames.

49. The results are also the same if we control for the variables that are unevenly distributed across experimental conditions and if we use ordered probit (see tables A4.4 and A4.7).

50. Druckman, Peterson, and Slothuus 2013.

51. The results are consistent if we control for variables that are unevenly distributed across experimental conditions and if we use ordered probit.

52. The interaction term is not significant in the DACA model ($p = 0.31$), though the sign is the same as in the DREAM Act analysis. The negative sign on the interaction term suggests that the amnesty condition has a stronger negative effect on both policies as respondents move from being Democrats to Republicans. Since the interaction terms are not directly interpretable, we discuss the change in mean support for both policies moving from the control wording to the amnesty wording by partisan group.

53. That the effects wash out for independents could be due to the higher collinearity introduced by adding more interaction terms.

54. The findings are similar if we control for variables that are unevenly distributed across experimental conditions (see tables A4.6 and A4.8) and if we run ordered probit.

55. We also find a moderating effect for some of the frames on support for DACA depending on whether the respondent had children. Among those without children, the episodic non-empathetic frame and the thematic empathetic frame increased support for the policy by about one-third of a unit ($p < 0.05$, two-tailed). The episodic empathetic frame is also close to statistically significant if a one-tailed test is used ($p = 0.085$, one-tailed).

56. The results are similar if we include controls for the variables that are unevenly distributed across experimental conditions (see tables A4.6 and A4.8) or if we use ordered probit.

57. Condon 2013.

58. Davis and Gomez 2013.

59. Murray 2014; *Tea Party News* 2013.

Chapter 5: Framing Deportations in the News Media and Public Opinion

1. Library of Congress, "Primary Documents of American History: Alien and Sedition Acts," available at: https://www.loc.gov/rr/program/bib/ourdocs/Alien.html (accessed May 10, 2016).

2. "An Act Concerning Aliens," facsimile version available at: http://www

.ourdocuments.gov/document_data/pdf/doc_016.pdf (accessed March 30, 2016).

3. Zolberg 2005.
4. While a historical study of immigration opinion is beyond the purview of this book, we tried to find polls of public opinion on deportation regarding Operation Wetback in the 1950s and Operation Gatekeeper in the 1990s, but found no examples from Gallup or other polling organizations.
5. Cooper and O'Neil 2005.
6. Illegal Immigration Reform and Immigrant Responsibility Act of 1996, Pub. L. No. 104-208, 110 Stat. 3889 (1996).
7. Gonzalez-Barrera and Krogstad 2014; Kliegman 2014.
8. Coe et al. 2008; Morris 2007; Feldman et al. 2011.
9. Two content analyses were used to supply the findings for this section. The quantitative content analysis included stories appearing between January 1, 2007, and December 31, 2013. The qualitative content analysis included stories from 2007, 2010, 2012, and 2013. Sample years were selected based on two criteria: years coinciding with our survey experiments and years in which "illegal" immigration was most salient. The search term used in Lexis-Nexis to supply the stories to code for qualitative content analysis was the following: hlead (deport!) for the *Washington Post*, the *Washington Times*, CNN, and Fox News; body (deport!) and body (immigra!) for MSNBC. MSNBC required a different, broader search term because of the small number of stories returned by the other search term. The quantitative analysis analyzed all stories resulting from this search (see table 5.1). Additionally, the qualitative analysis analyzed either a systematic random sample or all stories resulting from this search depending on the size of the search. Stories unrelated to deportation were thrown out. Full sets of stories were analyzed for WP 2007 ($n = 42$), 2010 ($n = 53$), 2012 ($n = 71$), and 2013 ($n = 46$); WT 2007 ($n = 41$), 2010 ($n = 13$), 2012 ($n = 43$), and 2013 ($n = 38$); FOX 2007 ($n = 39$), 2010 ($n = 13$), 2012 ($n = 17$), and 2013 ($n = 5$); MSNBC 2007 ($n = 24$), 2010 ($n = 43$), and 2012 ($n = 164$); CNN 2007 ($n = 28$), 2010 ($n = 33$), 2012 ($n = 123$), and 2013 ($n = 11$); NYP 2007 ($n = 17$), 2010 ($n = 19$), 2012 ($n = 35$), and 2013 ($n = 5$). Every third story was analyzed for MSNBC 2013 ($n = 90$). A random sample of stories was analyzed for NYT 2007 ($n = 50$), 2010 ($n = 50$), 2012 ($n = 50$), and 2013 ($n = 50$). The overall inter-coder reliability for qualitative coding on deportation stories was 92 percent for mainstream media sources and 93 percent for conservative news sources.
10. Following a grounded approach to qualitative coding, we arrived at the following scheme and observations: use of language or phraseology that cast undocumented immigrants in a positive or negative light. Following along the lines of previous work (Druckman and Parkin 2005), we decided to code tone by counting the number of positively and negatively slanted terms or combination phrases that appear within each immigration story. Those stories with more than a 55/45 percent positive/negative split were coded as positive. Those stories with more than a 55/45 percent negative/positive split were coded as negative. Those stories falling in between were coded as neutral. Inter-coder reliability for the tone of deportation stories was 88 per-

cent for mainstream media sources and 92 percent for conservative news sources.

11. Restrictiveness was measured on a scale from 1 to 5 where 1 = almost entirely restrictive (76 to 100 percent), 2 = restrictive (51 to 75 percent), 3 = even/neutral (50 percent), 4 = permissive (51 to 75 percent), and 5 = almost entirely restrictive (76 to 100 percent). "Restrictive" is defined as that which supports deportation policies that effectively or intentionally restrict migration to the United States. "Permissive" is defined as that which opposes deportation policies that effectively or intentionally ease or permit migration to the United States. We used a qualitative content analysis to derive the findings for this section on permissiveness.

12. Gulasekaram and Ramakrishnan 2015.

13. For more on empathy and our coding, see chapter 4, note 13. Inter-coder reliability for empathy evoked by deportation stories was 88 percent for mainstream media sources and 92 percent for conservative news sources.

14. CNN anchor Suzanne Malveaux and CNN senior Latin Affairs editor Rafael Allen, *Around the World*, CNN, June 12, 2013.

15. White (2010).

16. Haynes 2014.

17. On improving reader and viewer attitudes, see Batson et al. 1997. On increasing policy support among readers and viewers, see Haynes 2014.

18. We use a qualitative content analysis to derive the findings for this section on empathetic language.

19. We used a qualitative content analysis to derive the findings for this section on episodic and thematic framing. Inter-coder reliability for the episodic or thematic framing of deportation stories was 88 percent for mainstream media sources and 92 percent for conservative news sources.

20. All stories that were not coded as episodic were by default coded as thematic.

21. ICE field director Jim Hayes and correspondent Casey Wian, *Lou Dobbs Tonight*, CNN, August 20, 2007.

22. Host John Gibson and correspondent Heather Nauert, *The Big Story with John Gibson*, Fox News, October 16, 2007.

23. Antonio Villaraigosa and Ed Schultz, *The Ed Schultz Show*, MSNBC, February 6, 2013.

24. Differences in the use of empathetic frames between episodic and thematic news coverage are stronger in print media (60 percent versus 26 percent) than in the case of cable news media (58 percent versus 47 percent). In both instances, the differences are statistically significant ($p < .001$).

25. Although we attempt to conceptualize and provide examples isolating these arguments, in practice it is important to note that many of these arguments appear in combination with others. Inter-coder reliability for pro or con framing of deportation stories was 93 percent for mainstream media sources and 93 percent for conservative news sources.

26. Rep. Tom Tancredo (R-CO) and host Tucker Carlson, *Tucker*, MSNBC, December 5, 2007.

27. Host Neil Cavuto and guest Joseph Vento, *Your World with Neil Cavuto*, Fox News, August 25, 2010.

28. Bill O'Reilly, *The O'Reilly Factor*, Fox News, August 20, 2007.
29. Smith 2012.
30. Host Bill O'Reilly, *The O'Reilly Factor*, Fox News, October 15, 2007.
31. Dinan 2013.
32. Coders were instructed to denote when any of the pro- or con-deportation arguments appeared in a deportation story. The appearance of an argument consisted of a liberal strategy in which coders were instructed to count as an affirmative appearance instances in which the text of the story either explicitly made the argument or could have implicitly primed the argument by mentioning related terms or phrasing. Inter-coder reliability for this portion of the content analysis was 91 percent.
33. Senior Latin affairs editor Rafael Romo and guests Evelyn Rivera, Gorte Teodoro, and Renata Teodoro, *Around the World*, CNN, June 12, 2013.
34. *Washington Post* 2010b.
35. Host Chris Wallace and guests William Kristol and Joe Trippi, *Fox News Sunday*, Fox News, June 17, 2012.
36. Al Sharpton, *Politics Nation*, December 6, 2012.
37. Saslow 2012.
38. Seper 2012.
39. Cohen 2013a.
40. We use a qualitative content analysis to derive the findings for this section on pro- and con-deportation frames.
41. The extremely small number of deportation stories may explain why the *New York Post* does not fit the pattern established by the other sources.
42. Deparle 2011.
43. Cohen 2011, 2013a.
44. According to balance tests, individuals were only unevenly distributed across experimental conditions by education level. Controlling for this measure does not alter the results (see table A5.1).
45. As in prior chapters, we tested the perceived direction and effectiveness of the frames in a study run via Mechanical Turk in the spring of 2015. As expected, individuals perceived the first two frames as being supportive of deportations (legal mean = 5.18; security mean = 5.06) and the latter two frames as being opposed (families mean = 2.68; costs mean = 2.63). With respect to effectiveness, the families frame was viewed as most effective (mean = 4.86), followed by the costs frame (mean = 4.65), the legal frame (mean = 4.43), and the security frame (mean = 3.89).
46. There were conditions where the frames were pitted against each other, but with so many arguments, the results become difficult to present and interpret. For analysis with single versus competing frames, see table A5.2.
47. Masuoka and Junn 2013.
48. Ramakrishnan et al. 2010.
49. See note 45 for details.
50. Merolla, Ramakrishnan, and Haynes 2013.
51. Druckman and Leeper 2012.
52. The findings remain the same if we run a regression with dummy variables for exposure to the legal argument, the security argument, the families argument, or the cost argument, with no argument as the baseline (see table A5.1).

53. See column 2 of table A5.1.
54. Participants were evenly balanced across experimental conditions on a host of demographic and attitudinal variables, though we find an imbalance on political interest ($p = 0.03$) and partisanship ($p = 0.02$) and close to a significant imbalance on gender ($p = 0.08$). We also had a manipulation for the terms used to describe those without legal status, which we present in a later chapter.
55. As expected, individuals in our 2015 study perceived both frames as supportive of deportations (cultural mean = 4.49; economic frame mean = 4.97). The economic frame was perceived as slightly less effective (mean = 4.21) than the legal frame, but as more effective than the cultural frame (mean = 3.46) and the security frame.
56. The results are the same if we run a regression analysis with variables for each treatment condition and controls for the variables that are unbalanced across experimental conditions (See table A5.3). They are also the same if we use ordered probit instead of OLS.
57. Importantly, we find no significant evidence that family frames were prominent in news coverage, although people might have been exposed in other ways to the idea that deportations disrupt families.
58. Indeed, these time-based arguments have made their way into decisionmaking by judges (Preston 2014) as well as by U.S. Immigration and Customs Enforcement (Prine 2014). These arguments, in some key respects, take up the arguments made by Joseph Carens (2010).
59. Participants were evenly balanced according to a host of demographic and political attitudinal measures across experimental conditions. The one exception is that participants were unbalanced with respect to education on the 2012 study ($p = 0.03$). We run an analysis controlling for this variable in table A5.5; the results are the same as those presented in the text. The results are also the same if ordered probit is used instead of OLS.
60. These differences are significant according to an ANOVA ($p = 0.004$), though it is clearly the case that there is no significant difference between fifteen and twenty years.
61. Lupia and McCubbins 1998.
62. M. Cohen 2013; see also *New York Times*/CBS News poll, April 24–28, 2013.
63. Zaller 1992.
64. Merolla and Zechmeister 2009; Kim 1999.
65. Merolla et al. 2013.

Chapter 6: What's in a Name: Illegal, Undocumented, or Unauthorized?

1. Lakoff 2004; Fine 1992; Gilens 1999; Schram 1995; Eyben and Moncrieffe 2007.
2. Downes 2007.
3. National Association of Hispanic Journalists 2006; ColorLines, "Drop the I-Word. Don't Call People 'Illegals,'" available at: http://www.colorlines.com/droptheiword/take-action/charlotte-observer-action.html (accessed March 30, 2016).

4. ColorLines and Applied Research Center, "Drop the I-Word: Don't Call People 'Illegals,'" 2010, available at: http://www.colorlines.com/content /campaign-toolkit (accessed April 2, 2011).

5. Lelyveld 2006.

6. *Washington Times* 2010.

7. Bean and Lowell 2009, 70.

8. We include analysis of the *New York Times* and its conservative alternative, the *New York Post*, to add greater breadth to our findings.

9. One quantitative content analysis was used to supply the findings for this section. The sample years were selected primarily to correspond with when the survey experiments were fielded. This quantitative content analysis included stories appearing between January 1, 2007, and December 31, 2013. The search term used in Lexis-Nexis to supply the stories to code for the quantitative content analysis was the following: hlead ("immigra!" or "illegal alien" or "illegal aliens" or PLURAL ("illegals") or "deport" or "deported" or "deportation!" or "undocumented immigra!" or "unauthorized immigra!").

10. Sullivan 2012.

11. For example, in the *New York Times*, 22 percent of editorial-page content on immigrants without legal status between 2007 and 2013 used the term "undocumented," while only 3.2 percent of news stories did so. The overall average in the *New York Times* is 6.1 percent, as news stories on immigrants without legal status (1,260 stories) were so much more voluminous than editorial-page content on the issue (231 stories). In response to a 2012 campaign to get the Associated Press to "drop the I-word," the news organization noted that the term would no longer be a "preferred term" starting in 2011, but it remained part of the *Associated Press Stylebook*, a guide commonly used by journalists around the world(Weinger 2012).

12. Colford 2013; Rivas 2013b.

13. Sullivan 2012.

14. Haughney 2013.

15. Notably, of the two mentions of "illegal aliens" by Democratic senators in the congressional session, only one involved Senate bill 744, the comprehensive immigration reform bill; in a floor speech on June 24, 2013, Bill Nelson (D-FL) argued for more spending on maritime border protection. The other mention was on September 26, 2013, when Mary Landrieu (D-LA) mentioned "illegal aliens" in the context of continuing appropriations and funding for Customs and Border Patrol. In the *New York Times*, for example, use of "illegal immigrant" jumped from 27 percent in 2014 to 52 percent of stories on the unauthorized in 2015.

16. Results not shown. See also Sen 2015. Portions of this section were published in Merolla, Ramakrishnan, and Haynes (2013), though that paper used only the data from 2007. We have extended the analysis through additional experimental studies.

17. Druckman 2001, 2004.

18. Knoll, Redlawsk, and Sanborn 2010.

19. Masuoka and Junn 2013.

20. Ibid.

21. In the analyses that follow, we do not use survey weights for the 2007 and 2010 YouGov surveys given that it dramatically reduces our sample size. We do, however, use survey weights for the 2011 and 2012 YouGov studies. We do not have survey weights for the Mechanical Turk sample or the SSI sample.

22. These results hold up if we run regressions controlling for variables that are unevenly distributed across experimental conditions (see tables A3.1, A3.2, and A3.3).

23. The p-value among those in the first generation is 0.12 and among those in the second generation it is 0.15.

24. This result holds up in a regression with controls for the variables that are unevenly distributed (see table A3.6).

25. One question was on support for S744, the Senate bill we report on in the appendix to chapter 3, and the other was on the economic rationales for and against legalization, also reported in that chapter.

26. The results are the same if we add controls for the variables that are unevenly distributed across experimental conditions (see table A4.1).

27. This effect drops out in the regression analysis controlling for other experimental conditions (see table A4.2).

28. These results are the same with controls for variables that are unevenly distributed across experimental conditions (see table A4.2).

29. Mean support for DACA was as follows across the experimental conditions: illegal immigrant (mean = 0.297); undocumented immigrant (mean = 0.186); and illegal alien (mean = 0.088). The difference between the "illegal immigrant" and "illegal alien" conditions is statistically significant ($p = 0.038$) (see table A4.2).

30. See table A6.3 for full regression results. We also find a moderating effect for whether the respondent was Latino or not, with the undocumented frame increasing support among non-Latinos but not Latinos.

31. We find the same effect for the DACA question in that study.

32. The results are the same if we run a regression controlling for the other experimental conditions and the variables that are unevenly distributed across experimental conditions (see tables A5.3 and A5.5).

33. See Define American, "About Define American," available at: http://www .defineamerican.com/page/about/about-defineamerican (accessed March 30, 2016).

Chapter 7: Conclusions

1. One notable exception, which we discuss later, is the case of immigrant adults who react against the illegal frame and become even more supportive of legalization.

2. Iyengar 1991.

3. Arnold 1990; Hurley and Hill 2003; Druckman and Nelson 2003.

4. Waters and Pineau 2015.

5. On the default image of an "illegal immigrant" as a Mexican immigrant, see Ramakrishnan et al. 2010 and Pérez 2010. On the effect of cueing Latino in-

stead of European origins on the opinions of American voters, see Brader, Valentino, and Suhay 2008.

6. Lau 1982, 1985; Fiske 1980.
7. On the costs of different courses of action, see Geer 2006; Jones and McGillis 1976. On the motivation to avoid costs, see Kahneman and Tversky 1979; Lupia and McCubbins 1998.
8. Marcus, Neuman, and MacKuen 2000.
9. On the greater impact of frames to which we have not been exposed, see Druckman and Leeper 2012; Chong and Druckman 2007a. On frames from unexpected sources, see Lupia and McCubbins 1998.
10. Cullen, Fisher, and Applegate 2000; Miceli 2005; Oliver 2006; Zivkovic et al. 2010.
11. Bullock 2011; Druckman, Peterson, and Slothuus 2013; Zaller 1992.
12. On the presence of source cues, see Bullock 2011; Druckman, Peterson, and Slothuus 2013.
13. In later years, we also saw some evidence of those for whom the issue was high in relevance moving in the direction of cues that painted immigrants and immigration policies in a more positive light. In 2010, when asked about whether immigrants who had been in the United States longer should be given special consideration and not be deported, individuals in the first and second generations exposed to the undocumented frame became less supportive of deportations compared to their counterparts exposed to the illegal immigrant frame. That we found fewer differences on the positive frames may also reflect that these groups are generally more supportive of policies like legalization and the DREAM Act; thus, it is not very likely that positive frames would have pushed them much further.
14. Ramakrishnan and Silva 2015.
15. Byrne and Hart 2009; Hart and Nisbet 2011; Skurnik et al. 2005.
16. For suggestions on new policy dimensions, see Snow et al. 1986; see also our discussion in chapter 2.
17. Rivas 2013a.
18. Gray 2013.
19. Wang 2015.

Appendices

1. Massey, Durand, and Malone 2002.
2. Gulasekaram and Ramakrishnan 2015.
3. Passel 2006.
4. Massey, Durand, and Malone 2002.
5. Smith 2011.
6. Passel 2006.
7. Schmitt 2001.
8. Gulasekaram and Ramakrishnan 2015.
9. They are also consistent if ordered probit is used instead of OLS.
10. All of the results are consistent if ordered probit is used.

References

Abrajano, Marisa, and Simran Singh. 2008. "Examining the Link Between Issue Attitudes and News Source: The Case of Latinos and Immigration Reform." *Political Behavior* 31(1): 1–30.

Allen, Mike, and Jim Vandehei. 2013. "Behind the Curtain: Immigration Reform Heads for Slow Death." *Politico*, July 9.

Allport, Gordon W. 1954. *The Nature of Prejudice*. Cambridge, Mass.: Addison-Wesley.

Altemeyer, Bob. 1988. *Enemies of Freedom: Understanding Right-Wing Authoritarianism*. San Francisco: Jossey-Bass Publishers.

Arceneaux, Kevin, and Martin Johnson. 2013. *Changing Minds or Changing Channels? Partisan News in an Age of Choice*. Chicago: University of Chicago Press.

Archibold, Randal C. 2010. "On Border Violence, Truth Pales Compared to Ideas." *New York Times*, June 19.

Arnold, R. Douglas. 1990. *The Logic of Congressional Action*. New Haven, Conn.: Yale University Press.

Barreto, Matt. 2010. "Proving the Exit Polls Wrong—Harry Reid Did Win over 90% of the Latino Vote." Latino Decision, November 15. Available at: http://www.latinodecisions.com/blog/2010/11/15/proving-the-exit-polls-wrong-harry-reid-did-win-over-90-of-the-latino-vote/ (accessed March 30, 2016).

Bartels, Larry M. 2002. "Beyond the Running Tally: Partisan Bias in Political Perceptions." *Political Behavior* 24(2): 117–50.

———. 2008. *Unequal Democracy: The Political Economy of the New Gilded Age*. New York: Russell Sage Foundation.

Batson, C. Daniel, Marina P. Polycarpou, Eddie Harmon-Jones, Heidi J. Imhoff, Erin C. Mitchener, Lori L. Bednar, Tricia R. Klein, and Lori Highberger. 1997. "Empathy and Attitudes: Can Feeling for a Member of a Stigmatized Group Improve Feelings toward the Group?" *Journal of Personality and Social Psychology* 72 (1): 105–18.

Bauder, David. 2009. "Is Dobbs Doomed? Controversial CNN Host Challenges His Own Network." Associated Press, August 4.

Bean, Frank D., and B. Lindsay Lowell. 2009. "Unauthorized Migration." In *The New Americans: A Guide to Immigration Since 1965*, edited by Mary C. Waters and Reed Ueda. Cambridge, Mass.: Harvard University Press.

Berg, Justin Allen. 2009. "White Public Opinion Toward Undocumented Immigrants: Threat and Interpersonal Environment." *Sociological Perspectives* 52(1): 39–58.

Berinsky, Adam J., Gregory A. Huber, and Gabriel S. Lenz. 2012. "Evaluating Online Labor Markets for Experimental Research: Amazon.com's Mechanical Turk." *Political Analysis* 20(3): 351–68.

Billig, Michael, and Henri Tajfel. 1973. "Social Categorization and Similarity in Intergroup Behaviour." *European Journal of Social Psychology* 3(1): 27–52.

Birney, Mayling, Michael J. Graetz, and Ian Shapiro. 2006. "Public Opinion and the Push to Repeal the Estate Tax." *National Tax Journal* 59(3): 439–61.

Blalock, Hubert M. 1967. *Toward a Theory of Minority-Group Relations*. New York: Wiley.

Bloemraad, Irene, Els de Graauw, and Rebecca Hamlin. 2015. "Immigrants in the Media: Civic Visibility in the USA and Canada." *Journal of Ethnic and Migration Studies* 41(6): 874–96.

Blumer, Herbert. 1958. "Race Prejudice as a Sense of Group Position." *Pacific Sociological Review* 1(1): 3–7.

Brader, Ted, Nicholas A. Valentino, and Elizabeth Suhay. 2008. "What Triggers Public Opposition to Immigration? Anxiety, Group Cues, and Immigration Threat." *American Journal of Political Science* 52(4): 959–78.

Branton, Regina, and Johanna Dunaway. 2008. "English- and Spanish-Language Media Coverage of Immigration: A Comparative Analysis." *Social Science Quarterly* 89(4): 1006–22.

———. 2009. "Spatial Proximity to the U.S.–Mexico Border and Newspaper Coverage of Immigration Issues." *Political Research Quarterly* 62(2): 289–302.

Brewer, Marilynn B., and Madelyn Silver. 1978. "Ingroup Bias as a Function of Task Characteristics." *European Journal of Social Psychology* 8(3): 393–400.

Brewer, Paul R. 2001. "Value Words and Lizard Brains: Do Citizens Deliberate About Appeals to Their Core Values?" *Political Psychology* 22(1): 45–64.

Bullock, John G. 2011. "Elite Influence on Public Opinion in an Informed Electorate." *American Political Science Review* 105(3): 496–515.

Burns, Peter, and James G. Gimpel. 2000. "Economic Insecurity, Prejudicial Stereotypes, and Public Opinion on Immigration Policy." *Political Science Quarterly* 115(2): 201–25.

Byrne, Sahara, and P. Sol Hart. 2009. "The Boomerang Effect: A Synthesis of Findings and a Preliminary Theoretical Framework." *Communication Yearbook* 33: 3–37.

Campbell, Angus, Philip Converse, Warren Miller, and Donald Stokes. 1960. *The American Voter*. New York: John Wiley and Sons.

Card, David. 2001. "Immigrant Inflows, Native Outflows, and the Local Labor Market Impacts of Higher Immigration." *Journal of Labor Economics* 19(1): 22–64.

Carens, Joseph H. 2010. *Immigrants and the Right to Stay*. Cambridge, Mass: MIT Press.

Cargile, Ivy A. M., Jennifer L. Merolla, and Adrian D. Pantoja. 2014. "The Effects of Media Framing on Attitudes Toward Undocumented Immigration." In *Scholars and Southern Californian Immigrants in Dialogue: New Conversations in Public Sociology*, edited by Victoria Carty, Rafael Luévano, and Tekle Mariam Woldemikael. Lanham, Md.: Lexington Books.

Carroll, Chris. 2013. "U.S. House Declares Immigration Bill 'Dead on Arrival.'" *Times Free Press*, July 1.

Chavez, Leo R. 2013. *Shadowed Lives: Undocumented Immigrants in American Society*, 3rd ed. Fort Worth, Tex.: Harcourt Brace College Publishers/Wadsworth.

Chong, Dennis, and James N. Druckman. 2007a. "Framing Public Opinion in Competitive Democracies." *American Political Science Review* 101(04): 637–55.

———. 2007b. "Framing Theory." *Annual Review of Political Science* 10(1): 103–26.

———. 2007c. "A Theory of Framing and Opinion Formation in Competitive Elite Environments." *Journal of Communication* 57(1): 99–118.

Citrin, Jack, Donald P. Green, Christopher Muste, and Cara Wong. 1997. "Public Opinion Toward Immigration Reform: The Role of Economic Motivations." *Journal of Politics* 59(3): 858–81.

Citrin, Jack, Beth Reingold, and Donald P. Green. 1990. "American Identity and the Politics of Ethnic Change." *Journal of Politics* 52(4): 1124–54.

Coe, Kevin, David Tewksbury, Bradley J. Bond, Kristin L. Drogos, Robert W. Porter, Ashley Yahn, and Yuanyuan Zhang. 2008. "Hostile News: Partisan Use and Perceptions of Cable News Programming." *Journal of Communication* 58(2): 201–19.

Cohen, Elizabeth F. 2011. "Reconsidering U.S. Immigration Reform: The Temporal Principle of Citizenship." *Perspectives on Politics* 9(3): 575–83.

———. 2013a. "Who Would the Founding Fathers Deport?" *Washington Post*, February 3.

———. 2013b. "Should Illegal Immigrants Become Citizens? Let's Ask the Founding Fathers." *Washington Post*, March 12.

Cohen, Micah. 2013. "Signs of a Shift on Immigration Among GOP Rank-and-File." FiveThirtyEight (*New York Times* blog), February 8.

Colford, Paul. 2013. "'Illegal Immigrant' No More." Associated Press, The Definitive Source, April 2.

Condon, Stephanie. 2013. "Cantor Signals Shift on Immigration, Backs Dream Act Principles." CBS News, February 5.

Cooper, Betsy, and Kevin O'Neil. 2005. *Lessons from the Immigration Reform and Control Act of 1986.* Washington, D.C.: Migration Policy Institute.

Craig, Maureen A., and Jennifer A. Richeson. 2012. "Coalition or Derogation? How Perceived Discrimination Influences Intraminority Intergroup Relations." *Journal of Personality and Social Psychology* 102(4): 759.

———. 2013. "Not in My Backyard! Authoritarianism, Social Dominance Orientation, and Support for Strict Immigration Policies at Home and Abroad." *Political Psychology* 35(3) 417–29.

Cullen, Francis T., Bonnie S. Fisher, and Brandon K. Applegate. 2000. "Public Opinion About Punishment and Corrections." *Crime and Justice* 27: 1–79.

Davis, Susan, and Alan Gomez. 2013. "GOP Districts Have Become Whiter, More Conservative." *USA Today*, May 30.

DellaVigna, Stefano, and Ethan Kaplan. 2006. "The Fox News Effect: Media Bias and Voting." Working Paper 12169. Cambridge, Mass.: National Bureau of Economic Research.

Deparle, Jason. 2011. "The Anti-Immigration Crusader." *New York Times*, April 17.

Dinan, Stephen. 2012. "Deportation Statistics Said to Be Inflated." *Washington Times*, August 23.

———. 2013. "Illegals Snared as Immigration Debate Continues; Obama Pressed to Halt All Deportations," *Washington Times*, August 19.

Dover, Tessa L., Brenda Major, and Charyl R. Kaiser. 2016. "Members of High-Status Groups Are Threatened by Pro-Diversity Organizational Messages." *Journal of Experimental Social Psychology* 62(1): 58–67.

Dovidio, John F., and Samuel L. Gaertner. 2004. "Aversive Racism." In *Advances in Experimental Social Psychology*, edited by Mark P. Zanna. London: Elsevier Academic Press.

Downes, Lawrence. 2007. "What Part of 'Illegal' Don't You Understand?" *New York Times*, October 28.

Druckman, James N. 2001. "On the Limits of Framing Effects: Who Can Frame?" *Journal of Politics* 63(4): 1041–66.

———. 2004. "Political Preference Formation: Competition, Deliberation, and the (Ir)relevance of Framing Effects." *American Political Science Review* 98(4): 671–86.

———. 2010. "Competing Frames in a Political Campaign." In *Winning with Words: The Origins and Impact of Political Framing*, edited by Brian F. Schaffner and Patrick J. Sellers. New York: Routledge, 2010.

Druckman, James N., Cari Lynn Hennessy, Kristi St. Charles, and Jonathan Webber. 2010. "Competing Rhetoric over Time: Frames Versus Cues." *Journal of Politics* 72(1): 136–48.

Druckman, James N., and Cindy D. Kam. 2011. "Students as Experimental Participants." In *Cambridge Handbook of Experimental Political Science*, edited by James N. Druckman, Donald P. Green, James H. Kuklinski, and Arthur Lupia. Cambridge: Cambridge University Press.

Druckman, James N., Martin J. Kifer, and Michael Parkin. 2009. "Campaign Communications in U.S. Congressional Elections." *American Political Science Review* 103(03): 343–66.

Druckman, James N., and Thomas J. Leeper. 2012. "Learning More from Political Communication Experiments: Pretreatment and Its Effects." *American Journal of Political Science* 56(4): 875–96.

Druckman, James N., and Kjersten R. Nelson. 2003. "Framing and Deliberation: How Citizens' Conversations Limit Elite Influence." *American Journal of Political Science* 47(4): 729–45.

Druckman, James N., and Michael Parkin. 2005. "The Impact of Media Bias: How Editorial Slant Affects Voters." *Journal of Politics* 67(4): 1030–49.

Druckman, James N., Erik Peterson, and Rune Slothuus. 2013. "How Elite Partisan Polarization Affects Public Opinion Formation." *American Political Science Review* 107(1): 57–79.

Duckitt, John, and Chris G. Sibley. 2010. "Right-Wing Authoritarianism and Social Dominance Orientation Differentially Moderate Intergroup Effects on Prejudice." *European Journal of Personality* 24(7): 583–601.

Dunaway, Johanna, Regina P. Branton, and Marisa A. Abrajano. 2010. "Agenda Setting, Public Opinion, and the Issue of Immigration Reform." *Social Science Quarterly* 91(2): 359–78.

Dunaway, Johanna, Robert K. Goidel, Ashley Kirzinger, and Betina Cutaia Wilkinson. 2011. "Rebuilding or Intruding? Media Coverage and Public Opinion on Latino Immigration in Post-Katrina Louisiana." *Social Science Quarterly* 92(4): 917–37.

Dwyer, Devin. 2012. "Obama '08 NALEO Promises Still Works in Progress." ABC News, June 22.

Eberhardt, Jennifer L., Paul G. Davies, Valerie J. Purdie-Vaughns, and Sheri Lynn Johnson. 2006. "Looking Deathworthy: Perceived Stereotypicality of Black Defendants Predicts Capital-Sentencing Outcomes." *Psychological Science* 17(5): 383–86.

Eberhardt, Jennifer L., Phillip Atiba Goff, Valerie J. Purdie, and Paul G. Davies. 2004. "Seeing Black: Race, Crime, and Visual Processing." *Journal of Personality and Social Psychology* 87(6): 876–93.

Eccleston, Collette P., Cheryl R. Kaiser, and Lindsay R. Kraynak. 2010. "Shifts in Justice Beliefs Induced by Hurricane Katrina: The Impact of Claims of Racism." *Group Processes and Intergroup Relations* 13(5): 571–84.

Espenshade, Thomas J., and Charles A. Calhoun. 1993. "An Analysis of Public Opinion Toward Undocumented Immigration." *Population Research and Policy Review* 12(3): 189–224.

Everett, Burgess. 2013. "Bill O'Reilly Backs Immigration Deal." *Politico*, June 20.

Eyben, Rosalind, and Joy Moncrieffe. 2007. *The Power of Labelling: How People Are Categorized and Why It Matters.* London: Earthscan.

Farley, Robert. 2010. "Gov. Jan Brewer Talks of Beheadings in the Arizona Desert." PolitiFact, *Tampa Bay Times*, September 8.

Feldman, Lauren, Edward W. Maibach, Connie Roser-Renouf, and Anthony Leiserowitz. 2011. "Climate on Cable: The Nature and Impact of Global Warming Coverage on Fox News, CNN, and MSNBC." *International Journal of Press/Politics* (November 2), doi:10.1177/1940161211425410.

Feldman, Stanley, and Karen Stenner. 1997. "Perceived Threat and Authoritarianism." *Political Psychology* 18(4): 741–70.

Fine, Terri Susan. 1992. "The Impact of Issue Framing on Public Opinion: Toward Affirmative Action Programs." *Social Science Journal* 29(3): 323–34.

Fiske, Susan T. 1980. "Attention and Weight in Person Perception: The Impact of Negative and Extreme Behavior." *Journal of Personality and Social Psychology* 38(6): 889–906.

Fiske, Susan T., and Shelley E. Taylor. 1991. *Social Cognition*, 2nd ed. New York: McGraw-Hill.

Franklin, Benjamin. 1760. *The Interest of Great Britain Considered: With Regard to Her Colonies, and the Acquisitions of Canada and Guadaloupe: To Which Are Added, Observations Concerning the Increase of Mankind, Peopling of Countries, &c.* Printed in London, 1760; Reprinted in Boston by B. Mecom.

Gaertner, Samuel L., and John F. Dovidio. 1986. "The Aversive Form of Racism." In *Prejudice, Discrimination, and Racism*, edited John F. Dovidio and Samuel L. Gaertner. San Diego: Academic Press.

———. 2000. *Reducing Intergroup Bias: The Common Ingroup Identity Model.* Philadelphia: Psychology Press.

Gaertner, Samuel L., John F. Dovidio, Phyllis A. Anastasio, Betty A. Bachman, and Mary C. Rust. 1993. "The Common Ingroup Identity Model: Recategorization and the Reduction of Intergroup Bias." *European Review of Social Psychology* 4(1): 1–26.

Gamson, William A., and Andre Modigliani. 1987. "The Changing Culture of Affirmative Action." In *Equal Employment Opportunity: Labor Market Discrimination and Public Policy*, edited by Paul Burstein. Piscataway, N.J.: Transaction Publishers.

———. 1989. "Media Discourse and Public Opinion on Nuclear Power: A Constructionist Approach." *American Journal of Sociology* 95(1): 1–37.

Geer, John Gray. 2006. *In Defense of Negativity: Attack Ads in Presidential Campaigns*. Chicago: University of Chicago Press.

Gentzkow, Matthew, and Jesse M. Shapiro. 2010. "What Drives Media Slant? Evidence from U.S. Daily Newspapers." *Econometrica* 78(1): 35–71.

Gilens, Martin. 1999. *Why Americans Hate Welfare: Race, Media, and the Politics of Antipoverty Policy*. Chicago: University of Chicago Press.

Goff, Phillip Atiba, Jennifer L. Eberhardt, Melissa J. Williams, and Matthew Christian Jackson. 2008. "Not Yet Human: Implicit Knowledge, Historical Dehumanization, and Contemporary Consequences." *Journal of Personality and Social Psychology* 94(2): 292–306.

Goffman, Erving. 1974. *Frame Analysis: An Essay on the Organization of Experience*. Cambridge, Mass: Harvard University Press.

Golan, Guy. 2006. "Inter-Media Agenda Setting and Global News Coverage." *Journalism Studies* 7(2): 323–33.

Gonzalez-Barrera, Ana, and Jens Manuel Krogstad. 2014. "U.S. Deportations of Immigrants Reach Record High in 2013." Washington, D.C.: Pew Research Center.

Gorak, David. 2010. "DREAM Act Just the Tip of the Iceberg." *Washington Times*, November 2.

Gray, Eliza. 2013. "Roger Ailes's Border War: Can the Fox News CEO Make His Network More Latino-Friendly?" *The New Republic*, February 11.

Gregory, David. 2013. "Marco Rubio Talks Immigration, Gun Control." *Meet the Press*, April 14.

Groseclose, Tim, and Jeffrey Milyo. 2005. "A Measure of Media Bias." *Quarterly Journal of Economics* 120(4): 1191–1237.

Gross, Kimberly. 2008. "Framing Persuasive Appeals: Episodic and Thematic Framing, Emotional Response, and Policy Opinion." *Political Psychology* 29(2): 169–92.

Gulasekaram, Pratheepan, and S. Karthick Ramakrishnan. 2015. *The New Immigration Federalism*. New York: Cambridge University Press.

Haider-Markel, Donald P., and Mark R. Joslyn. 2001. "Gun Policy, Opinion, Tragedy, and Blame Attribution: The Conditional Influence of Issue Frames." *Journal of Politics* 63(2): 520–43.

Hainmueller, Jens, and Michael J. Hiscox. 2010. "Attitudes Toward Highly Skilled and Low-Skilled Immigration: Evidence from a Survey Experiment." *American Political Science Review* 104(1): 61–84.

Hainmueller, Jens, and Daniel J. Hopkins. 2014. "Public Attitudes Toward Immigration." *Annual Review of Political Science* 17(1): 225–49.

Hamilton, James. 1998. *Channeling Violence: The Economic Market for Violent Television Programming*. Princeton, N.J.: Princeton University Press.

———. 2004. *All the News That's Fit to Sell: How the Market Transforms Information into News*. Princeton, N.J.: Princeton University Press.

Hart, P. Sol, and Erik C. Nisbet. 2011. "Boomerang Effects in Science Communi-cation: How Motivated Reasoning and Identity Cues Amplify Opinion Polar-ization About Climate Mitigation Policies." *Communication Research:* 0093650 211416646.

Haughney, Christine. 2013. "The Times Shifts on 'Illegal Immigrant,' but Doesn't Ban the Use." *New York Times*, April 23.

Haynes, Chris. 2014. "Vying for Conservative Hearts and Minds: Changes in Media Frames on Immigration Since 2000." In *Scholars and Southern Californian Immigrants in Dialogue: New Conversations in Public Sociology*, edited by Victoria Carty, Rafael Luévano, and Tekle Mariam Woldemikael. Lanham, Md.: Lex-ington Books.

Hopkins, Daniel J. 2010. "Politicized Places: Explaining Where and When Immi-grants Provoke Local Opposition." *American Political Science Review* 104(1): 40–60.

Hurley, Patricia A., and Kim Quaile Hill. 2003. "Beyond the Demand-Input Model: A Theory of Representational Linkages." *Journal of Politics* 65(2): 304–26.

Islam, Mir Rabiul, and Miles Hewstone. 1993. "Dimensions of Contact as Predic-tors of Intergroup Anxiety, Perceived Out-group Variability, and Out-group Attitude: An Integrative Model." *Personality and Social Psychology Bulletin* 19(6): 700–710.

Iyengar, Shanto. 1991. *Is Anyone Responsible? How Television Frames Political Is-sues*. Chicago: University of Chicago Press.

Iyengar, Shanto, and Kyu S. Hahn. 2009. "Red Media, Blue Media: Evidence of Ideological Selectivity in Media Use." *Journal of Communication* 59(1): 19–39.

Iyengar, Shanto, and Donald R. Kinder. 1987. *News That Matters: Agenda Setting and Priming in a Television Age*. Chicago: University of Chicago Press.

Jachimowicz, Maia. 2004. "Bush Proposes New Temporary Worker Program." Washington, D.C.: Migration Policy Institute.

Jackman, Mary R. 1978. "General and Applied Tolerance: Does Education In-crease Commitment to Racial Integration?" *American Journal of Political Science* 22(2): 302–24.

Johnson, Bryan R., and Cardell K. Jacobson. 2005. "Contact in Context: An Ex-amination of Social Settings on Whites' Attitudes Toward Interracial Mar-riage." *Social Psychology Quarterly* 68(4): 387–99.

Jones, Edward E., and Daniel McGillis. 1976. "Correspondent Inference and the Attribution Cube: A Comparative Appraisal." In *New Directions in Attribution Research*, edited by John H. Harvey, Robert F. Kidd, and William John Ickes. Vol. 1. Hillsdale, N.J.: Erlbaum.

Kahneman, Daniel, and Amos Tversky. 1979. "Prospect Theory: An Analysis of Decision under Risk." *Econometrica* 47(2): 263–92.

Kaiser, Cheryl R., and Jennifer S. Pratt-Hyatt. 2009. "Distributing Prejudice Un-equally: Do Whites Direct Their Prejudice Toward Strongly Identified Minori-ties?" *Journal of Personality and Social Psychology* 96(2): 432–45.

Kaiser, Cheryl R., and Clara L. Wilkins. 2010. "Group Identification and Preju-dice: Theoretical and Empirical Advances and Implications." *Journal of Social Issues* 66(3): 461–76.

Kalkan, Kerem Ozan, Geoffrey C. Layman, and Eric M. Uslaner. 2009. "'Bands of

Others'? Attitudes Toward Muslims in Contemporary American Society." *Journal of Politics* 71(3): 847–62.

Kam, Cindy D. 2005. "Who Toes the Party Line? Cues, Values, and Individual Differences." *Political Behavior* 27(2): 163–82.

Kerwin, Donald. 2010. "Getting It Right: Legalization in the United States." Washington, D.C.: Migration Policy Institute.

Key, V. O., Jr. 1949. *Southern Politics in State and Nation.* New York: Vintage Books.

Kim, Claire Jean. 1999. "The Racial Triangulation of Asian Americans." *Politics and Society* 27(1): 105–38.

Kim, Seung Min. 2014. "Eric Cantor Loss Kills Immigration Reform." Politico, June 10.

Kinder, Donald R., and Lynn M. Sanders. 1990. "Mimicking Political Debate with Survey Questions: The Case of White Opinion on Affirmative Action for Blacks." *Social Cognition* 8(1): 73–103.

———. 1996. *Divided by Color: Racial Politics and Democratic Ideals.* Chicago: University of Chicago Press.

Kinder, Donald R., and David O. Sears. 1981. "Prejudice and Politics: Symbolic Racism Versus Racial Threats to the Good Life." *Journal of Personality and Social Psychology* 40(3): 414–31.

Kliegman, Julie. 2014. "Activist Janet Murguía Calls Obama 'Deporter-in-Chief,' Says He Has Deported More Immigrants Than Other Presidents." PolitiFact, *Tampa Bay Times*, March 17.

Knoll, Benjamin R., David P. Redlawsk, and Howard Sanborn. 2010. "Framing Labels and Immigration Policy Attitudes in the Iowa Caucuses: 'Trying to Out-Tancredo Tancredo.'" *Political Behavior* 33(3): 433–54.

Lakoff, George. 2004. *Don't Think of an Elephant! Know Your Values and Frame the Debate: The Essential Guide for Progressives.* White River Junction, Vt: Chelsea Green Pub. Co.

Lau, Richard R. 1982. "Negativity in Political Perception." *Political Behavior* 4(4): 353–77.

———. 1985. "Two Explanations for Negativity Effects in Political Behavior." *American Journal of Political Science* 29(1): 119–38.

Lau, Richard R., Lee Sigelman, and Ivy Brown Rovner. 2007. "The Effects of Negative Political Campaigns: A Meta-analytic Reassessment." *Journal of Politics* 69(4): 1176–1209.

Ledgerwood, Alison, and Amber E. Boydstun. 2014. "Sticky Prospects: Loss Frames Are Cognitively Stickier Than Gain Frames." *Journal of Experimental Psychology: General* 143(1): 376–85.

Lee, Jennifer, and Min Zhou. 2015. *The Asian American Achievement Paradox.* New York: Russell Sage Foundation.

Lelyveld, Joseph. 2006. "The Border Dividing Arizona." *New York Times*, October 15.

Levendusky, Matthew S. 2013. "Why Do Partisan Media Polarize Viewers?" *American Journal of Political Science* 57(3): 611–23.

Luntz, Frank. 2005. "Respect for the Law and Economic Fairness: Illegal Immigration Prevention." Arlington, Va.: Luntz, Maslansky Strategic Research.

Lupia, Arthur, and Mathew D. McCubbins. 1998. *The Democratic Dilemma: Can*

Citizens Learn What They Need to Know? Cambridge: Cambridge University Press.

MacKuen, Michael. 1984. "Exposure to Information: Belief Integration, and Individual Responsiveness to Change." *American Political Science Review* 78(2): 372–91.

Marcus, George E., W. Russell Neuman, and Michael MacKuen. 2000. *Affective Intelligence and Political Judgment.* Chicago: University of Chicago Press.

Massey, Douglas S., Jorge Durand, Nolan J. Malone. 2002. *Beyond Smoke and Mirrors: Mexican Immigration in an Era of Economic Integration.* New York: Russell Sage Foundation.

Masuoka, Natalie, and Jane Junn. 2013. *The Politics of Belonging: Race, Public Opinion, and Immigration.* Chicago: University of Chicago Press.

McCaffrey, Dawn, and Jennifer Keys. 2000. "Competitive Framing Processes in the Abortion Debate: Polarization-Vilification, Frame Saving, and Frame Debunking." *Sociological Quarterly* 41(1): 41–61.

McClain, Paula D., Niambi M. Carter, Victoria M. DeFrancesco Soto, Monique L. Lyle, Jeffrey D. Grynaviski, Shayla C. Nunnally, Thomas J. Scotto, J. Alan Kendrick, Gerald F. Lackey, and Kendra Davenport Cotton. 2006. "Racial Distancing in a Southern City: Latino Immigrants' Views of Black Americans." *Journal of Politics* 68(3): 571–84.

McCombs, Maxwell E., and Donald L. Shaw. 1972. "The Agenda-Setting Function of Mass Media." *Public Opinion Quarterly* 36(2): 176–87.

Merolla, Jennifer L., Adrian D. Pantoja, Ivy A.M. Cargile, and Juana Mora. 2013. "From Coverage to Action: The Immigration Debate and Its Effects on Participation." *Political Research Quarterly* 66(2): 322–35.

Merolla, Jennifer L., S. Karthick Ramakrishnan, and Chris Haynes. 2013. "'Illegal,' 'Undocumented,' or 'Unauthorized': Equivalency Frames, Issue Frames, and Public Opinion on Immigration." *Perspectives on Politics* 11(3): 789–807.

Merolla, Jennifer L., and Elizabeth J. Zechmeister. 2009. *Democracy at Risk: How Terrorist Threats Affect the Public.* Chicago: University of Chicago Press.

Miceli, Melinda S. 2005. "Morality Politics vs. Identity Politics: Framing Processes and Competition Among Christian Right and Gay Social Movement Organizations." *Sociological Forum* 20(4): 589–612.

Miller, Joanne M., and Jon A. Krosnick. 2000. "News Media Impact on the Ingredients of Presidential Evaluations: Politically Knowledgeable Citizens Are Guided by a Trusted Source." *American Journal of Political Science* 44(2): 301–15.

Morris, Jonathan S. 2007. "Slanted Objectivity? Perceived Media Bias, Cable News Exposure, and Political Attitudes." *Social Science Quarterly* 88(3): 707–28.

Morris, Rachel. 2006. "Borderline Catastrophe: How the Fight over Immigration Blew up Rove's Big Tent." *Washington Monthly* (October).

Murray, Mark. 2014. "Eric Cantor a Casualty of Immigration Reform." NBC News, June 11.

Mutz, Diana C. 2006. *How the Mass Media Divide Us.* Washington, D.C.: Brookings Institution Press.

National Association of Hispanic Journalists. 2006. "NAHJ Urges News Media to Stop Using Dehumanizing Terms When Covering Immigration." April 3. Available at: http://www.nahj.org/nahjnews/articles/2006/March/immigration coverage.shtml (accessed February 20, 2011).

Nelson, Thomas E., Rosalee A. Clawson, and Zoe M. Oxley. 1997. "Media Framing of a Civil Liberties Conflict and Its Effect on Tolerance." *American Political Science Review* 91(03): 567–83.

Nelson, Thomas E., and Donald R. Kinder. 1996. "Issue Frames and Group-Centrism in American Public Opinion." *Journal of Politics* 58(4): 1055–78.

Nelson, Thomas E., and Zoe M. Oxley. 1999. "Issue Framing Effects on Belief Importance and Opinion." *Journal of Politics* 61(4): 1040–67.

Nelson, Thomas E., Zoe M. Oxley, and Rosalee A. Clawson. 1997. "Toward a Psychology of Framing Effects." *Political Behavior* 19(3): 221–46.

Newman, Benjamin J. 2013. "Acculturating Contexts and Anglo Opposition to Immigration in the United States." *American Journal of Political Science* 57(2): 374–90.

Ngai, Mae M. 2004. *Impossible Subjects: Illegal Aliens and the Making of Modern America.* Princeton, N.J.: Princeton University Press.

Nyhan, Brendan, Jason Reifler, and Peter A. Ubel. 2013. "The Hazards of Correcting Myths About Health Care Reform." *Medical Care* 51(2): 127–32.

Oliver, J. Eric. 2006. *Fat Politics: The Real Story Behind America's Obesity Epidemic.* New York: Oxford University Press.

Oliver, J. Eric, and Janelle Wong. 2003. "Intergroup Prejudice in Multiethnic Settings." *American Journal of Political Science* 47(4): 567–82.

Ottaviano, Gianmarco I. P., and Giovanni Peri. 2012. "Rethinking the Effect of Immigration on Wages." *Journal of the European Economic Association* 10(1): 152–97.

Oxley, Julianna C. 2011. *The Moral Dimensions of Empathy: Limits and Applications in Ethical Theory and Practice.* New York: Palgrave Macmillan.

Pantoja, Adrian. 2006. "Against the Tide? Core American Values and Attitudes Toward U.S. Immigration Policy in the Mid-1990s." *Journal of Ethnic and Migration Studies* 32(3): 515–31.

Paolini, Stefania, Jake Harwood, and Mark Rubin. 2010. "Negative Intergroup Contact Makes Group Memberships Salient: Explaining Why Intergroup Conflict Endures." *Personality and Social Psychology Bulletin* 36(12): 1723–38.

Passel, Jeffrey S. 2006. "Size and Characteristics of the Unauthorized Migrant Population in the U.S.: Estimates Based on the March 2005 Current Population Survey." Washington, D.C.: Pew Hispanic Center (March 7).

Passel, Jeffrey S., D'Vera Cohn, and Ana Gonzalez-Barrera. 2013. "Population Decline of Unauthorized Immigrants Stalls, May Have Reversed." Washington, D.C.: Pew Hispanic Center (September 23).

Patler, Caitlin, and Roberto G. Gonzales. 2015. "Framing Citizenship: Media Coverage of Anti-Deportation Cases Led by Undocumented Immigrant Youth Organisations." *Journal of Ethnic and Migration Studies* 41(9): 1453–74.

Payne, B. Keith. 2001. "Prejudice and Perception: The Role of Automatic and Controlled Processes in Misperceiving a Weapon." *Journal of Personality and Social Psychology* 81(2): 181–92.

Payne, B. Keith, Alan J. Lambert, and Larry L. Jacoby. 2002. "Best Laid Plans: Effects of Goals on Accessibility Bias and Cognitive Control in Race-Based

Misperceptions of Weapons." *Journal of Experimental Social Psychology* 38(4): 384–96.

Pérez, Efrén O. 2010. "Explicit Evidence on the Import of Implicit Attitudes: The IAT and Immigration Policy Judgments." *Political Behavior* 32(4): 517–45.

Peri, Giovanni. 2011. "Rethinking the Area Approach: Immigrants and the Labor Market in California." *Journal of International Economics* 84(1): 1–14.

Pettigrew, Thomas F. 1997. "Generalized Intergroup Contact Effects on Prejudice." *Personality and Social Psychology Bulletin* 23(2): 173.

Pettigrew, Thomas F., and Linda R. Tropp. 2006. "A Meta-analytic Test of Intergroup Contact Theory." *Journal of Personality and Social Psychology* 90(5): 751–83.

Pew Research Center. 2006. "The Latino Electorate: An Analysis of the 2006 Election." Washington, D.C.: Pew Research Center (July 24).

Pierson, Paul. 2001. "The Prospects for Democratic Control in an Age of Big Government." In *Politics at the Turn of the Century,* edited by Arthur M. Melzer, Jerry Weinberger, and M. Richard Zinman. Lanham, Md: Rowman & Littlefield.

Preston, Julia. 2014. "Advocates Voice Dismay over Delay on Immigration." *New York Times,* September 8.

Prine, Carl. 2014. "Faces of Immigration Vary in W. Pa." *Pittsburgh Tribune Review,* August 17.

Prior, Markus. 2007. *Post-Broadcast Democracy: How Media Choice Increases Inequality in Political Involvement and Polarizes Elections.* New York: Cambridge University Press.

———. 2013. "Media and Political Polarization." *Annual Review of Political Science* 16(1): 101–27.

Quinnipiac University Poll. 2012. "American Voters Say Health Care Law Is a Tax Hike, Quinnipiac University National Poll Finds; Most Want Arizona-Type Immigration Law in Their State." Hamden, Conn.: Quinnipiac University Polling Institute (July 12).

Rahman, Mizanur. 2008. "Clinton and Obama Talk Immigration in Debate." *Houston Chronicle,* February 22.

Rahman, Rema. 2012. "DREAM Act Protesters Occupy Obama Campaign Office." Associated Press, June 7.

Ramakrishnan, Karthick, Kevin Esterling, Michael Neblo, and David Lazer. 2010. "Illegality, National Origin Cues, and Public Opinion on Immigration." Paper presented at the annual meeting of the Midwest Political Science Association, Chicago (August 22–24).

Ramakrishnan, S. Karthick, and Andrea Silva. 2015. "The News That Didn't Bark: Media (Non)Coverage of the Unaccompanied Minor Crisis." Presentation at the UC Immigration Conference, Riverside, February 19.

Rattan, Aneeta, Cynthia S. Levine, Carol S. Dweck, and Jennifer L. Eberhardt. 2012. "Race and the Fragility of the Legal Distinction Between Juveniles and Adults." *PLoS ONE* 7(5): e36680.

Republican National Committee. 2013. *The Growth and Opportunity Project.* Available at: http://goproject.gop.com/ (accessed March 30, 2016).

Richeson, Jennifer A., and J. Nicole Shelton. 2007. "Negotiating Interracial Interactions: Costs, Consequences, and Possibilities." *Current Directions in Psychological Science* 16(6): 316–20.

Rivas, Jorge. 2013a. "Leaked Memo Urges GOP to Say 'Undocumented Immigrants.'" Colorlines, January 29.

———. 2013b. "USA Today 'Will No Longer Use the Term Illegal Immigrant.'" Colorlines, April 11.

Saad, Lydia. 2014. "More in U.S. Would Decrease Immigration than Increase." Gallup. Available at: http://www.gallup.com/poll/171962/decrease-immigration-increase.aspx (accessed June 1, 2016).

Santa Ana, Otto. 2002. *Brown Tide Rising: Metaphors of Latinos in Contemporary American Public Discourse.* Vol. 1. Austin: University of Texas Press.

———. 2013. *Juan in a Hundred: The Representation of Latinos on Network News.* Austin: University of Texas Press.

Saslow, Eli. 2012. "Virginia Teen Can Remain in Country." *Washington Post,* June 12.

Scheve, Kenneth F., and Matthew J. Slaughter. 2001. "Labor Market Competition and Individual Preferences over Immigration Policy." *Review of Economics and Statistics* 83(1): 133–45.

Schildkraut, Deborah J. 2001. "Official-English and the States: Influences on Declaring English the Official Language in the United States." *Political Research Quarterly* 54(2): 445–57.

———. 2005. *Press One for English: Language Policy, Public Opinion, and American Identity.* Princeton, N.J.: Princeton University Press.

Schmitt, Eric. 2001. "Two Amigos Visit Toledo and Court Its Mexicans." *New York Times,* September 7.

Schneider, Bill. 2008. "Analysis: McCain's Uphill Battle on Illegal Immigration." CNN, June 21.

Schram, Sanford. 1995. *Words of Welfare: The Poverty of Social Science and the Social Science of Poverty.* Minneapolis: University of Minnesota Press.

Schuman, Howard, Charlotte Steeh, and Lawrence Bobo. 1997. *Racial Attitudes in America: Trends and Interpretations.* Cambridge, Mass: Harvard University Press.

Sen, Rinku. 2015. "Let's Drop the I-Word—Again." Colorlines, November 6.

Seper, Jerry. 2012. "Immigration Group Sues Arizona; Driver's License Restriction by Gov. Brewer Is at Issue." *Washington Times,* November 30.

Shahid, Aliyah. 2010. "Damage Control: Brewer Admits She Was Wrong on Headless Nodies." *New York Daily News,* September 4.

Shain, Michael. 2009. "Source: CNN Wanted Lou Out." *New York Post,* November 16.

Sherman, Steven J., Diane M. Mackie, and Denise M. Driscoll. 1990. "Priming and the Differential Use of Dimensions in Evaluation." *Personality and Social Psychology Bulletin* 16(3): 405–18.

Shirley, Craig, and Donald Devine. 2010. "Karl Rove Is No Conservative, as His Memoir Shows." *Washington Post,* April 10.

Sigelman, Lee, and Susan Welch. 1993. "The Contact Hypothesis Revisited: Black-White Interaction and Positive Racial Attitudes." *Social Forces* 71(3): 781–96.

Skurnik, Ian, Carolyn Yoon, Denise C. Park, and Norbert Schwarz. 2005. "How Warnings About False Claims Become Recommendations." *Journal of Consumer Research* 31(4): 713–24.

Small, Mario Luis. 2002. "Culture, Cohorts, and Social Organization Theory: Understanding Local Participation in a Latino Housing Project." *American Journal of Sociology* 108(1): 1–54.

———. 2004. *Villa Victoria: The Transformation of Social Capital in a Boston Barrio.* Chicago: University of Chicago Press.

Smith, Lamar. 2012. "Obama Puts Illegals Ahead of Americans; 'Record' Deportation Numbers Don't Add Up." *Washington Times,* September 12.

Smith, Rogers M. 1993. "Beyond Tocqueville, Myrdal, and Hartz: The Multiple Traditions in America." *American Political Science Review* 87(3): 549–66.

———. 1997. *Civic Ideals: Conflicting Visions of Citizenship in U.S. History.* New Haven, CT: Yale University Press.

———. 2011. "Living in a Promiseland? Mexican Immigration and American Obligations." *Perspectives on Politics* 9(3): 545–57.

Sniderman, Paul M., and Sean M. Theriault. 2004. "The Structure of Political Argument and the Logic of Issue Framing." In *Studies in Public Opinion: Attitudes, Nonattitudes, Measurement Error, and Change,* edited by Williem E. Saris and Paul M Sniderman. Princeton, N.J.: Princeton University Press.

Snow, David, and Scott Byrd. 2007. "Ideology, Framing Processes, and Islamic Terrorist Movements." *Mobilization: An International Quarterly* 12(2): 119–36.

Snow, David A., E. Burke Rochford, Steven K. Worden, and Robert D. Benford. 1986. "Frame Alignment Processes, Micromobilization, and Movement Participation." *American Sociological Review* 51(4): 464–81.

Stenner, Karen. 2005. *The Authoritarian Dynamic.* New York: Cambridge University Press.

Stephan, Walter G., et al. 2002. "The Role of Threats in the Racial Attitudes of Blacks and Whites." *Personality and Social Psychology Bulletin* 28(9): 1242–54.

Stroud, Natalie Jomini. 2007. "Media Use and Political Predispositions: Revisiting the Concept of Selective Exposure." *Political Behavior* 30(3): 341–66.

Sullivan, Margaret. 2012. "Readers Won't Benefit If Times Bans the Term 'Illegal Immigrant.'" Public Editor's Journal (blog), *New York Times,* October 2.

Tajfel, Henri. 1982. "Social Psychology of Intergroup Relations." *Annual Review of Psychology* 33(1): 1–39.

Tajfel, Henri, and John C. Turner. 1979. "An Integrative Theory of Intergroup Conflict." *The Social Psychology of Intergroup Relations* 33(47): 74.

Tarman, Christopher, and David O. Sears. 2005. "The Conceptualization and Measurement of Symbolic Racism." *Journal of Politics* 67(3): 731–61.

Tea Party News. 2013. "Cantor Crafting Dream Act–Like Amnesty Bill." *Tea Party News,* July 11. Available at: http://www.teaparty.org/cantor-crafting-dream-act-like-amnesty-bill-26316/ (accessed March 25, 2016).

Todd, Andrew R., Galen V. Bodenhausen, Jennifer A. Richeson, and Adam D. Galinsky. 2011. "Perspective Taking Combats Automatic Expressions of Racial Bias." *Journal of Personality and Social Psychology* 100(6): 1027–42.

Turner, John C. 1985. "Social Categorization and the Self-concept: A Social Cognitive Theory of Group Behavior." *Advances in Group Processes: Theory and Research* 2: 77–122.

Tversky, Amos, and Daniel Kahneman. 1981. "The Framing of Decisions and the Psychology of Choice." *Science* 211(4481): 453–58.

————. 1986. "Rational Choice and the Framing of Decisions." *Journal of Business:* S251–78.

U.S. Department of Homeland Security (DHS). Office of Immigration Statistics. 2013. 2012 Yearbook of Immigration Statistics. Washington: DHS (July).

Vedantam, Shankar. 2010. "Deportation Delay Brings Celebration." *Washington Post,* December 1.

Voss, Kim, and Irene Bloemraad, eds. 2010. *Rallying for Immigrant Rights.* Berkeley: University of California Press.

Wallsten, Peter. 2012. "Marco Rubio's Dream Act Alternative a Challenge for Obama on Illegal Immigration." *Washington Post,* April 25.

Wang, Frances Kai-Hwa. 2015. "Fiorina Slams 'Festering Problem' of Chinese Maternity Tourism." NBC News, August 31.

Washington Post. 2010a. "Dream Act Could Save Immigrant Students from Deportation" (editorial). *Washington Post,* August 12.

Washington Post. 2010b. "Immigration impasse ahead" (editorial). *Washington Post,* December 29.

Washington Times. 2010. "Illegal Aliens Are Illegal and Alien" (editorial). *Washington Times,* December 29.

Waters, Mary C., and Marisa Gerstein Pineau, eds. 2015. *The Integration of Immigrants into American Society.* Washington, D.C.: National Academies Press.

Weaver, David A., and Joshua M. Scacco. 2012. "Revisiting the Protest Paradigm: The Tea Party as Filtered Through Prime-Time Cable News." *International Journal of Press/Politics* (October 25): doi:10.1177/1940161212462872.

Weiner, Rachel. 2012. "Sean Hannity: I've 'Evolved' on Immigration." *Washington Post,* November 8.

Weinger, Mackenzie. 2012. "Vargas to AP, NYT: End 'Illegal Immigrant.'" Politico, September 21.

Weprin, Alex. 2012. "MSNBC Adding New Show Hosted by Melissa Harris-Perry to Weekend Lineup." *Adweek: TVNewser,* January 5.

White House, The. 2010. "Remarks by the President on Immigration." June 15.

White, Josh. 2010. "Eight Area Jurisdictions Join in Immigration Checks; ICE Program Aims to Deport Jail Inmates." *Washington Post,* April 22.

Yancey, George. 1999. "An Examination of the Effects of Residential and Church Integration on Racial Attitudes of Whites." *Sociological Perspectives* 42(2): 279–304.

Young, Alford A. 2010. "New Life for an Old Concept: Frame Analysis and the Reinvigoration of Studies in Culture and Poverty." *Annals of the American Academy of Political and Social Science* 629(1): 53–74.

Zaller, John. 1992. *The Nature and Origins of Mass Opinion.* Cambridge: Cambridge University Press.

Zavestoski, Stephen, Kate Agnello, Frank Mignano, and Francine Darroch. 2004. "Issue Framing and Citizen Apathy Toward Local Environmental Contamination." *Sociological Forum* 19(2): 255–83.

Zivkovic, Tanya, Megan Warin, Michael Davies, and Vivienne Moore. 2010. "In the Name of the Child." *Journal of Sociology* 46(4): 375–92.

Zolberg, Aristide. 2005. *A Nation by Design.* Cambridge, Mass.: Harvard University Press.

Index

Boldface numbers refer to figures and tables.